Baseball's
Greatest Comeback

Baseball's Greatest Comeback

The Miracle Braves of 1914

J. Brian Ross

ROWMAN & LITTLEFIELD
Lanham • Boulder • New York • Toronto • Plymouth, UK

Published by Rowman & Littlefield
4501 Forbes Boulevard, Suite 200, Lanham, Maryland 20706
www.rowman.com

10 Thornbury Road, Plymouth PL6 7PP, United Kingdom

British Library Cataloguing in Publication Information Available

Library of Congress Cataloging-in-Publication Data
Ross, J. Brian
  Baseball's greatest comeback : the miracle Braves of 1914 / J. Brian Ross.
    pages cm
  Includes bibliographical references and index.
  ISBN 978-1-4422-3606-6 (cloth : alk. paper) — ISBN 978-1-4422-3607-3 (ebook)
  1. Boston Braves (Baseball team)—History. I. Title.
  GV875.B59R67 2014
  796.357'64097446109041—dc23

                                                                    2014006298

♾️™ The paper used in this publication meets the minimum requirements of
American National Standard for Information Sciences—Permanence of Paper
for Printed Library Materials, ANSI/NISO Z39.48-1992. Printed in the United States
of America

For Toni

Contents

Preface

This book tells the story of the baseball's greatest comeback, a spectacular last-place-to-first-place rise by one of baseball's feistiest group of ballplayers, the "Miracle Braves." The word *miracle* suggests a change from the possible to the impossible; it refers to an event so incredible that only divine intervention can produce the end result. In 1914, Americans, many of whom held a rational, progressive outlook, did not openly profess that Providence was shaping the outcome of a baseball season, but they did acknowledge that they were witnessing a highly implausible event: a boisterous, highly superstitious manager, assisted by a star player who had faced painfully difficult times, guiding a group of castoffs and misfits to rise from 15 games back in mid-July to a three-month stretch of improbable victories. And Americans were observing this baseball miracle while Europeans were engaged in the brutal initial battles of World War I, including one of the war's crucial moments, a battle that despite tens of thousands of casualties, earned the designation "Miracle of the Marne." The 1914 baseball season, especially when contrasted with the horrors of World War I, allowed Americans to pause, wonder, and enjoy their national pastime.

The baseball fans who most appreciated the miraculous workings of the Braves rooted for them at Boston's Fenway Park, a stadium built for the Red Sox in 1912, and the temporary home of the Braves in late summer 1914. At a much later date, Fenway Park served as my home field, too. When my father, Robert M. Ross, finished his work at Hanscom Field Airport in Lexington, he would arrange for us to attend Red Sox games at Fenway. We would usually sit near left field so that we could cheer on his fellow World War II pilot, Ted Williams, and later Williams's protégé, Carl Yastrzemski. It was during these special moments that I acquired an affection for Boston baseball. And it was driving with my father to historical sites in Boston—he often showed me the place where the British captured Paul Revere—that sparked my boyhood interest in history. This affection for the subject grew exponentially over time and sustained me through graduate school, where I followed a scholarly path to the Progressive Era, a time period whose characters and events burst out of the Victorian past. As a graduate student at the University of Michigan, Professor Sydney Fine strongly encouraged me to read every book in existence on the time period, and later, at Case Western Reserve University, Professor David Hammack helped me shape my ideas and research into a dissertation, a study of Progressive philanthropy. In the past 15 years, ever since I organized a baseball history conference on the 50th anniversary of Jackie Robinson's entering the major leagues, I began to absorb marvelous baseball literature. This book, *Baseball's Greatest Comeback*, then, connects three of my affections: memories of growing up in Boston, the Progressive Era, and baseball's past.

Acknowledgments

My research has benefitted from librarians and archivists upon whom I relied so often. I thank Winfree Segal and Steve Carter-Lovejoy at the Tuckahoe Library in Henrico County Virginia; Sean Casey at the Boston Public Library; Anne Benham and Barbara Selby at the University of Virginia Alderman Library; and Freddy Berowski and Tim Wiles from the A. Bartlett Giamatti Research Library at Cooperstown's National Baseball Hall of Fame & Museum. I am especially grateful to my colleagues at Collegiate School: Ben Lamb, Allen Chamberlain, and Melanie Barker, who answered my frequent and unexpected queries on every possible subject.

I appreciate those who helped me track down images of Boston and its Braves: Barbara Natanson at the Library of Congress; Karen Shafts and Jane Winton at the Boston Public Library; John Horne of the A. Bartlett Giamatti Research Library at Cooperstown's National Baseball Hall of Fame & Museum; and Alison Moore and Mark Rucker of the Rucker Archive.

My gratitude extends to Marilyn Shaw who offered countless helpful suggestions, and I am deeply indebted to the editorial staff at Rowman & Littlefield, especially Christen Karniski, who responded with wisdom and reassurance to each of my requests.

And I give my deepest, most heartfelt thanks to my family: Colleen and Joe; Jessica and Tim; Cat, Josh, and Oliver; and, of course, Toni. Upbeat, and compassionate, she reviewed my words with insight, support, and kindness.

Introduction

The Guns of August, Barbara Tuchman's dramatic, Pulitzer Prize–winning narrative on the early months of World War I, has shaped our collective memory of the summer of 1914. Those who reflect on the early months of World War I invariably connect that summer to the assassination of Archduke Francis Ferdinand, the diplomatic blundering that led to World War I, and the Battle of the Frontiers, where millions of soldiers were mobilized to fight what military historians have called one of the bloodiest battles in history. Tuchman and other historians have seized our historical imaginations with the "August Madness," where, after the announcement of war declarations, high-spirited crowds in London, Paris, Vienna, St. Petersburg, and Berlin shouted, raised flags, and jubilantly sang patriotic songs.

But in the summer of 1914, crowds in the United States often devoted their energies to a madness of a different sort: a baseball pennant race, a pennant race in which the Boston Braves, a perennial woeful team, rose from the ashes of last place—15 games behind in early July—and battled for the National League crown against the New York Giants, one of the most dominant teams of all time. Americans delighted in the Braves' "Miracle" season; they savored their Deadball Era baseball heroes, players who, instead of smashing home runs, stole bases and sacrificed base runners across home plate. They cheered wildly and sang fervently from the first pitch to the final out in such new concrete and steel stadiums as Chicago's Wrigley Field and Boston's Fenway Park.

Fenway Park signified a growing, changing, turn-of-the-century Boston. The city had recently constructed a new fine arts museum and a symphony hall; it had invested millions to revitalize the harbor. The bustling port had offered thousands of jobs to the Irish as they immigrated to Boston in the nineteenth century. At the turn of the new century, thousands of immigrants poured in from Southern Europe and Eastern Europe. Italians and East European Jews founded new neighborhoods in Boston, and, by 1910, the city's population had mushroomed to 670,000. City politicians ceaselessly strove to cope with the problems caused by rapid urbanization. Political bosses adhered to the old formula based on ethnic loyalties and the neighborhood ward system; others formed a Progressive Good Government Association that sought to eliminate waste and corruption in city hall. Shrewd bosses turned to progressivism, often promoting genuine reform, at times expressing vote-getting political rhetoric. In 1906, John Francis "Honey Fitz" Fitzgerald, a ward boss in the North End and Boston's first Irish Catholic mayor, campaigned for the city's top office on a Progressive platform of efficiency and businesslike principles.[1]

Once elected, Fitzgerald operated municipal services in the manner of the urban boss. He consumed his days negotiating with office seekers, lobbyists, and contractors; he spent his evenings attending wakes, banquets, and public celebrations.[2] Honey Fitz, the great patriarch of the Kennedy political family, had little inclination to pursue progressive reform. Progressive reform is an amorphous concept that historians still grapple to understand, but many agree that progressive reformers attempted to regulate business, improve working conditions, and mitigate class conflict, and that they promoted a set of middle-class values based on rationality and professionalism. Most scholars concur that progressivism reached its peak in the years before World War I. Progressives at the local and state levels won elections, and, in 1912, Woodrow Wilson, a Progressive Democrat, defeated the Republican William Howard Taft and Teddy Roosevelt, founder of his new Progressive Party. By 1914, the year of the Braves' success, Wilson had signed into law a series of Progressive measures like the Clayton Antitrust Act, which sought to stop anticompetitive practices, and the Federal Reserve Act, which set up the country's central banking system.

It was during the Progressive Era that baseball emerged as the national pastime. Successful minor leagues sprouted up throughout the country; attendance at major-league games soared. Baseball magnates capitalized on the trend as they witnessed the value of major-league teams shoot upward. Baseball publications, flooding the market, promoted the notion that the game offered a healthy, morally sound way of life.[3] As historian Steven A. Riess notes, "The baseball creed coincided with the prevailing broad-based progressive ethos that promoted order, traditional values, efficiency, and Americanization by looking back to an idealized past."[4] Woodrow Wilson, a college player, attended 11 major-league games during his two terms in office and, in 1915, became the first president to attend a World Series.[5]

In 1914, progressives and their counterparts delighted in the Braves' success. Americans enjoyed the rise of the Boston Braves, in part because it was so unexpected, in part because the experience reflected traditional values of hard work and determination, and also because Americans, who were well aware of the death and destruction in Europe, found solace in their peaceful national pastime. As the "Guns of August" maimed and killed thousands of young European soldiers, American sports fans discovered the Braves, a team of likeable, determined, and highly unconventional ballplayers. Baseball fans rooted so enthusiastically for the Braves because the team followed the lead of Walter "Rabbit" Maranville, Johnny "The Crab" Evers, and George "Big Daddy" Stallings, three of the most memorable characters in baseball's past. Rabbit Maranville, the cheerfully madcap, brilliant fielding shortstop, Johnny "The Crab" Evers, an obsessively driven, yet highly sensitive, team captain, and George "Big Daddy" Stallings, a clever, yet fanatically superstitious manager, pulled together a band of youthful players, almost all of whom had met a similar fate from other major-league teams: rejection. And the Boston Braves played like rejects for the first half of the 1914 baseball season. They found themselves 15 games out of first place on July 4; three days later, the Braves lost to a minor-league team in an exhibition game.

In July and August, the Braves fought back, finishing the season with a miraculous 68–24 record as they battled such competitive teams as the Chicago Cubs and John McGraw's powerful New York Giants. The Giants were led by the crusty John McGraw, sometimes tagged "Little Napoleon." McGraw, a brilliant strategist and ruthless competitor, had guided his team to three pennants in the last four years. McGraw publicly cursed owners, baited umpires, and brawled with opposing players and fans. Fans so vehemently disliked McGraw's Giants that they fired stones and bottles at his team as they rode carriages to the ballpark. Yet, even if the Braves could achieve victory over the Giants, the Braves knew that they would most likely meet the great Philadelphia Athletics, who, in late August, stood 13 games ahead of the second-place Boston Red Sox. Connie Mack, the A's manager, coached a team so talented that they had won three out of the last four World Series, including a 1913 victory over the Giants.

The rise of the 1914 Boston Braves is the core of this book. Although this volume surveys the 1914 season chronologically, it weaves in glimpses of the time period, the early battles of World War I, and the events of the Progressive Era. More importantly, this book examines five major figures from the summer of 1914: George Stallings, Johnny Evers, "Rabbit" Maranville, John McGraw, and Connie Mack. These five men reflect the values of progressive era baseball; all five helped to produce a joyous baseball season—the season of the "Miracle Braves."

· 1 ·

Pains, Aches, and Hopefulness

$\mathscr{P}$laying against the New York Giants on May 9, 1914, Boston Braves pitcher George "Lefty" Tyler "kicked" at umpire Cy Rigler. "Kicking," in early twentieth-century baseball jargon, signified not a physical action, but a player's strident complaining: his shouting, brow-beating, and intimidating an umpire. Tyler had allowed the Giants' John "Chief" Meyers to double in Fred Merkle and Fred Snodgrass, players who, by 1914—and later in the annals of sports history—had committed two of baseball's greatest blunders, and he blamed Rigler for his misfortunes. The assertive 240-pound Rigler judged the Braves pitcher's kicking as offensive and "exiled Tyler to the clubhouse." Tyler's team-mate, Braves' captain Johnny Evers, experienced a similar rage. Evers "started to kick in the first inning and was still kicking when the game was over."[1] Fans expected players like Tyler and Evers to kick; in fact, kicking was so much a part of turn-of-the-century baseball that the era's most celebrated manager, the Giants' John McGraw, deemed "judicious kicking" just as valuable to a team as baserunning or bunting.[2] But Tyler and Evers were not kicking judiciously. They were protesting frantically and furiously, reacting to a day of humiliation in a spring of bad breaks, missed opportunities, and gut-wrenching losses. By May 9, Tyler and Evers began to complain, snarl, and kick at umpires because the Braves—despite a successful spring training—had won 3 and lost 11 (.214 winning percentage) and sat 10 games out of first place. Their fury deepened as the season took a turn for the worse, and, by July 4, the 26–40 Braves lingered 15 games behind the first-place Giants. On July 7, their ineptitude plunged to a new low: They lost an exhibition game to a minor-league team.[3]

But then Tyler and Evers and the rest of the Braves players began to transform their rage into a relentless, unbeatable force. Climbing out of last place, they won 66 of their last 89 games, rushed past the previous year's

1

pennant winners, the New York Giants, and stood ready to face one of baseball's great dynasties, the Philadelphia Athletics. How did the Braves, not only desperately behind in July, but also a notoriously weak team for more than a decade, manage to carry out one of baseball's greatest comebacks? The indispensable man in the Braves' revival was 46-year-old George Stallings. Stallings, the turnaround specialist, the chief executive officer on the field, the baseball genius, and the master psychologist, rallied these failing, kicking, and initially ineffectual ballplayers. An impeccably dressed Southern gentleman, Stallings acted like any skilled turnaround specialist. He generated assets out of liabilities—among his many weak outfielders he selected a few that he could "platoon"; he found opportunities that others had disregarded. He discovered a core of starting pitchers whom others had overlooked, and he anointed a new co-leader to carry out his mission, second baseman Johnny Evers. Indeed, Stallings simply reinvented his product, the Boston Braves.

THE GENTLEMAN

Stallings appears in the annals of baseball as an overly emotional, verbally abusive martinet. Yet, accounts of the Braves' "Miracle Man" rarely reveal his contradictory nature. The dark-eyed "Gentleman George" lived an intensely private life, while he skillfully manipulated public relations; he spoke in a courteous manner to friends and family, even though he abusively berated players and umpires, and he carefully calculated the probabilities of every at bat, even though he devotedly followed a set of improbable superstitions.

Born in Georgia just two years after the Civil War had ended, Stallings, by some accounts, attended Virginia Military Institute and considered medical school, but he could not draw himself away from his passion, baseball; he then suffered a less-than-mediocre career as a professional ballplayer. A journeyman minor leaguer, Stallings appeared just briefly on the major-league circuit, where he knocked in two hits in just 20 at bats.[4] Like other great managers, from Connie Mack to Tony La Russa, Stallings, perhaps because of his inadequacies as a player, taught himself the finer points of the game. As George Will noted in *Men at Work: The Craft of Baseball*, "A lot of excellent managers were marginal players. Which is to say, they made playing careers out of the margin that mind could give them."[5]

FROM TAMMANY HALL TO BOSTON

Stallings joined the Braves' organization in 1913, at the invitation of owner James Gaffney. Gaffney, a former New York City policeman, ascended the ranks of New York City politics through his connections with political boss Charles F. Murphy. In 1902, Murphy had risen to the boss of New York City's political machine, Tammany Hall. Tammany Hall, named after a Lenape (Delaware) Indian sachem, started as a patriotic society in 1789, and, in the course of the nineteenth century, evolved into a political machine that offered services to immigrants in exchange for political support. The service-for-political-support exchange offered endless opportunities for political entrepreneurs, and Tammany bosses, including Boss Tweed and Richard Croker, earned notoriety for their graft and corruption. Yet, Murphy, a hard-nosed, crafty politician, opened up Tammany to a diverse set of political interests as he moved away from the corrupt practices of his predecessors. Although he followed the tradition of providing immigrant services in exchange for votes, Murphy, in the spirit of the Progressive Era, pushed for child labor laws and factory legislation. He also recruited professionally trained experts in health, education, and finance. Murphy mentored a new kind of Tammany politician in such reputable and reform-minded candidates as Al Smith, who, four years after Murphy's death, served as the Democratic Party nominee for president.[6]

Braves president James Gaffney, another Murphy apprentice, climbed up through the Tammany Hall political machine, which labeled its various parts with Indian names: The meeting hall was a "wigwam," and the leaders were "sachems." Amassing financial wealth as a building contractor, by 1913, Gaffney had achieved sufficient financial leverage to buy the National League's professional ball club in Boston. Gaffney, who started his career as a policeman and later won election as city alderman, moved his way up to serve as president of the New York Construction Company, a company that garnered contracts for excavating Pennsylvania Station and Grand Central Terminal.[7] Displaying affection for the Tammany "Braves," Gaffney rechristened the Boston team with its new nickname. The Braves namesake, he hoped, would please the fans, who had suffered the failures of the Boston Beaneaters, Doves, and Rustlers, teams that in the previous 10 years had only known losing seasons.[8] (See table 1.1.) Like a good Tammany Hall politician, Gaffney sought to please his constituents: He anointed the team the "Braves"; renovated the South End Grounds ballpark (while seeking a site for a new stadium); and revamped the Braves uniforms, emblazoning them with the image of a Native American warrior. Most important, he replaced manager Johnny Kling with George Stallings.

Competing with the owners of the Yankees, Bill Devery and his old friend Frank Farrell, who also had connections to Tammany, Gaffney sought to rapidly build a winning baseball team. Stallings, he concluded, could immediately transform the Braves. Stallings had earned a reputation as a strong minor-league manager capable of revitalizing losing teams.[9] Gaffney's advisers also pointed to Stallings's record of competence. Under Stallings's

Table 1.1. Boston Braves: The Ten Years before the 1914 Season

Year	Team Name	Finished	Won	Lost	Manager	Attendance (League Rank)
1904	Boston Beaneaters	7th	55	98	Al Buckenberger	140,694 (8th)
1905	Boston Beaneaters	7th	51	103	Fred Tenney	150,003 (8th)
1906	Boston Beaneaters	8th	49	102	Fred Tenney	143,280 (8th)
1907	Boston Doves	7th	58	90	Fred Tenney	203,221 (7th)
1908	Boston Doves	6th	63	91	Joe Kelley	253,750 (7th)
1909	Boston Doves	8th	45	108	Mike Bowerman, Harry Smith	195,188 (8th)
1910	Boston Doves	8th	53	100	Fred Lake	149,027 (8th)
1911	Boston Rustlers	8th	44	107	Fred Tenney	116,000 (8th)
1912	Boston Braves	8th	52	101	Johnny Kling	121,000 (8th)
1913	Boston Braves	5th	69	82	George Stallings	208,000 (7th)

Note: The National League included eight teams. Earlier names for the Boston organization were Beaneaters, Doves, and Rustlers. *Source*: http://www.baseball-reference.com.

guidance, players had regularly improved, and although he had faced controversies, his teams had risen in the standings. Immediately after hiring the vibrant, determined Stallings, Gaffney offered the new manager unconditional support. He spelled out his views on managerial authority, saying, "C-A-R-T-E- B-L-A-N-C-H-E—That's carte blanche. It means full and unquestioned authority. That's what you will have with the Braves. I think you're the greatest manager in baseball."[10]

In 1913, the term *carte blanche* meant full control of the team, trades, and player development; it equaled the twenty-first-century positions of manager, general manager, and director of minor-league operations. Still, it did not mean that Stallings could purchase, for instance, the contract of a Walter Johnson or Christy Mathewson, the two greatest pitchers of the era. But Gaffney's offer of full control, at the very least, provided Stallings with the power to shape his team at will, and that level of power inspired confidence in Stallings: "Give me a club of only mediocre ability," he said, "and if I can get the players in the right frame of mind, they'll beat the world champions."[11]

Johnny Evers, a onetime player-manager who possessed encyclopedic baseball knowledge, knowledge that he and coauthor Hugh Fullerton set out in the meticulously detailed book *Touching Second*, claimed, "Mr. Stallings knows more baseball than any man with whom I have ever come in contact during my connection with the game."[12]

BASEBALL MAGIC

Yet, the analytical, baseball-by-the-numbers Stallings often conjured up a host of superstitious powers that he hoped would carry his team to victory. Most managers and ballplayers followed superstitious rituals, for example, wearing the same socks throughout a hitting streak or performing the same rites at each at bat. Players knew not to pass a funeral procession before a game; they thought it bad luck to touch the catcher's mitt when at the plate. John McGraw fought off the "hoodoo" by not pitching superstar pitcher Christy Mathewson on Opening Day; Ty Cobb always swung three bats while waiting on deck; and Hall of Fame second baseman Eddie Collins stood at bat with his gum placed on top of his ball cap—unless he got two strikes, and then he stuck the gum back in his mouth.[13]

But George Stallings practiced superstitious rites at the most advanced level ever witnessed in Major League Baseball. He issued a prohibition against the color yellow—a color associated with bad luck in sports. He forbade yellow clothing amongst his players, and he banned yellow ads at the ballpark. "Get that damn sign out of here or paint it over," he once fumed.[14]

He arranged the dugout according to his prescribed set of ritualized practices: Bats were placed in exact order, never to be tampered with, and the drinking cup always found itself hanging in precisely the same manner from the water spigot. And trash, too, if it did not bring bad luck, upset the order of the dugout. Because Stallings would shout angrily when he caught sight of debris on the ground, opposing players provoked him before games by stealthily littering the dugout premises with bits of paper and peanuts (pigeons then regularly befriended the Braves' dugout).[15]

In one instance, Stallings's observations of rituals resulted in self-inflicted back pain. According to baseball lore, when the Braves started a rally, Stallings would freeze, maintaining his posture until the next out. In one game, a Braves batter smashed a hit through the infield just as Stallings halted, hunched over. Stallings remained stationary for the length of the rally—30 minutes—and then found himself locked into this hunched position, needing to be carried off the field.[16]

Stallings, a practitioner of a superstitious, "reverse psychology," suffered painfully when outsiders wished him well. Supporters who offered encouragement and hope, he believed, only courted disaster. When before a game a group of fans brought a flowered horseshoe to the plate—a common practice during this era—he lamented, "My God, we're jinxed."[17] He experienced grief when Braves players on the field were offered flowers or trophies, also Dead-ball Era traditions. And worst of all was the simple admonition, "Good luck." Attempting to avoid well-wishers before the team left on a road trip, Stallings would arrive at a train station far ahead of departure time and board the train immediately, before any fan could jinx him with a friendly "Good luck" or any words of encouragement. Because fans would inevitably wish him well, there was only one escape from baseball hoodoo; to avoid jinxes he carried a small, extremely smooth triangular object, as well as a ragged, worn-out, and well-rubbed rabbit's foot, a talisman that could protect him from both well-wishers and practitioners of superstitious evil. If litter and words of support brought chaos and defeat, lucky charms and talismans delivered blessings and victory. In a trunk that he brought to Braves' games, Stallings held his collection of amulets, the most important of which was a 10-cent charm blessed by a witch doctor from Cuba.[18]

It is no surprise that baseball players and managers have been highly superstitious. Disciples of "baseball magic," according to anthropologist and baseball scholar George Gmelch, behave like ritualistic Trobiander fishermen from the South Seas. These Pacific island fishermen, who drew their primary sustenance from the sea, found little help from superstitious rites when fishing in secure, regularly abundant fishing waters of the inner lagoon. Yet, when fishing in the dangerous open seas, where the daily catch was highly unpredictable, Trobianders resorted to an elaborate set of rites. The Trobiander fisherman, like a professional batter striding to the plate, knew that his livelihood depended on successfully plying his trade. When the ballplayer wears the same socks that he wore two days ago, during the last victory, when he tugs on his cap, when he pulls on his sleeves, he, like the Trobiander out on the high seas, practices magic that might give him success, especially in a demanding environment.[19] The player performs a ritual that just might edge him toward success. Modern batters, who generally fail 7 out of 10 times to get a hit, experience remarkably demanding conditions. And success for the batter was especially rare in the Deadball Era. In the early twentieth century, pitchers held the advantage over batters because of their arsenal of trick pitches, especially the spitball. Pitchers rarely threw a new baseball; instead they tossed a "deadball." They served up to batters a cut, tobacco-stained, dirt-worn, uneven, spit-laden sphere so unhittable that teams scored only a few runs per game.[20] Stallings, trying to press out every possible run, relied on his own superstitious rites.

BY THE NUMBERS

Despite his excessive observance of superstitious practices, Stallings followed baseball by the numbers. He never composed a "guide to baseball statistics" (although his great admirer, Johnny Evers, produced a systematic treatise on the game), but Stallings's colorful commentary on walks or "bases on balls" suggests that he would have understood the twenty-first-century mathematical, or "moneyball," dimension of the game. Disdainful of any pitcher who could not throw strikes, he claimed, "It would be just my luck to go to hell and be chained to a bases on balls pitcher."[21] In 1928, close to death because of cardiac arrest, Stallings answered a physician who asked if he knew the source of his heart problem by saying, "Bases on balls, you son of a bitch, bases on balls."[22] Stallings, who displayed disgust when a fielder committed an error, when a pitcher yielded a home run, or when a batter missed a signal, feared, above all else, bases on balls. His "bases-on-balls-in-hell imagery" was founded on the seemingly simple baseball principle that not only hits, but walks, yielded run production. In 1914, Stallings clearly understood the modern notion of on-base percentage. On-base percentage, a statistic that came into prominence through the advocacy of renowned baseball statistician and scholar Bill James, was well received by fans and journalists only around 2000. In 2000, Paul Podesta, as described in Michael Lewis's *Moneyball*, claimed, moreover, that on-base percentage was the single most important offensive statistic. An assistant to Oakland A's general manager Billy Beane, Podesta, in the words of Lewis, concluded, "A player's ability to get on base—especially when he got on base in unspectacular ways—tended to be dramatically underpriced in relation to other abilities."[23] Well before 1914, Stallings understood the value of the unspectacular walk; he had acquired a profound understanding of baseball probabilities.

According to James, Stallings was one of the first managers to promote the idea of platooning, recognizing the statistical advantage of righty–lefty and lefty–righty offensive advantages. When a manager platoons, he inserts into the lineup a right-handed position player to face a left-handed pitcher (or vice versa). This notion of platooning, according to some students of baseball history, originated with the Yankees' Casey Stengel, who started his managerial career with the Brooklyn Dodgers in the 1930s. Yet, it seems that Stallings and his contemporary, manager of the Giants, John McGraw, initiated the practice as far back as the 1910s.[24]

Does platooning even work? On the surface, the practice appeals to a baseball strategist's common sense, but, in recent years, the authors of *Baseball between the Numbers* have questioned the idea. The *Baseball between the Numbers* statisticians claim that a manager might be much better off playing a good curveball hitter, regardless of his handedness, against a curveball pitcher.[25] Yet, managers have occasionally been blessed with seasons of successful platooning, and Stallings, in 1914, rotated in a series of outfielders who produced timely runs. The platooning endeavor proved Stallings at his best. He would take calculated risks, attempting a relatively new practice, and he could detect talent and adapt it to his needs.

In the summer of 1914, he discovered outfielders for his platoon system whose specialized talents matched team needs: left-handed hitters, for instance, who could hit righties. He also knew how to provide psychological support for the platooned players, players who suffer slight wounds to their egos when relegated to the role of part-timer. The professional ballplayer whose sense of self was easily offended when required to take on the platooning role—the role, after all, implied that the player failed to succeed as a starter—might find solace through the support of a psychologically astute manager like George Stallings.

In baseball, a game in which there is a fine line between winning and losing, managers like Stallings sought any possible means to achieve the upper hand: platooning players, limiting walks, or wearing an amulet. In *Men at Work*, Will comments on Tony La Russa managing a modern team, writing, "Even a very good team like the 1988 Athletics has only a slim advantage. . . . To get that edge, often a manager must fret constantly."[26] And Stallings, although fearful that a particular omen—a black cat or a speck of yellow—would bring misfortune, remained adamant that he and his players would create their own luck. "Breaks," he complained, "I'll break the next man that talks to me about breaks. You make your own breaks in baseball."[27]

THE BOSS

Stallings had also earned a reputation for his iron will, his determination to stand up to any player—even owners who might undermine his position. In 1909, Stallings took command of the New York Highlanders (later renamed the Yankees), who, in 1908, finished dead last. By mid-season 1910, Stallings's Highlanders team had risen to second place to challenge the powerful Philadelphia A's. Even as the team moved up in the standings, Stallings was forced to stand his ground against the attacks of the highly accomplished and notorious Hal Chase.

Chase, described in Eric Rolfe Greenberg's novel *The Celebrant* as a "broad-shouldered, bull-necked rowdy," proved himself as one of the best defensive first basemen in history: a slick fielder who could play far off the bag, snatching up with ease sacrifice bunt attempts.[28] Because he was such an artful fielder, both contemporaries and baseball chroniclers have overlooked his prowess as a hitter and base stealer. Yet, Chase excelled at manufacturing runs: He stole bases (twice second in the American League), and he often advanced teammates along the base paths with the hit-and-run. In the American League, he finished in the top 10 in RBIs four times and in batting average three times; in 1916, he won the National League batting title (.339) and finished second in slugging percentage (.459). Refined and skillful as a ballplayer, "Prince Hal" caroused his way through New York's theater districts, consorting with the likes of singer Al Jolson, playwright George M. Cohan, and billiards champion Willie Hoppe. Although reaching stardom in his eight and a half seasons as a Yankee, Chase suffered from a gambling habit that persisted throughout a 15-year professional baseball career and earned him a reputation as one of the most corrupt ballplayers in the game's history.[29]

During Chase's career, fans, players, and managers accused him of dishonesty on the playing field. When he took his position at first base, fans regularly shouted, "Well, Hal, what are the odds today?"[30] His managers publicly decried him for unethical behavior. In 1916, Cincinnati Reds manager Christy Mathewson, widely respected for his integrity and honesty, suspended Chase for "indifferent play and insubordination." Mathewson suspected Chase of bribing Giants pitcher Bill Perritt before a game at the Polo Grounds. And John McGraw, although he curiously hired the talented first baseman in 1919, years later explained that Chase had paid Giants' players to intentionally lose games. Late in the 1910 season, when Stallings charged that Chase was throwing games, Chase gained the support of the Highlanders' (Yankees) club president, Frank Farrell. Farrell, a noted gambler with strong ties to Tammany Hall, fired Stallings, replacing him with Chase. The Highlanders failed to win the pennant and, in 1911, plummeted to sixth place.[31]

Never yielding to Farrell or Chase, never willing to give up his honor and authority, Stallings proclaimed, "I've got to be the boss. . . . Boss all the way."[32] Certainly Stallings's need to act as the unassailable "boss" helped him shape the youthful 1914 Braves into a winning team. But more important, his willingness to stand up to the likes of a star player, Hal Chase, and a prominent owner, Frank Farrell, proved an impenetrable integrity, a quality that inspired his players to battle relentlessly. Despite his very evident flaws—his explosive temper, offensive language, and fanatical devotion to superstition—Stallings earned the respect of his players.

Stallings, although disgusted with Chase's "laying down," would suspect that more than a few players threw games during the first two decades of the twentieth century. Gamblers, after all, had stalked baseball's diamonds since the New York Knickerbockers played on the Elysian Fields in the 1840s. And after the World Series of 1905, suspicion arose that gamblers had influenced Rube Waddell, the A's outrageous, gifted, man-child pitcher. Waddell, a 26-win pitcher in 1905, mysteriously injured his pitching shoulder when roughhousing with teammates just before the World Series.[33] Before the renowned 1908 Giants–Cubs playoff game that had grown out of the "Merkle's Boner," Giants' team physician Joseph M. Creamer attempted to bribe umpires Bill Klem and Jimmy Johnstone with a sum of $2,500 each (more than $64,000 in 2012 dollars) to ensure a Giants victory. Creamer was later banned from organized baseball, and baseball fans learned 16 years after the 1908 season that members of the Philadelphia Phillies had been offered $40,000 (more than $1 million in 2012 dollars) if they relaxed their standards and let the Giants win.[34] The Phillies' catcher, Red Dooin, claimed, "The money was placed in my lap by a noted catcher of the New York Giants while I was in a railroad station."[35] During the Deadball Era, fans often joined gambling pools and bet on every angle of the game. Daily newspapers printed the odds. Gamblers, who had easy access to bountiful sums of cash, might easily tempt a player who was scrambling for his next dollar. Stallings disdained gambling, and, in Buffalo, as a minor-league manager, he posted "No gambling" signs throughout the stadium and, according to one chronicler, hired plainclothes policemen to watch for fans gambling.[36]

After the 1919 World Series scandal, when gamblers and members of the Chicago White Sox, most likely assisted by Chase, breached the stronghold of the World Series, the sport—at least temporarily—lay in ruins. Yet, many Americans had great affection for baseball, largely because they believed it was relatively incorruptible. Indeed, throughout the early 1900s, most Americans believed that because baseball, unlike boxing or horse racing, was assembled from so many varied parts, cheating was nearly impossible. In 1910, John Montgomery Ward, a founding father of the major leagues, claimed, "No player would dare to be dishonest, no matter how willing he might be." The usually caustic Rollin Hartt, a writer for *Harper's Weekly*, was convinced that despite incidental acts of gambling, "[i]t is the very certainty that no such roguery can be practiced that makes a ball game so popular."[37]

Throughout the Deadball Era, most Americans, like Ward and Hartt, hoped for a pure national pastime. This need to protect the integrity of the game reached high drama after the 1919 World Series scandal, when baseball commissioner Kenesaw Mountain Landis decided to permanently ban eight Chicago "Black Sox" from baseball for fixing the World Series—despite their acquittal in court. Landis's decision, so unbending, so permanent, reflected this deep-rooted belief that the United States must disassociate baseball from gamblers and uphold the honor of the game.

BEHIND THE SCENES

Stallings, principled and resourceful, also earned acclaim for his skill as a shrewd baseball tactician. Tom Daly, a catcher for eight years during the Deadball Era who later coached the Red Sox for 14 years, claimed, "Stallings knows baseball better than Einstein knows algebra. It was a privilege to just sit and listen to him talk baseball."[38] Stallings's greatest admirer was Braves second baseman Johnny Evers, one of baseball's shrewdest minds. Evers, who had been at the helm of the Chicago Cubs in 1913, regarded managers as crucial planners and decision makers. At times, powerful managers, according to Evers, manipulated players as if they were marionettes. These behind-the-scenes managers dangled their puppets/players over the ballpark. Players on the field reacted to every move, sign, or voice command; indeed, an astute manager altered every swing, steal, catch, or throw. Yet, spectators, wrote Evers, rarely comprehended the planning and gamesmanship in baseball. "They imagine, most of them, that the players are individuals who walk to the plate, hit or miss the ball, and make a safe hit or out; they do not know that behind the way the man hits, behind the movements of the base runner, behind the position the men take, are hidden a code of signals and a series of orders to be obeyed without question, for the general good."[39]

Turning toward a military metaphor, Evers asserted that the manager, like a general leading in battle, could devise a strategy that, if followed unquestionably and unfailingly by his charges, could bring victory. Evers and other top strategists in the 1900 to 1919 Deadball Era, a time when the assortment of trick pitches (and, it seems, a loosely wrapped ball) meant few home runs but countless "manufactured" runs, understood the importance of "waiting on pitches," a practice strongly endorsed by the most modern of twenty-first-century general managers, Billy Beane of the Oakland A's. The practice, lucidly described in Lewis's *Moneyball*, requires that players show "plate discipline," holding off on pitches out of the strike zone until they find just the right pitch to hit. Even if he has two strikes, the ballplayer should foul off pitches, achieving a "good at bat," which, if nothing else, drives up the pitch count and wears down the opposing pitcher.[40]

Deadball Era managers never concerned themselves with pitch counts or innings pitched—in 1903, during a one-month span, Joe McGinnity, the first real "iron man," three times pitched both games of a doubleheader and won all six games. In 1904, he pitched 408 innings. In 1908, Christy Mathewson pitched 391 innings, and Ed Walsh, 464. Today, a starting pitcher, if healthy, throws 200 innings per year.[41] Yet, Deadball Era managers kept a close watch on pitchers, looking for the slightest indication of a tired arm. And they encouraged their batters to wait, knowing that when the pitcher was worn out, it was the optimal moment to attack.

In 1908, in the opinion of Johnny Evers, wearing down an opposing pitcher brought a World Series victory to the Chicago Cubs. Implementing the wait-for-the-right-pitch strategy, Chicago Cubs manager Frank Chance, the "Peerless Leader," in the second game of the World Series, engineered a victory that, in the eyes of Evers, elevated Chance to the level of a "baseball Napoleon." (At the time Evers was writing, John McGraw had already earned the title "Little Napoleon.") Chance, alerted before the game that "Wild Bill" Donovan would pitch for the Tigers, concisely expressed his strategy to his Cubs, "Wait." Succeeding, according to Evers, in "one of the most beautiful, strategic struggles ever fought," players "[w]aited—waited—waited, while the huge crowd went wild as inning after inning reeled away and neither side was able to score a run." The Tigers' Donovan was formidable. He threw a blazing, moving fastball and a powerful, sharp-breaking curve. As Chance sent each player to face Donovan, a "human Gatling gun," he steadfastly issued the command, "Wait."[42]

And, claimed Evers, the manager's loyal soldiers strode to the plate and patiently endured "[o]ne strike, one ball, two strikes, a foul, two balls, foul, foul, sometimes three strikes, sometimes a weak fly that netted nothing." Players only hit when forced to do so; instead, they extended their at bats, causing Donovan to offer as many pitches as possible. In the top of the seventh, Chance sensed that the Detroit pitcher was beginning to tire. In the eighth, Art "Circus Solly" Hofman (known for his acrobatic fielding) pushed the count to the maximum and then desperately scratched a single into left field. During Hofman's at bat, Chance observed Donovan wearily lowering his pitching arm. Determined that Donovan was tiring himself out with hard fastballs, Chance commanded, "Switch." Joe Tinker, the next batter, complied faithfully and knocked the next ball into a sign above the right-field seats. The Cubs, "like soldiers attacking a breached wall . . . rushed to the assault, and, before the inning was over, they made six runs and their waiting game had won."[43]

THE PSYCHOLOGIST

Like Frank Chance, Stallings, in Evers's judgement, could lead the baseball troops to victory. Evers recognized Stallings as a brilliant baseball manager, not only because of Stallings's grasp of tactics, strategy, and statistical nuance, but also because of his profound understanding of human psychology. Baseball, Evers contended, "is almost as much psychological as it is athletic." By 1914, the term *psychology* had secured its place within the vocabulary of educated Americans. The first professional psychology organization, the American Psychological Association, elected G. Stanley Hall as its first president in 1892. Hall, a Johns Hopkins professor, published his book on adolescent psychology in 1904, five years before he invited Sigmund Freud to guest lecture in the United States. When they wrote their 1910 baseball handbook *Touching Second*, Evers and Fullerton certainly had a sense for the subject; yet, for them, "baseball psychology" meant "motivation" and "momentum."[44]

Psychology, used in the broadest sense by Evers and Fullerton, explains why a weaker team can consistently beat a stronger one, why a batter will hit three doubles one day and strike out four times the next, and why a pitcher, dominant over powerful teams, can give up 10 runs to a weaker opponent. The victor in the classic struggle in baseball—the conflict between pitcher and batter—can decisively solve baseball's "psychological problems." Evers and Fullerton concluded that Cubs shortstop Joe Tinker, an average batter, had cracked the psychological mystery behind one of baseball's greatest pitchers, the Giants' Christy Mathewson: the Mathewson of the 373 victories and a 2.13 ERA, the Mathewson with the virtually unhittable "fadeaway" or screwball. In 1908, Tinker, a mere .266 hitter, acquired sufficient psychological resolve so that he could regularly beat Mathewson.[45] So confident was Tinker, so "imbued with the idea that he could hit Mathewson's pitching at will, in four games against the Hall of Famer he crushed four game-breaking hits."[46]

Tinker's crucial at bats against Mathewson exemplified the psychological nature of baseball at its deepest level. "The psychological instant," asserted Evers, is the crisis point, the key play in the game in which all is won or lost. Evers added,

> Twenty men on the bench are watching closely and intently every move of the pitcher. The tide of battle rises, ebbs—and then suddenly, at the start of some inning, something happens. What it is no one outside the psychic sphere of influence ever will understand, but the silent, tight-lipped, alert fellow on the bench sees something or feels something, and the mysterious "break" has come.[47]

Frank Chance sensed this turning point, or "break," when he ordered his Cubs to "Switch." During another crucial game in the 1908 pennant drive, the Cubs defeated the Giants when Chance sensed the "break," or "psychological instant." Chance "won the game from the bench when he lifted his cap from his head," signaling the delayed double steal. As Harry Steinfeldt sprinted toward second, the catcher threw to second, and then, Frank "Wildfire" Schulte dashed home.

> An instant later, in a whirling cloud of dust, a runner [Schulte] pivoted around the plate, his foot dragging across the rubber just as the ball, hastily hurled back to the catcher, came down upon his leg. The umpire's hands went down. The run had scored. The game was won. The crowd, in a tumult of enthusiasm, roared and screamed and shrilled its joy.[48]

AN ACT OF RAGE

Managers like Chance and George Stallings intuitively grasped this psychological phenomenon, and managers like Chance and Stallings best understood the psychological underpinnings of their players. Yet, managers—except for Connie Mack—also included in their psychological repertoire both an unrelenting caustic commentary and ironfisted disciplinary tactics. Chance often exploded into a tirade, and most accounts of Stallings refer to fiery temperament and abusive language. Journalist Edwin Pope said his language could "sear asbestos" and cited Hub Perdue, a pitcher traded away by the Braves in mid-season 1914,

> He [Stallings] is all-fired strenuous in his talk. When I first went to the Braves I told him, "Mr. Stallings, I'm a southern boy like you, but I don't

cotton to your kind of talk; I jest isn't been raised that way." Well, Mr. Stallings's answer was just about the most fearsome string of cusses I ever did hear.[49]

Braves' historian Harold Kaese wrote that Stallings "[r]aved and raged like a maniac, sliding up and down the bench, bouncing his nervous foot furiously, and fining his players recklessly."[50]

However, most players interpreted Stallings's anger as his singular form of encouragement, in other words, an act, part of the game. In the early twentieth century, the game of baseball transformed itself into a relatively civilized pastime, yet it kept a strong element of rowdiness. With few exceptions, managers, through an assortment of fines, penalties, and harsh, humiliating language, sought to transform unruly young toughs into a disciplined team. The Cubs' Frank Chance threatened to bench players or "plaster" (fine) them, and when a pitcher walked a batter in a close game, or when a position player committed a careless error, he kicked the ball bag, scattering baseballs from the bench to the foul line.[51] John McGraw, the National League's most successful manager, "plastered" his players for any listless effort, or he might leave a player at home on a road trip. McGraw was confident that he could control "Turkey Mike" Donlin, the carousing, pistol-shooting, often-jailed outfielder. McGraw suspended the outfielder and even ejected him from the Giants' hotel.[52] Few players would stand up to a manager who, according to umpire Arlie Latham, "ate gunpowder every morning and washed it down with warm blood."[53] The league suspended McGraw for 15 games in 1905, for fighting with Pittsburgh manager Fred Clarke and then cursing at Pittsburgh owner Barney Dreyfuss. Umpire James Johnstone ejected McGraw for protesting a call in nasty, crude language.[54]

BIG DADDY

George Stallings earned a reputation for profanity that nearly matched McGraw's. Stories of Stallings's colorful, caustic criticisms of players have been passed along in Braves' baseball lore for nearly 100 years. But his tirades formed only one device in his arsenal of psychological weaponry. Stallings's ability to encourage individual players caused Evers to judge him as the "greatest genius in baseball."[55] Evers respected Stallings for his aggressive approach to baseball. In Evers's view, no other major-league manager—and Evers had played for two managers before Stallings—attacked the game with more determination. Evers held deep reverence for Stallings as a motivator who adapted to each player's personality: "Stallings handles men very skillfully. First he sizes up a player, and if thinks he is of the type that will have the spirit broken by 'riding,' he encourages him, jollies him along, and does little scolding." But, if Stallings noticed a tough, thick-skinned player giving less than 100 percent, noted a player interviewed for an article in the October 14, 1914 installment of the *New York Times*, "[h]e can give him one of the best tongue-lashings I have ever heard, and I have listened to a good many." Evers, capable of handing out a vicious tongue-lashing himself, witnessed a year in which Stallings transformed players "inclined to loaf" into "some of the best ballplayers in the business." Stallings could push and pull the right psychological levers. His coarse language, impetuous fines, and timely encouragement brought out the best in the Braves. Stallings knew just when to stop riding a player. He instilled confidence—not boastfulness, arrogance, or false pride. "He had the knack of inspiring confidence in a player and making him believe that he was as good as any man that has ever put on a uniform without letting him lose his head."[56]

The success of Stallings's communication skills was rooted in his adaptability and pragmatism. "I believe," he once asserted, "something could be done with him [any player] if he were handled right."[57] When Stallings issued a fine, he wanted to draw attention to a player's shortcoming. He had no intention of cutting into a player's salary. Stallings's players knew, for instance, that he would levy excessive fines that would never be paid. His assessment of fines turned into a game. If he shouted out, "$500 fine!" to a player who missed a sign, the player would up the ante with "make that a thousand," only to hear Stallings roar back, "Now it's $1,500."[58] (John McGraw, who operated in a similar fashion, might have even quietly paid back the expense of a fine.) The Braves viewed Stallings not as an abusive tyrant, but as a kindly authority figure: It was no wonder that players referred to him as both a commander, when they called him "Chief," and an affectionate father, calling him "Big Daddy."[59]

But during spring training in 1914, players were more apt to view Stallings as an oppressive ruler than a kindly father. Spring training brought heat, strenuous conditioning, and bodily suffering, and yet the promise that a team might return home with a pennant or World Series title. "Under the blossoming magnolia trees," wrote Cait Murphy in her colorful account of the 1908 season, *Crazy '08*, "every one of the sixteen major-league teams can believe that this year will be better than the last; that rookies will sparkle and veterans prosper; that fans will pour through the gates; and that luck will be all good."[60] In the spring of 1914, Stallings, the hopeful, demanding "master psychologist," would enter his second year of full command of the Braves.

SCIENTIFIC TRAINING

Stallings, like his counterparts Branch Rickey as manager of the St. Louis Browns and Charles Comiskey, owner of the Chicago White Stockings, approached spring training with a Progressive Era mind-set. In his renowned synthesis of the Progressive Era, Robert Wiebe, in *The Search for Order*, explained this new mind-set when he described the transformation of the United States from 1877 to 1920. The United States, said Wiebe, shifted from a set of "island communities" with late nineteenth-century small-town traditions to a more complex, interconnected, twentieth-century urbanized society. The American middle class, influenced by a progressive reform impulse toward professionalism and a new emphasis on scientific management, adopted a new set of values that allowed citizens to recapture a sense of order.[61]

Reflecting this faith, in 1911, Frederick Winslow Taylor, an engineer and efficiency expert, wrote *The Principles of Scientific Management*. The book outlined "Taylorism," a process where factory managers categorized workers' specialized tasks, describing optimal performance standards, a "series of discrete steps which workers performed repeatedly and quickly to the rhythm of machines."[62] Taylor conducted time and motion studies in which he broke down jobs to the hundredths of a second. He proposed the "art and science" of shoveling, where workers used up to 10 different shovels,

> each one appropriate to handling a given type of material, not only so as to enable the men to handle an average load of 21 pounds, but also to adapt the shovel to several other requirements which become perfectly evident when this work is studied as a science.[63]

Although somewhat arbitrary and often based on "rules of thumb," and never in a true sense "scientific," Taylor's work encouraged more systematic business practices.

In the spring of 1914, George Stallings's counterpart, Branch Rickey, took the helm of the St. Louis Browns and applied scientific management, or "Taylorism," to his spring training routines. Rickey, who wanted to prepare his players for the long season ahead, transformed the spring training regime through his "scientific" practices: "I shall have three batting cages," he announced in camp, "three handball courts, one sliding pit, and a place for running dashes at the training camp . . . whether anyone approves of it or not. If this is theory, it is blamed good practical theory." Rickey also added a Progressive Era, professional element to baseball, requiring his players to study new nuances of the game. Rickey, the "professor," although facing a few rebellious students, required attendance at long blackboard discussions where he probed the skills of sliding and the art of base stealing.[64]

Brushing up on baseball tactics, and, more important, following a set of rigorous exercises, yielded better ballplayers. Players, often scraping by on their baseball salaries, took on nonathletic occupations during the off-season. They found little time for winter conditioning. While such celebrities of the game as Christy Mathewson and John McGraw played the highly lucrative

Vaudeville circuit, most ballplayers engaged in more mundane tasks: insurance sales, piano moving, and, in the case of Johnny Evers, operating a shoe store. These jobs cut back on the time available to keep in shape. Players were also reluctant to pursue other sports; the 1914 contract barred players from playing in off-season athletic contests, including softball, baseball, football, or any other sport that could cause serious injury.[65]

Finding few opportunities to maintain playing shape in the off-season, players understood the reason for spring training. Yet, the physical ordeal of spring workouts went unnoticed by fans, at least in the eyes of Johnny Evers. In his view, fans neglected the need for conditioning; they believed that players' success depended solely on innate ability: "Most fans think baseball is merely a question of natural speed of foot, quickness of eye, strength of arm, and accuracy of throwing." Fans seemed to feel that players could just appear every spring and immediately throw, run, pitch, and catch; Northern fans (in 1914 there were no major-league teams in the South) surveyed the morning sports sections and concluded that spring training equaled a "pleasure junket," or "one long, jubilant period of hopefulness." The players' reality remained far from the fans' imagination; spring training meant "hard work . . . pains, aches, strenuous self-denial, and hours of thought."[66]

PROFESSIONALISM

At its inception in the 1890s, spring training involved constant barnstorming: Major-league teams played against minor-league and local teams. By 1910, the annual tradition had evolved into three distinct rites: a few weeks of conditioning, a few weeks of scheduled contests, and, finally, a long, winding journey home, a trip filled with games against semipro teams and minor-league affiliates. At turn of the last century, major-league teams, reflecting the Progressive Era ethos, sought to raise the level of baseball professionalism and set up permanent training camps by buying land for ballparks, baths, and gymnasia.[67] Baseball shifted away from a game of amateurs to a sport dominated by skilled, well-trained professionals.

The initial rite of spring training—conditioning—resembled a curious blend of boot camp and health spa. Veterans and rookies endured hours of rigorous drills and exercises, and then spent equally long sessions recovering through heat and massages. Players on their first spring training day tried to slip gently into a regimen of exercise, only to have their tender sinews and muscles experience sharp, unrelenting pain. Describing the first moments of spring training, Evers wrote,

The sun is shining brightly, the air soft and redolent of the scent of growing things, spikes sink into the warm earth. Before 10 o'clock, 30 or more
men, let loose from the snow drifts of the North and a long winter of
inactivity, race out on the open, filled field for the first time, and begin
throwing a dozen balls around.

A relaxed game of toss then shifted to the torture of "high-low," a "ballplayer's
invention for tormenting the body and limbering the muscles." Players would
toss the ball short distances just too high, too low, too far left, or too far right.
The "principal skill lies in looking at the top of Jones's head and throwing the
ball at Smith's feet," added Evers. The lightest of exercises, within five minutes
of rapid playing, "high-low" brought the uninitiated to near exhaustion.[68]

Players, wearing heavy flannels and sweaters and working hard at this
game of baseball, were expected to engage in a vigorous workout, and all
would pursue their own set of exercises: gymnastic stretching, jogging, or
another throwing drill. Toward the end of the three-hour training session,
carried out in the heat of the day, the manager would order his charges to run
two miles back to the bathhouse, where they would enjoy showers and "throw
themselves down, one after another, for a hurried massage by the overworked
trainer." The trainer/masseuse—and there was only one—received unceasing
calls for help, both in the evening and morning, from these tender-armed,
limping, cranky athletes, who, "knowing they would have to undergo the
soreness and stiffness all over again, moped in the hotel."[69]

Just into the second day of practice, according to Evers and Fullerton,
players arrived at the training ground. They wrote, "A thin, red line of crip-
ples hobbles into the park, limps onto the diamond like a G.A.R. [Federal
Civil War Veterans] parade, and the sound of creaking muscles and groaning
swear words arises." Yet, both players and managers appreciated the rationale
for training: "Condition is the biggest asset of any club in the first six weeks of
the season." In the course of the first week, soreness, and then stiffness, would
gradually vanish. For most, the bodily pain decreased with a steady ritual of
conditioning drills. Pain management also required the health spa treatment:
"Massage, baths, and the use of every conceivable device goes on steadily 14
hours a day during the preparatory season."[70]

In the early 1900s, players were convinced that they could reach the
highest level of conditioning through dietary habits and weight-loss pro-
grams. Players consumed large doses of treacle, a viscous, dark-brown mo-
lasses that dietary lore promised would preserve arm strength if consumed
twice daily. Highly aware that too much weight limits agility, a pitcher like
Cubs great Orval Overall—he won a key game in the 1908 Cubs' World
Series victory—proclaimed at the opening of spring training in 1909 that he
intended to lose 25 pounds and keep his weight down to 194. "A team of

30 men arriving at the spring camp," wrote Fullerton and Evers, "is usually between five and six hundred pounds heavier than it will be at mid-season."[71] Players assumed that they could sweat off weight, and in the rooms of the hotel spa, Evers and Fullerton would find "half a dozen players swathed like puffy mummies in blankets, sweaters, and flannels until they looked as if they were starting on an Arctic journey." Other players, covered by half a dozen blankets, would sit on the radiators of hotel bathrooms that had been transformed into Turkish baths. Players shaped their abs by pressing 20-pound cannonballs and iron rolling pins across their abdomens or repeating elaborate, 13-step leg-raiser drills.[72]

After two weeks of physical therapy and strenuous physical exercise—the final workouts lasting as long as five hours—the majority of the team (pitchers kept up with the conditioning) directed all of their energies toward their true joy, batting. "About all [a player] wants to do during that period is bat," notes Evers. "A ballplayer would get up at two o'clock any morning to bat." Batting drills were soon complemented with team play, as the "Regulars" took on the "Yanigans" (players trying to make the team) in games so competitive that "there is enough squabbling and fighting and noise to fill a championship season."[73]

Stallings planned for a Braves training camp, which, according to J. C. O'Leary of the *Boston Globe*, was "second to none in the South and elsewhere." Reserving a large suite on the ninth floor of the Dempsey Hotel, in Macon, Georgia, Stallings would arrange for two rooms with shower baths and massage tables. Braves players, subject to Stallings's demands for tough physical workouts, would at least receive the right care for relaxation and recovery. Pitchers, often complaining about Stallings's absolute rule, were required to run four miles per day. Says O'Leary, in 1913, "He ran the Braves in spring training until they hated him."[74] Players would be expected to meet and discuss baseball tactics and strategy before heading to the ballpark. Stallings clearly conveyed that he was the commander, the man in charge. Yet, he encouraged players to offer suggestions, even questions, on any aspect of training camp.[75]

In 1914, Stallings, quite the realist, expressed his hope for progress in the year ahead. In his first year, 1913, he had unequivocally asserted the following to the *Boston Globe*: "The National League would have to furnish another team for the tail-end position."[76] Although journalists and fans had considered 1913 a rebuilding year, Stallings surprised critics as the Braves rose out of the basement and grabbed the fifth spot in the standings. At the outset of spring training in 1914, he proclaimed that the team would rise even higher, finding a place in the first four teams in the National League's eight—in other words, the first division. The Braves, he predicted, would find only one competitive opponent, the New York Giants.[77]

THE BRAVES ON THE MOUND

Four pitchers, Stallings believed, could endure the rigors of spring training and then lift the team into the first division: Bill James, Dick Rudolph, George "Lefty" Tyler, and "Hub" Perdue. None of these players had achieved star designation; still, Braves fans, influenced by the hopeful aura of spring training, might see the group's "potential."

Bill James, a rugged, six-foot, three-inch, 195-pound, 22-year-old from California, inspired considerable optimism. A highly touted prospect, in 1912, James had pitched as a minor leaguer for Seattle in the Northwestern League, where he posted a 26–8 record, with a 2.17 ERA, at one point winning 16 consecutive games. In his first major-league season, 1913, "Seattle Bill" went 6–10, but he earned a respectable 2.79 ERA, showing a good spitball, changeup, and an outstanding fastball.[78]

Rudolph, like so many of the Braves, entered the 1914 season as a second-year man. After four solid years as a minor-league pitcher, he had performed miserably in a tryout with McGraw's Giants in 1910. He then headed back to the minors, playing for Toronto of the International League, where he seemed destined for a strong, although never-ending, minor-league career. But Rudolph knew that his weak performance at the McGraw-directed tryout differed dramatically from his pitching prowess. Aware of his skills on the mound, he promoted himself relentlessly. (Promotion and advertising were ingrained in American culture, and the early 1900s represented a new era in marketing with the growth of Macy's Department Store, the Sears catalog, and soaring corporate advertising budgets.) Rudolph networked among major leaguers, including Braves third-base coach Fred Mitchell, and, in 1913, he risked all by imposing upon himself an ultimatum: the majors or nothing. Rudolph succeeded. After he announced his decision to quit Toronto in May 1913, Jim McCaffery, the Toronto owner and a friend of Fred Mitchell, sold him to the Braves. For the remainder of 1913, Rudolph learned to skillfully mix his pitches—a spitball and a sharp curveball—and earned a 14–13 record, with a 2.92 ERA. Hailed years earlier by Toronto manager Joe Kelley as potentially "as great as Mathewson," Rudolph looked extremely promising in the spring of 1914.[79]

Lefty Tyler, the pitcher with the longest tenure on the Braves, joined the club in 1910. Less than mediocre with his first managers, he flourished under Stallings's guidance. In 1913, he threw four shutouts, while posting a 16–17 record, with a 2.79 ERA. He had acquired a 5.06 and 4.18 ERA in the previous two seasons, respectively, and, in 1912, with his 12–22 record, he had led the National League in losses. With his unorthodox "crossfire" delivery (since banned by Major League Baseball) and a deceiving "slowball" (changeup), he would, in 1913, lead the Braves pitching staff in innings pitched, with 290, strikeouts, with 143, and games started, with 34. By modern standards, he compiled a respectable 1.216 WHIP, or walks plus hits per inning pitched (Stallings at had at least an intuitive, if not actual, grasp of this statistic). And most impressive, by any standard, was his National League–leading 28 complete games.[80]

The Braves had high expectations for the courteous Tennessean, Hub Perdue (named after a vegetable, hubbard squash). Joining the Braves as a 29-year-old rookie in 1911, he pitched reasonably well in 1912 (13–16), and turned in a stellar pitching performance in 1913. The Braves placed their hopes in Perdue because in 1913, he pitched 212 innings and earned a 16–13 record—the team's best win–loss percentage—a 3.26 ERA, and an outstanding 1.13 WHIP.[81]

In addition to James, Rudolph, Tyler, and Perdue, the Braves had acquired a number of serviceable pitchers who might throw a few innings of relief or spot start. These included the "towering" Texan Eugene Cocreham, a six-foot, four-inch right-hander who had pitched one inning for the Braves in 1913; Dick Crutcher, a 24-year-old rookie right-hander from Kentucky; Ensign Cottrell, a southpaw from Syracuse University who had just 15 innings of major-league experience prior to 1914; Paul Strand, another left-hander, 20 years old, drafted from a Spokane, Washington, minor-league team; and, finally, the eight-year veteran Otto Hess.[82] Born in Switzerland, Hess had won 20 games for Cleveland in 1906. Yet, he had a reputation for inconsistency and unpredictability. Hess could pitch brilliantly for five innings, only to implode and lose.[83]

IN THE OUTFIELD

In 1913, Stallings tried to shape a winning team by experimenting with 46 different players, including 12 outfielders. From that pool of outfielders he chose as his left fielder his most versatile player: Joe Connolly. Connolly, the ninth of 11 children of Irish immigrants and a native of nearby Rhode Island, entered the big leagues in 1913, as a 29-year-old rookie. The five-foot, eight-inch Connolly, a serviceable minor-league pitcher who had suffered arm ailments, resurrected his career when he switched to the outfield and joined the Braves in 1913. Despite breaking an ankle near the end of the season, he proved himself as the Braves' best hitter: 79 runs, 57 RBIs, 11 triples, a .281 batting average, and a .410 slugging percentage. A stalwart left fielder, Connolly offered Stallings a swift player with a solid bat: having swiped 18 bases in 1913, the left-handed batter would hit third in Stallings's lineup.[84]

Twenty-three-year-old Leslie Mann also endured the trials of 1913, and secured the role as backup outfielder. Mann, a student of the game, took copious notes on each pitcher. A star athlete in football, baseball, and track at Springfield College, Mann could achieve baseball's most exciting hit, the triple (more than 100 in his career), and platoon against left-handers. Emil Yde, a left-handed pitcher for the Pirates, once labeled Mann the "greatest hitter in the world against left-handed pitchers." Yde added, "If I knock him down with one pitch, Mann gets up and hits the next pitch against the fence." In 1913, Mann played in 120 games and batted .243.[85]

Opening the season in center field was 22-year-old Larry Gilbert, a player whom the *Boston Globe*, in the hopeful spring of 1914, judged to be a potential star. A former pitcher, like Connolly, Gilbert had shifted to the outfield for the minor league Milwaukee club in 1913, where he showed potential as a power hitter. While playing for Double-A Milwaukee, he earned a .395 slugging percentage and hit 10 homers, outstanding in a year when Frank "Home Run" Baker of the Philadelphia A's led the majors with 12 home runs.[86]

THE REST OF THE FIELD

Joining these three second-year players was the tall, pleasant, and unassuming catcher Hank Gowdy. Gowdy, with more time as a Brave than any other player, had joined the team in 1912. Before he signed with the Braves, he had seen action at first base for most of his career. When Gowdy played for the Giants in 1910, John McGraw had encouraged him to switch to catcher because 20-year-old Fred Merkle appeared to be the Giants' first baseman of the future. Traded to the Braves in 1911, the six-foot, two-inch, 180-pound Gowdy played backup for one year at first base, and, in 1912, Stallings dispatched him to the minors to master the art of catching. The 24-year-old redhead entered the 1914 season, like most of his teammates, a novice at his position.[87]

Like Gowdy, the corner infielders lacked significant major-league experience. At third base, the Braves played a virtual rookie, 22-year-old Charlie Deal (present-day rookie status is defined by a 130 at bats threshold; Deal managed 192 at bats before joining the Braves).[88] Deal, who had participated in only 68 major-league games in three years, including two seasons with the Detroit Tigers, played most of 1913 for Providence at the minor-league level, but he batted .312 in Providence and showed a glimmer of potential at the end of the season, when, as a member of the Braves, he earned a .306 average in 10 games. The young man from Pennsylvania would attend third base skillfully.[89]

Deal would fire across the diamond to a large target at first base: Charles "Butch" Schmidt. Described in the *Boston Globe* as the "largest man playing baseball today . . . yet a wonderfully fast man for his size," Schmidt had also served a short apprenticeship in the majors—27 games with just 80 at bats.[90] Like so many of Stallings's charges, the 25-year-old had switched positions. The six-foot, one-inch, 200-pound Schmidt had first tried out with Stallings's 1909 New York Highlanders (Yankees) as a pitcher. Stallings, again coaching Schmidt when he pitched for Buffalo in the International League in 1912, had moved this large, unmistakable target to first base.[91] Having made a favorable impression in the last few games of the 1913 season, Schmidt arrived at camp early and in superb condition.[92]

Throwing to first from his shortstop position was the acrobatic, flamboyant, determined Walter "Rabbit" Maranville. Another second-year player, Rabbit had earned the nickname from a seven-year-old girl who, during a minor-league game, observed the five-foot, five-inch, 155-pound shortstop hopping around second base. This practical-joking, basket-catching shortstop joined the Braves in spring training of 1913. When Stallings first evaluated Maranville, he judged him sufficiently athletic to be a backup, but lacking the physical tools for everyday play. Yet, Maranville persisted in his quest to be a starter. In the spring of 1913, when Maranville learned that Stallings was prepared to choose nephew Art Bues as shortstop, he retorted, "If I couldn't play ball better than that guy I would quit." Maranville, although regularly enduring Stallings's verbal outbursts, stayed with the team, and when, on the last day of spring training, Bues turned intensely ill, Maranville found his opportunity. Asked to start on Opening Day against the Giants' superstar Christy Mathewson, Maranville told Stallings, "Yes, and you will never get me out of there." Rabbit punched three singles in a Braves 8–3 victory, played 143 games that season, and entered the 1914 season as the Braves' starting shortstop.[93]

In the spring of 1914, Maranville, like all of the young Braves, learned the nuances of the game from 31-year-old, newly acquired veteran Johnny Evers. Said Maranville, "Evers, with his brains, taught me more baseball than I ever dreamed about. He was psychic. He could sense where a player was going to hit if the pitcher threw the ball where he was supposed to."[94] Evers's reputation as a zealous, brainy, confrontational, and highly skilled ballplayer preceded his tenure with the Braves. Always recognized as the second baseman in Franklin Pierce Adams's poem "Tinker to Evers to Chance," or "Baseball's Sad Lexicon," he also achieved notoriety for realizing that Fred Merkle, of the famed "Merkle's Boner," had, during a crucial Cubs–Giants game, failed to touch second base, thus preventing the New York Giants from winning the celebrated pennant race of 1908. Evers, the square-jawed, nervous, 125-pound, 12-year veteran, had served as player-manager for the Cubs in 1913, but at the end of that season, the Cubs and crosstown rivals the White Sox had played in the Chicago Series, an alternate playoff series for teams that failed to reach the World Series—and the Cubs lost. With the Cubs' defeat, controversial team owner Charles W. Murphy, who, in the 1908 World Series, placed the press in the grandstands while he set up a ticket-scalping scheme, and who had already expressed antagonism toward his intense and sometimes impulsive manager, found a reason for firing Evers. "We ought to have beaten the White Sox easily," groused Murphy, "and would have if the team had been properly handled. Evers's bad judgment cost us the series and cost me about $60,000." The Cubs then traded Evers—as a player—to the Braves for second baseman Bill Sweeney. When Evers threatened to join the newly formed Federal League, the Braves offered the contractually freed Evers $25,000, a sum too difficult for Evers to refuse. And when the Braves signed him, George Stallings immediately appointed Evers as captain.[95]

The Braves entered the 1914 season with much promise. Most of their hopes rested on the team's captain, Johnny Evers, the star second baseman and a former manager, and on comeback specialist George Stallings. Stallings, now in his second year of shaping the team, had taken Gaffney's "carte blanche" offer to heart: Stallings had selected almost every member of the team. He had searched the minors; conducted trades; brought in players, including Bill James from the Northwestern League; and even signed "free agent" Johnny Evers. Except for Evers and Otto Hess, a spot starter, few players had significant major-league experience. Many of the players were not yet 25 years of age. But Stallings believed that his team could become one of the top four teams, and *Boston Globe* writers remained hopeful that Stallings could deliver. The 1913 team had offered a touch of hope—after nine previous years of misery. They judged Stallings as a shrewd decision maker who could develop talent, and they believed that he had selected "materials that looks good." As O'Leary concluded, "There is no doubt that the present Boston team is the strongest one, considered from every angle, that has represented the city in the National League in 10 years."[96]

• 2 •

Losing with "the Crab"

$\mathscr{T}$he Boston Braves' second baseman, Johnny Evers, reached baseball immortality in part because of his role in the notorious "Merkle's Boner." A pivotal moment in the 1908 pennant race, it centered around the New York Giants' Fred Merkle's failure to touch second on a walk-off hit. Merkle's Boner is an affair in baseball history that has received infinite interpretations, yet, at its core, the event showed two of Evers's brilliant traits: his unyielding determination and his belief that baseball players can win by studying every dimension of the game: angles, distances, and the rules. Without Evers's baseball genius, a combination of his intimate knowledge of the game and lightning-quick response time, no such event would have taken place. Baseball reporters labeled the episode "Merkle's Boner," but they would have been more accurate had they tagged it "Evers's Brilliance."

The incident took place on Wednesday, September 23, 1908, when Evers (pronounced Eh–vers) played second for the Chicago Cubs.[1] In a fiercely contested pennant race, the Cubs, one of the most dominant teams of the early 1900s, had moved to one and a half games ahead of the Giants, who, along with the Pirates, ruled as one of the National League's superpowers. The Giants had captured the National League pennant in 1904 and 1905, the Cubs in 1906 and 1907, and the Pirates in 1903 and 1909. The 1908 season served as a scorching battleground for these three formidable teams.

Tempers between the Giants and Cubs had flared the previous day, when the Cubs' tough, forceful player-manager, Frank Chance, had spiked Giants second baseman Buck Herzog.[2] On the afternoon of the Merkle moment, 20,000 New Yorkers filled the stands at the Polo Grounds to watch the Cubs' side-wheeling southpaw, Jack Pfiester, duel the great Christy Mathewson, the most celebrated athlete of the era. Giants fans rooted fiercely for the six-foot, two-inch, 195-pound Mathewson, who was headed toward a 37–11 season, with a 1.43 ERA.[3] He pitched his usual masterful game for eight innings, committing only one mistake. In the fourth inning, he left a fastball on the outside corner of the plate to his longtime nemesis Joe Tinker, who drove the ball past the desperately lunging right fielder, Mike Donlin, into deep center, just up to the back edge of the Polo Ground outfield. Tinker scrambled around the bases for an inside-the-park home run. It was the only home run hit off Mathewson since July 17.

Later in the game, the Giants scraped together a few hits to score a run in classic Deadball Era fashion. In the sixth inning, Herzog reached first on an infield single, second on a throwing error, third on a Roger Bresnahan sacrifice bunt, and then home on a Mike Donlin RBI single.[4] Yet, the Giants were hard pressed to score more than one run because they faced the Cubs' unassailable strengths: extraordinary pitching and skillful defense. The 1908 Cubs, with a pitching staff that posted a 2.14 ERA, led the National League in fielding percentage (.969).[5] Three times, the Cubs' defense—Joe-Tinker-to-Johnny-Evers-to-Frank-Chance double plays—thwarted Giants rallies. Cubs pitcher Jack Pfiester, who would earn a 2.02 ERA throughout eight seasons, regularly annihilated the Giants lineup. Pfiester, who would acquire a 15–5 record against the Giants, including seven shutouts, had defeated John McGraw's team three times in the 1908 season (twice in a four-day time span). After a late August victory over New York, I. E. Sanborn of the *Chicago Tribune* wrote, "Pfiester, the spelling of which has been the occasion of as many wagers as mispronunciations, will be dropped as meaningless and inappropriate, and for the rest of time and part of eternity, Mr. Pfiester of private life will be known to the public and the historians as Jack the Giant Killer."[6]

But during the September 23 Merkle game, the "Giant Killer" had suffered a near lethal baseball wound: a dislocated arm. Accounts suggest that Pfiester pitched the entire game with a severely injured arm, an injury that Evers described, saying, "A large lump had formed on Pfiester's forearm, the muscle bunching. He could not bend his arm, and to pitch a curve brought agony."[7] Each time he threw a curve—only three times in the game—teammates helped him to the bench. The Giants, alert to Pfiester's frailty, rallied in the bottom of the ninth. With one out, Art Devlin singled, and the next batter, "Moose" McCormick, hit a slow roller to Evers, who tossed the ball to Tinker for a force-out at second; however, because of Devlin's knee-crunching slide into the second baseman, Tinker could not relay it to Chance for the double play. Moose trudged safely to first.[8]

The crowd scarcely recognized the next batter, Fred Merkle, a 19-year-old rookie. Like his fellow players, he displayed no name or number on his back, and now, in September, he was starting in his first major-league game.

Merkle often received accolades for both his intelligence and curiosity to grasp the nuances of baseball, matters that he had learned by standing in the dugout close to baseball's shrewd mastermind, John McGraw. Described by a New York journalist as a "fellow who uses intelligence in everything he does," Merkle drew similar praise from his friends and teammates. Friends labeled him a "gentleman" and a "scholar," and a "voracious reader." Giants catcher John "Chief" Meyers described him as the "smartest man on the club."[9] Merkle had displayed great baseball potential: Wrote Bozeman Badger of the *Chicago Tribune*,

> Suppose Fred Tenney should be crippled. That would be a calamity, wouldn't it? Yes, it would in one way, but it wouldn't keep the Giants from winning the pennant. There is a young fellow on the bench named Fred Merkle who can fill that job better than nine-tenths of the first basemen in the league. He is crying for a chance to work.[10]

Yet, the odds stood against Merkle. He was a rookie with about 40 at bats, he had grounded out twice that day, and he faced nearly agonizing pressure at this pivotal moment in a heated pennant race between two archrivals. There were two outs—and two strikes—as he stared down the Giant Killer, Jack Pfiester, but Merkle cleanly lined a base hit to right. With Merkle on first and McCormick on third, the crowd cheered on the next batter, Al Bridwell, who smashed Pfiester's first pitch, a single to center. As McCormick plodded across the plate, the crowd swarmed onto the field. Merkle headed for second, but then, avoiding the fans and sensing victory for the Giants, he acted as nearly every other player would have at the time: He veered toward the clubhouse—the peculiarly located right-field clubhouse at the Polo Grounds—before ever touching second base. Merkle, Giants players, and Giants fans exulted in victory. The pennant appeared within reach.[11]

NOT SO FAST

Despite the excitement of the apparent "walk-off" hit, regardless of the frenzied Giants throng mobbing the field, and notwithstanding the confusion among the players as to whether the game was actually finished, Evers kept his cool and remembered the basic baseball rule: "A run is not scored if the runner advances to home base during a play in which the third out is made . . . by any runner being forced out."[12] Then he unwaveringly sought to seek justice. Evers, who, according to baseball lore, reviewed the baseball rulebook nightly, realized that because Merkle had never touched second, he could fetch the ball himself, touch second, and nullify the run. As recently as September 4, during a Cubs–Pirates game, Evers had faced a nearly identical situation. With two outs in the ninth, he noticed that rookie Warren Gill had failed to touch second as a winning run scored. Evers retrieved the ball, touched second, and then adamantly proclaimed to umpire Hank O'Day that Gill was out and that the run should be nullified. But O'Day overruled Evers. O'Day, focused on the runner at home, had not witnessed the scene at second base. O'Day later encountered Evers by chance at a hotel and found the opportunity to explain his rationale. O'Day understood Evers's view but could not issue a call because he had not seen the offense. Now Evers had earned a second chance, because Hank O'Day was officiating the Cubs–Giants game.[13]

Amid the turmoil of the September 23 contest between the Cubs and Giants, Evers had to track down the ball, and this time he had to step on second in front of O'Day, who could witness the event. For Evers, hunting down the ball in the midst of hundreds of high-spirited, yelling, rushing fans (and in the face of Giants players who knew his design) proved a complicated, but not impossible, task. Where did the ball go? The fog of baseball, like the fog of war, is blurred by myth and legend. Reporters and eyewitnesses have offered multiple, conflicting views on this part of the story. As writer Cait Murphy observes, "There are tens of thousands of eyewitnesses, but they all see different things, mostly what they wish to see."[14]

Apparently, "Iron Man" McGinnity, coaching first base that day for the Giants (three Giants pitchers—McGinnity, Wiltse, and Mathewson—also recalled coaching first base), snared the ball in right field and heaved it into the stands to a fan, a well-dressed brown bowler type, who almost immediately lost a battle with two Cubs players who ripped the ball away and tossed it to Joe Tinker, who threw it to Evers. Evers jumped up and down on the bag madly, arms uplifted, signaling to umpire O'Day. And O'Day, in concurrence with fellow ump Bob Emslie, ruled that Merkle was out, that the run did not count, and that the score was tied. Did Mathewson or any of the Giants actually see Merkle touch second? Did Tinker or, perhaps, third baseman Harry Steinfeldt grab the original ball from the stands, or did Evers find another ball in right field? Newspaper accounts and players' later recollections (some of Evers's earlier stories are at odds with his later renditions) differ on most matters, but in nearly all cases, three truths emerge: 1) Merkle never touched second; 2) Evers held a ball as he stood on second; and 3) O'Day testified that points one and two did occur.[15]

The incident ignited journalistic fires in Chicago and New York, earning front-page coverage. The next day, when the teams played again, fans taunted O'Day. An anxious Evers hired a security guard, but fans ripped off the guard's badge, smeared his hat with mud, and stole his billy club. Later, as the pennant race intensified, the Merkle affair transcended its real importance; after all, Pittsburgh still was contending, not just New York and Chicago, and the fans for each team had already witnessed about 150 other games that season, each of which proved as important as the Merkle game. Nevertheless, when, at the end of the season, the Giants and Cubs finished with identical league-winning records, all eyes were directed at one play, the September 23 Merkle's Boner. The Giants had lost, 4–2, in the pennant-deciding Cubs–Giants playoff game, a game so electrifying that more than 100,000 New York fans swarmed to the Polo Grounds—a game, according to Mathewson that ". . . stands out from everyday events like the battle of Waterloo and the assassination of Abraham Lincoln."[16] Yet, fans did not turn their attention to the playoff loss, but instead thought of the one misdeed of rookie first baseman Fred Merkle.[17]

JOHNNY EVERS, "THE CRAB"

Evers's key role in the incident represented his brand of baseball. He played with passion, determination, and intelligence. Although on the day of Merkle's Boner Evers went 1-for-4, with no runs and no RBIs, and although he had fumbled a ball and later failed to complete a good throw on a double play in the crucial ninth—unlikely mishaps for so brilliant a defender—he shook off the mistakes, and then, at the decisive point in a key game, amid a raucous, unruly, swarming-all-over-the field crowd, kept his baseball wits. He understood that a minor rule might have been broken, and knew that he would need evidence—a ball and an official member of the judiciary, umpire Hank O'Day. And O'Day's ruling, "perhaps the single most courageous call a baseball umpire ever commits on the field of play," was prompted by Evers's baseball shrewdness.[18]

Who was this clever, knowledgeable, in-your-face Cubs second baseman? The son of Irish immigrants Ellen Keating Evers and John Evers Sr., Johnny Evers was born in South Troy, New York, in 1881. Johnny Evers grew up in a culture defined by baseball. His father, a government clerk (and president of the school board), uncles, and six brothers all played the game. In 1884, his uncle Thomas played for the twenty-first-century equivalent of a Double-A team, batting .232 for the Washington Nationals. His younger brother Joe was skilled enough to earn a tryout with the New York Giants.[19]

Players like Johnny Evers, second generation Irish Americans, dominated baseball in the late nineteenth century, perhaps making up 40 percent of professional rosters.[20] Frank Deford notes that "there developed the same sort of backlash against the Irish in baseball as, say, was directed at blacks in the 1970s, when they began to dominate the National Basketball Association."[21] The "Sons of Erin," as the *Sporting News* called them, found baseball as a means of economic mobility. In *Past Time: Baseball in History*, historian Jules Tygiel examined three sons of Irish immigrants—Connie Mack, Charles Comiskey, and John McGraw—all of whom rose up and realized wealth and fame as baseball magnates.[22]

Baseball opened a path upward for Evers. A sign painter and a factory hand at a shirt collar plant, he drew from his factory earnings and, in 1900, organized his own amateur team, the "Cheer-ups." Evers seized an opportunity to play on the local professional Troy team in 1902. Before an exhibition game against the Albany Giants, the Troy manager complained that his shortstop had suddenly fallen ill. The diminutive Evers, sitting in the stands when he heard the complaint, vaulted over the park railing and volunteered his services. Accepted as a team member, the 21-year-old, dressed in an oversized shirt and cap, appeared as an ill-prepared, gangly youth amongst the men of Troy. "Take the child out," yelled one fan, and, "Yes, I saw him there; I saw him go under," jeered another.[23] But Evers played skillfully.

After he dug out a few hard grounders and hit a bases-loaded double, he earned a starting role and a $60 a month contract. He kept his job in the shirt collar factory while playing against teams in the New York State League. By midsummer, the *Sporting News* reported, "Johnny Evers, who is playing short, is considered by baseball writers in every city where he has appeared to be the find of the season. He has more than made good."[24]

Scouts from the major leagues regularly toured the New York State League, and the talented Troy team produced a few major leaguers, including Ed Hilley, Alex Hardy, Chick Robitaille, and George "Hooks" Wiltse. Toward the end of the 1902 season, Chicago Colts' (later Cubs') manager Frank Selee sent George Huff, a scout, to evaluate Troy pitchers. Huff recruited Evers when he saw a "wiry little bunch of nerves and muscle" who "gave the unmistakable signs of a possessing a 'baseball' brain in his head."[25] Selee, who had lost second baseman Bobby Lowe because of a leg injury, purchased Evers's contract from Troy for $200 and offered the short, scrawny young man with a protruding jaw a salary of $100 a month if he would play for the Chicago club.[26] Signing with Selee required minimal reflection on Evers's part. He could make more money than ever before, and he had a chance to play major-league ball.

Remaining on a major-league club demanded recognizable talent—no one at the major-league level had seen him play before—and Evers believed that his first playing opportunity would be a career-shaping public trial. He faced this challenge only 10 days after his father passed away. Unable to spend time grieving his loss, Evers boarded an overnight train from Albany so that he could join the club in Philadelphia. Resting uncomfortably in a smoker car, chewing black cigars to stave off hunger, he arrived hungry and exhausted at the ballpark. Suited up in an oversized uniform, the emaciated Evers inspired little confidence among teammates. "This kid will be killed, and we'll all be accessories," lamented a teammate to Selee. Selee rearranged his infield, moving Joe Tinker from second to third and placing Evers at short. Evers, undoubtedly tired, anxious, and distracted, muffed three grounders and threw wildly to first base.[27]

But, according to biographer Gil Bogen, Evers's teammates surprised him with their empathy, and Selee reacted with unexpected restraint. Evers had expected Selee to send him back to the minors. "Then, you're not going to can me after the fizzle I made?" queried Evers. Selee patiently looked beyond Evers's failed audition: "I heard of you riding down from Troy in the smoker without eating anything except a sandwich. No wonder you had a bad afternoon. I'll bet that you will have a better day tomorrow." The next day, Selee placed Evers at second and moved Tinker to short. Said Bogen, he "sensed a smoothness in the way they handled double plays together." Evers finished the year with only a .225 average, but he proved himself as a quick, energetic, mentally tough second baseman. When spectators watched him field grounders, they saw elbows, knees, and a Habsburg-like oversized jaw, all moving nervously near the ground. When they saw umpires make unfavorable calls, they witnessed an unyielding, griping, "kicking" Johnny Evers. Both his crablike movements and his irritable temperament inspired Chicago baseball writer Charles Dryden to label Evers "The Crab."[28]

And major-league managers saw the skills offered by Evers, this active, omnivorous, five-pair-of-legs crustacean. "They claim he is a crab, and perhaps they are right," said Cleveland Naps manager Joe Birmingham, who managed the Cleveland team (later Indians) from 1912 to 1915. "But I would like to have 25 such crabs playing for me. If I did, I would have no doubts over the pennant. They would win hands down."[29]

The fiery and determined Evers was a kinder, slightly gentler version of Ty Cobb. Both Cobb and Evers tried to get on base by any means necessary, and if they failed, or if they perceived that they were treated unfairly, they bickered stridently with players, managers, and umpires. While Cobb earned a reputation as nasty, Evers warranted his "crabby," highly irritating status. Evers's physical presence, his thin, bony frame highlighted by his trademark jaw, suited the player who, when next to an umpire, was always "jawing." A "keen little umpire-fighting bundle of nerves," as one reporter depicted him, Evers was tossed out of more ball games than any player in the twentieth century, with 52 ejections.[30]

EVERS AND THE SCIENCE OF BASEBALL

Evers's incessant "jawing" was matched by his unrelenting drive to reach base. He refused to go down swinging, and "by the end of his career he had been first or second in most at bats per strikeout six times."[31] Regularly earning the league's highest walk-to-strikeout ratio, Evers ranked among the National League's top 10 in runs scored four times, and on-base percentage five times.[32] Second in the league with walks, with 108 in 1910, and always calculating how to get on base, he learned the value of the base on balls: "I am convinced that in my own career I could usually have hit 30 points higher if I had made a specialty of hitting. . . . In my own case I frequently faced the pitcher when I had no desire whatever to hit. I wanted to get a base on balls."[33]

And once on base, he aggressively, although methodically, stole bases. Among the National League's top 10 in steals three times, he stole 49 bases in 1906. Although he only averaged 13 stolen bases a year between 1912 and 1914, he was always a threat.[34] Pitchers knew that Evers understood distances and times, in other words, the science of base stealing. Articulating the progressive, scientific attitude, he composed, just a year before Frederick W. Taylor penned *The Principles of Scientific Management*, an account of how to steal third base:

> Figures prove positively that the runner can go 32 feet up the line toward third, and, if he starts back quickly enough, can beat the throw back to second. If he goes the other way, he has 58 feet to run and must slide only 23 feet farther, and the ball must travel almost twice as far and be relayed perfectly to catch him. If he makes the play correctly, the fastest possible handling of the ball will only catch him by three feet, unless he is blocked off the base.[35]

How about Evers's defense? Most baseball fans are familiar with his fielding prowess because of Franklin Pierce Adams's poem "Baseball's Sad Lexicon," or "Tinker to Evers to Chance":

> These are the saddest of possible words:
> "Tinker to Evers to Chance."
> Trio of bear cubs, and fleeter than birds,
> Tinker and Evers and Chance.
> Ruthlessly pricking our gonfalon bubble,
> Making a Giant hit into a double—
> Words that are heavy with nothing but trouble:
> "Tinker to Evers to Chance."

Adams, a Chicagoan, composed the poem in New York City, on the way to a 1910 Cubs–Giants game at the Polo Grounds. Better known as "FPA," his pen name for the *New York Evening Mail*, in 1910, Adams ignited one of baseball poetry's all-time hits.[36] The poem has endured, earning places in both general American pop culture and baseball lore. Baseball scholar Daniel Okrent discusses the poem in Ken Burns's *Baseball* documentary and suggests that the trio of infielders earned their fame more because of the poem than their actual fielding abilities.[37]

Although the group did not stand at the top in terms of yearly, total double plays (in part because Chicago pitchers walked relatively few batters), Tinker, Chance, and Evers fielded brilliantly. Chance, according to baseball historian Bill James, was an "exceptional defensive first baseman."[38] Baseball scholars Gary Mitchem and Mark Durr claim that "[a]ll three had career fielding percentages and range factors above the league average. And in the 11 seasons with the Cubs, Evers or Tinker would finish in the National League in the top for Fielding Wins seven times, twice making the list together."[39] Leading all National League shortstops in 1906 with a .944 fielding percentage, Tinker led National League shortstops in the same category five times; he stood at the top in range factor four times and double plays twice.[40]

Evers's ability, too, matched Adams's description in "Baseball's Sad Lexicon." Throughout his career, Evers earned an above average fielding percentage, and he was ranked by Bill James in 2001 as the 25th best all-time second baseman in Win Shares, a statistic that determines a player's offensive and defensive contributions to team victories. Writes James, "Evers deserved the Gold Glove as the National League's best second baseman in 1904, 1906, and 1907."[41] But what raised Johnny Evers to another level was his fielding intelligence, the baseball brilliance behind the statistics and schemes in the book *Touching Second*. It was his shrewdness in the Merkle's Boner incident. It was, according to the Braves' keystone partner, Walter (Rabbit) Maranville, a form of baseball clairvoyance, a skill so special that "it was just Death Valley, whoever hit a ball our way."[42]

Evers's brilliant knowledge of the game allowed the Cubs to play a connected, collaborative defense, a defense similar to the one described in George Will's *Men at Work*:

> But imagine taut elastic bands connecting every player behind the pitcher. As the pitcher begins his delivery, every player should impart some slight change in the tension of the band, a change that would radiate through the team. Most of the change would be a slight movement, or leaning, denoting the essence of a defensive play—anticipation.[43]

Evers and Tinker could anticipate, "sometimes through signals, more often through a glance or a nod or sheer intuition," what was going to happen on the field.[44] Evers's success was rooted in his tireless baseball intellect, his resourcefulness and far-reaching knowledge of the game.[45]

THE EVERS–TINKER FEUD

Baseball enthusiasts remember Johnny Evers for more than just his great fielding, determination, braininess, and incessant scolding of umpires. They also recall his hypersensitivity, a defensiveness expressed through both anger and despondency. Baseball scholars are quick to point out that the Johnny Evers of "Tinker to Evers to Chance" fame refused to talk to shortstop Joe Tinker during two of the Cubs' greatest seasons. Reporters and players from the time have generally agreed that the two players of baseball's most renowned keystone combination despised one another. For much of their career as Cubs, whenever team members met, Evers would peer at Tinker with a vicious, glazed look. Beginning in 1905, Evers and Tinker stopped talking to one another off the field, stopping all dialogue until a final reconciliation—30 years later.

What so angered the two? And how could two seemingly compatible fielders even be angry? In *Baseball Magazine*, F. C. Lane describes Evers and Tinker as the "Siamese twins of baseball," because "they play ball as if they were one man, not two."[46] Baseball author Gil Bogen comments that "Evers would make a lightning dash, scoop up a seemingly impossible grounder, and make a throw to second for the start of a double play without looking to see if anyone was there. It was as if he knew Tinker would be there." In turn, Tinker could also snare a sharp grounder and "throw it to second for a lightning double play knowing Evers would be there."[47]

Baseball experts have disputed the source of the friction. In *Baseball*, Geoffrey C. Ward and Ken Burns point to a "dispute over cab fare."[48] David Shiner, in *Deadball Stars of the National League*, discussed a brawl between the two. "One day early in 1905, he threw me a hard ball; it wasn't any farther than from here to there," Evers claimed, pointing to a lamp about 10 feet from where he sat. "It was a real hard ball, like a catcher throwing to second." The throw bent back one of the fingers on Evers's right hand.[49] But Bogen, who has conducted the most in-depth account of the incident, suggests that this mutual loathing found its origins in a combination of factors: the dispute over cab fare; Tinker's anger-laden, close-range throw; and a resulting on-field brawl.[50]

According to Tinker, in September 1905, before an exhibition game in Bedford, Indiana, Evers left the hotel in the only taxi available, leaving Tinker and his teammates behind. Evers's negligence at the hotel probably led to both Tinker's whipping a "hard ball" at Evers and the ensuing fistfight. But after both players were pulled apart, they agreed to a permanent truce, and, according to Tinker, "I said to Evers, 'Now listen: If you and I talk to each other we're only going to be fighting all the time. So don't talk to me, and I won't talk to you. You play your position and I'll play mine, and let it go at that.'" "That suits me," said Evers.[51]

EVERS AROUSES SYMPATHY

While the silent feud with Tinker gained Evers notoriety among baseball fans, his missing nearly an entire baseball season because of a "nervous breakdown" aroused their sympathy. Evers took temporary leave of the majors, not because of his irascibility, but because of profound mental anguish stemming from a severe injury, business bankruptcy, and personal trauma. Toward the end of the 1910 season—the season when Franklin Pierce Adams penned "Tinker to Evers to Chance"—Evers, in a game against Cincinnati, raced home from second base after Sol Hofman's single to center. Evers sprinted down the third-base line, began to slide, and then held up when he noticed the low, poorly thrown ball from center. But as he hesitated, as he cut short his slide, he caught his cleat in the hard ground near the plate and tumbled to his side. Throughout the ballpark, fans heard his lower leg snap. Evers's ankle cracked, and he yelled, "Oh my God, my ankle's all gone to hell," yet he made sure to touch the plate and score.[52]

The break caused Evers to miss the rest of the season, and the Cubs, now without their iron-willed, star second baseman, hobbled into the World Series. After five games against Connie Mack's A's, they fell to defeat. The Cubs missed Evers's fielding and his teamwork with Tinker. The team needed his aggressiveness and, above all, his baseball intelligence, his ability to coach on the field. Heartbroken because he had not played for the Cubs in the World Series, the infielder thought that the injury was so severe that his baseball future stood in jeopardy. Later, only weeks after the break, Evers learned that his career beyond baseball, his investments in a Troy shoe store that he had begun to expand into a "Shoe Emporium" in Chicago, had collapsed. When he limped into Troy on crutches, he found that his former business partner had ripped out key pages of accounting ledgers and fled, leaving Evers with losses of around $25,000, an overwhelming sum in an era when a skilled craftsman earned $1,200 a year and a baseball player $3,000.[53]

Evers, who had thought that the shoe store investment would achieve a "comfortable" life for his family, with or without baseball, now found himself broke, nearly destitute, unable to support his family, and, perhaps, too severely injured to resume his baseball career. He commented, "It is no pleasant thing to find the savings of the best years of your life swept away and yourself in a crippled and uncertain physical condition to face the long climb again, once more penniless and without resources." Evers seemed to suffer from depression, saying, "I won't disguise the fact that that was a dark winter for me."[54]

But Evers began to recover physically and saw hope both in his baseball and financial future. He anticipated a possible financial turnaround, largely because of the generosity of controversial owner Charles W. Murphy, a baseball magnate beloved for his great success—the Cubs' four pennants and two world championships—yet despised for his impetuous verbal attacks on players and managers, brazen defiance of league rules, and insolent treatment of the press. Years earlier, Murphy had blundered through a series of ill-timed, inappropriate statements during the Merkle incident. He once asserted, "We can't supply brains to the New York club's dumb players."[55] Despite a league order, he refused to build a visiting clubhouse at Chicago's West Side Park, and during the 1908 World Series, Murphy, a former reporter himself, consigned the press to the very back row of the grandstand.[56]

In Evers's opinion, Murphy demonstrated rather obvious failings, yet they were failings that were common among baseball owners of the time:

> I am not claiming that Murphy is a saint by any means, but I am saying that many things that Murphy had done for which he has been criticized have been supplicated by every other magnate in the game without that criticism. Murphy has his faults, but so have the rest, and fair play is only fair play.[57]

Murphy showed Evers his beneficent side when he offered Evers encouragement, a fully paid ocean cruise, and the "best contract for the ensuing season" that he had ever sent him.[58] The contract buoyed Evers's hopes during his dark winter. He fought his way back into playing shape. His leg healed markedly in the spring of 1911, and he was soon back at second base.

But five weeks into the season, he faced even greater adversity. On May 20, after a Brooklyn–Chicago rainout, Johnny Evers drove out of Chicago's West Side Park with his brother Joe and two passengers, including his friend, Chicago journalist George McDonald. After colliding with a trolley, the car rolled onto its side. Although Evers and two passengers were spared, McDonald received a crushing blow to his skull and died later that day.[59] Evers, who "felt like a murderer," spiraled downward again, probably reaching a state of clinical depression. "The shock of that sudden death was more than I could stand. I again had a bad case of nervous prostration and was laid up for a very long time," said Evers. He lost interest in baseball and life: "It didn't seem to me that anything mattered." No longer able to play, often suffering from sleeplessness, he acquired a fear of going to the second floor of any building. He once commented, "I don't believe anyone who has never suffered from nervous disorders will understand the moods or action of one who has."[60]

The Cubs provided a support group for the star second baseman. Murphy took Evers on road trips with the team and sat with him in the grandstands. Manager Frank Chance raised his spirits and allowed players to sit with the sleepless Evers well beyond curfew. Chance, notorious for his mental toughness on the field—he did not allow Cubs players to shake hands with opponents—displayed uncommon kindness, gently listening to Evers, cheerily supporting him, and sympathetically guiding him toward rehabilitation. According to Evers, "He sent me away to the mountains. I never did knew who did it, but when I arrived at Troy there was a big automobile waiting for me that took me direct to Camp Totem, where I spent several weeks. I lived out in the open air and went to bed every night at eight o'clock and slept."[61] Evers managed to play a few games toward the end of the 1911 season and was fully recuperated by the following spring.

EVERS'S STAR RISES

In 1912, Evers willed his way to healthiness and performed at a peak level, batting .341 and second in the National League with a .431 on-base percentage.[62] He said, "Then I made up my mind that the only thing I could do under the circumstances was to do my best, and I did. In many ways it was my best season."[63] His season was so strong and his knowledge of the game so profound that at the end of 1912, when the Cubs sought a new manager, Charles Murphy turned to Evers. Murphy needed a new manager because longtime skipper Frank Chance was incapacitated. Deaf in one ear, partially deaf in the other, experiencing violent headaches, and suffering from blood clots in the brain, Chance was in need of brain surgery. A prizefighter in the off-season, and a player who had endured numerous beanings because of his bold crowding of the plate, Chance received his release from Murphy after both sides issued charges in the Chicago newspapers. Murphy, who had once called Chance the "greatest manager in the past quarter century," made public his disappointment as Chance recovered in the hospital, accusing the "Peerless Leader" of having lost control of the team because he had failed to enforce a prohibition clause in the players' contracts. Quick to the defense, Chance labeled Murphy an "ingrate" and a "cheap liar." When the Cubs lost to the White Sox in an end-of-season intercity rivalry, Murphy refused to renew Chance's contract.[64]

After Murphy offered Evers a four-year player-manager contract, Evers reluctantly accepted. Evers admired Chance, who had supported him through championship seasons and personal losses. He did not want to take the position at Chance's expense. Evers, just a year since the pain of bankruptcy, severe injury, and the death of a friend, knew his own fragile state of mind, stating, "At first I did not think I could carry the burden of managing. I thought I would break down under it, and I will not deny that I thought so for the first month or so of my work." When he was certain that Chance would never return to the Cubs, when he saw the opportunity of a $10,000 salary increase, he stood ready to seize the opportunity.[65]

EVERS AND THE PROGRESSIVE ERA

Evers brought to his new position a cast of mind shaped by the Progressive Era. In an era of such Progressive presidents as Theodore Roosevelt, Evers's baseball mind-set reflected one of the basic tenets of the movement: the quest for efficiency. Roosevelt displayed this way of thinking in his conservation policies, rooted not only in his belief in conserving the environment, but also in his faith in "national efficiency." Saving our resources would, he believed, prove to be cost effective.[66] Branch Rickey had exhibited this efficiency-first outlook in his approach to spring training exercises.

The movement toward efficiency manifested itself most prominently in Henry Ford's noteworthy achievement: the assembly line. Ford initiated the assembly line in 1913, at first arranging for his workers to produce magneto coils in a systematic, sequential process. Ford later mass assembled crankcases, camshafts, and then the famous Model Ts. When reporter Julian Street visited Ford Motor's Highland Park factory in 1914, he noted that "there was system—relentless system—terrible 'efficiency.'"[67] It was not simply that Henry Ford had "invented" the assembly line. Ford employees had absorbed the assembly line concept when they had earlier visited slaughterhouses in Chicago, where they had witnessed animals passing through a "disassembly" process. As observers at a Swift meatpacking plant, Ford's employees noted the gruesome yet efficient process by which slaughtered swine moved from station to station, and were transformed from pig into pork.[68] Indeed, industrial efficiency infused the workplace atmosphere of the Progressive Era United States.

About the same time Henry Ford ramped up the assembly-line process in Highland Park, Johnny Evers and Hugh Fullerton published their book, *Touching Second*. Baseball fans from the twenty-first century rarely judge baseball from 100 years ago as "scientific." When they observe photos from 1914, they see players with oversized bats, undersized gloves, and baggy uniforms. Baseball enthusiasts read baseball histories that describe pitchers tossing filthy, worn-out, inaccurate spitballs, and show fans swarming out onto the fields at any moment. The twenty-first-century fan perceives an antiquated Deadball Era.

Yet, in 1910, Evers and Fullerton were convinced that baseball had been evolving for 70 years, reaching a scientific pinnacle so great that the 1910 version of the game was in danger of being reduced to a mechanical science, and that the game might lose its individualistic expression. "The game," they wrote, "is the most highly developed, scientific, and logical form of athletic pastime evolved by man, and the ultimate evolution of the one universal game."[69] Other cultures throughout the world, from the Hottentots to the Australian bushmen, might toss and catch a "spheroid," but inventive Americans had forged the near-perfect game: baseball. If the distance from home to first were 88 feet, players would score constantly; if the distance were 92 feet, few if any runners would score. But 90 feet proved ideal. Evers concludes,

> The game is the only one played which is founded upon exact and scientific lines. The playing field is laid out with such geometrical exactness, and with such close study of the natural speed of foot and power of arm of the human animal, as to give the defensive team an equal chance with the attackers, and to compel both attacker and defender to approach the extreme limit of human speed and agility in every close play.[70]

CONCERNS ABOUT THE MODERN GAME

Echoing the views of entrepreneurs like Henry Ford and such efficiency experts as Frederick Taylor, Evers and Fullerton saw the game progressing toward specialization. In the nineteenth century, they observe, most players entered the game as pitchers and catchers. Then, failing at these two key positions, they might sign on as a third baseman or right fielder.[71] But in the twentieth century, "because baseball is one of the most highly specialized of all trades," players early on sought mastery of a specific set of skills: "A second baseman is as distinct from a shortstop as a paying teller of a bank is from the individual ledgerman. . . . The right fielder may be able to play left field, but not nearly so well as he can his own position."[72] Highly specialized players found their way to the majors because of a modern scouting system. Organized at a national level, and staffed by veteran players and retired owners, the system relied on "dragnet methods."[73] Baseball authorities would inspect and review "league after league and club after club," seeking men like Evers, the former shirt collar factory worker from Upstate New York.[74]

In 1909, as the scouting system mushroomed, and as the number of recruits swelled, the major clubs felt compelled to impose a limit on each team's recruits, and Evers and Fullerton feared that the modern scouting system would bulldoze the old, informal, flexible network. Players would no longer be "discovered"; there would be no serendipitous findings on the baseball fields of Iowa. The new scouting system kept track of all the clubs, of all the players' "habits, dispositions, speed, hitting ability, and intelligence."[75] Now a team could diagnose the strengths and weaknesses of a minor leaguer and, before a player reached the majors, acquire intimate knowledge of his baseball skills. In 1908, Fullerton and Evers noted that when a Braves batter arrived from the minors, the Cubs already knew his "peculiarities, batting habits, and disposition."[76] Before the game, pitchers and coaches reviewed in detail the player's "position at bat, the way he swung at a ball, the kind of ball he could hit, and what he could not, and exactly how he could reach first base."[77]

Evers regarded players as professionals who had successfully passed a "postgraduate course of a moral and physical training," and who played the game in a style radically different from 15 years earlier; however, in 1911, the old informal network still complemented the new system.[78] The Giants' Fred Snodgrass noted that Deadball Era managers had not abandoned the traditional way of scouting: "The way they got young players was by direct observation themselves. Or some friend of the club would tip off John McGraw, or other managers, that here was a likely kid, and they would bring him and look him over."[79]

Analyzing a pitcher's skills was essential. Evers and Fullerton could dissect the action of each pitcher, and, in the manner that Henry Ford broke down the tasks of magneto coil production, they evaluated the "slow ball," the twentieth-century version of the changeup:

> It was discovered that if the ball be held far back in the palm of the hand, with the little finger and on the third finger on one side and the thumb on the other, with the other fingers held so as not to touch the ball at all, the result could be attained.[80]

The pitcher, gripping the ball tightly at the point of release, swinging his arm in full force, could toss a slightly wobbly, nonrotating ball that stopped by air pressure, "obeys the call of gravity, and drops quickly toward the earth after expending its force."[81] And pitching was complicated in 1910. As Bill James and Rob Neyer point out in their 2004 book on pitching, "By 1903, not literally but generally speaking, the pitchers were throwing everything we throw now. The forerunner of every modern pitch was in use somewhere by 1910."[82]

While Evers understood the physics of baseball, he also quite clearly mastered what he called "geometric baseball." Evers and Fullerton had concluded that each ball field held five infield "grooves" and four outfield "grooves." If a batter knocked a ball down this groove or lane, he had a reasonably good chance of earning a hit—only a spectacular play might stop him. Evers knew that there was a seven-and-a-half-foot gap between the first and second basemen, but an eight-and-a-half-foot gap between the shortstop and third baseman, "because the ball goes faster in that direction, and the space between the third baseman's extreme limit of finer reach and the foul line is a foot and a half."[83] Fullerton took highly detailed notes of games, marking grounders with wavy lines—a wave for each time the ball hit the ground—and marking, for instance, if the ball went to the left of the shortstop. It was the early twentieth-century way of videotaping a game. Evers comprehended these calculations, and Fullerton noted his friend's astuteness in the field. The best testimonial to the ability of Johnny Evers, of the Chicago club, to fill these grooves was given on the bench of opposing team last summer: "Hit 'em where they ain't," growled one player to another, who had been thrown out by Evers. "I do, but he is always there," retorted the other.[84]

Scientific baseball players, Evers believed, stood on the shoulders of earlier players: "The modern player has the benefit of the accumulated experience of a dozen baseball generations to study before he even starts to play."[85] But approaching baseball via physics and geometry, the forming of a "scientific pastime" presented dangers to the game: Players might be reduced to industrial automatons, operating in a "machine-like" fashion. Like many in the early twentieth century, Evers and Fullerton feared bureaucratic structures and corporate efficiency. The only salvation rested in the "fighting, aggressive player," the Ty Cobb, or perhaps Evers himself, the "exponents of the unexpected," those who stirred up the others, created new plays, and broke the rules.[86]

In the view of Evers and Fullerton, aggressive individuals exhibited a toughness rarely displayed by the modern, indulged player. Players acted in such a highly pampered style that they could ignore the manager and general rules of society.

> The public does not realize that the manager is dealing with 22 ultra-independent athletes, vulgarly healthy, frankly outspoken, and unawed by any authority or pomp. Only persons who have one child, that possesses four grandparents, twenty or thirty aunts all trying to spoil it, can understand in full the difficulties of the manager's job.[87]

Ballplayers, according to Evers, were mere youths who rose from low wages to comfortable salaries in a matter of weeks. They acted like "grown children" who received unceasing flattery and praise:

> It is no wonder that the major-league players become spoiled. The hotel arrangements are all made for them; their baggage is checked, the train connections, berths, and carriages are all arranged for by the manager or secretary. The player is told when to go, where to go, and how to go, and some players, after years of traveling, are almost as helpless as if they had never been on a train.[88]

Dealing with the players/children of 1910 produced a prematurely gray Cubs manager in Frank Chance, who was "battered, grizzled, careworn, and weary" at the age of 32. The manager as father was "forced to soothe their injured feelings, condole with them in their troubles, cheer them in their blues, and check them in their exuberance."[89]

Evers and Fullerton witnessed a modern baseball game in which players received not only unwarranted praise, but also unparalleled opportunities to enhance their income. By the first decade of the twentieth century, baseball players were earning endorsements for sweaters, socks, razors, and Coca-Cola. The popular beverage earned a label of "wholesomeness" through its endorsement by national idol Christy Mathewson. And players, including Mathewson, enhanced their celebrity status when, during the off-season, they performed on the vaudeville stage. Mathewson, the great American sports hero, performed comedy sketches in 1910, at New York's Hammerstein Theater, clearing $1,000 per week, earnings far greater than his salary of $10,000 per year. And Mathewson's celebrity brought him other income opportunities as well: He wrote a newspaper column during the 1911 World Series; put together a how-to baseball book entitled *Pitching in a Pinch*; authored a play, *The Girl and the Pennant*; endorsed a series of short stories for boys, the "Matty Books"; and even took on a feature role in the 1913 film *Breaking into the Big Leagues*.[90] With players performing as vaudeville actors, movie stars, and authors, Evers and Fullerton saw themselves as part of an era dominated by commercialization.[91]

MANAGING IN 1912

In 1912, Evers faced the challenges of the modern manager. Although he managed with even more ferocity than he played, his passion for the game could not compensate for a below-average Cubs team. A third-place finish that year, despite 91 victories, yielded moderate fan support for a team that had attained first or second place each year from 1906 to 1911, and that had, in 1907 and 1908, claimed World Series victories. As soon as Evers was hired, Joe Tinker, Evers's double-play partner/nemesis, quit; then other Cub weaknesses surfaced. A Chicago reporter assessed Evers's Cubs: "His pitching staff is a wreck. He has only one good catcher. His outfield needs rejuvenation. All in all, Johnny has taken on an enviable task, but we wish him well."[92]

Evers fared better at complaining than leading. As a first-time manager, the anxious, combative adversary of major league umpires sometimes failed to effectively command his charges. A reporter from the *Chicago Gazette* pointed out that Evers was following a great managerial act, and "All this works on the mind of Evers, who even as a player was high-strung and sensitive. With the added responsibilities, he is irritable, nervous, and lacking in patience . . . nature did not endow him with the disposition of a natural leader, hence his tendency to crab."[93] Umpires reacted to Evers's irritability and tossed him out with regularity. Murphy offered him a new suit if he could avoid an ejection for two weeks, and at one point, Evers behaved appropriately, earning the suit; yet, umpires ejected him a day after the two-week time limit had lapsed. In 1913, Evers's edginess contributed to a third-place, 88–63 record. Another third-place finish, despite a strong last six weeks, proved inadequate for Murphy, and when the Cubs failed to defeat the White Sox in Chicago's all-important intercity series, Murphy fired the hot-headed leader.[94]

Evers's dismissal and Murphy's apparent breaking of a questionably worded contract provoked reactions throughout the National League. National League owners judged Murphy as an outrageous, out-of-control owner who might push one of the brightest stars out of the league. A few American businessmen, seeking a piece of the baseball industry, had begun in the fall of 1913 to organize the Federal League. Magnates from the new league set their sights on National League and American League players who felt shackled by baseball's reserve clause, a contractual arrangement that allowed owners to secure a player on a team in perpetuity.[95]

Evers, like other major leaguers, was tempted by a lucrative Federal League contract: five years at $15,000 a year and a $30,000 signing bonus. The upstart league had already secured contracts from minor leaguers, semi-pro players, and major leaguers who were past their prime. American League and National League executives feared that the Federal League's higher salaries and reserve clause–free contracts would appeal to major-league players. Owners wanted to block the flow of star players to the new league and offered huge salary increases to such players as Ty Cobb, Eddie Collins, Tris Speaker, and Christy Mathewson.[96] But Evers's case was peculiar: His dismissal from the Cubs, compounded by a botched trade attempt by Murphy, allowed him to become, in many respects, baseball's first free-agent star. A Federal League official tantalized Evers, depositing thousands of dollars of hard cash in front of him at New York's Knickerbocker Hotel. Evers resisted the temptation, envisioning himself as a well-paid National Leaguer, and offered himself to the Boston Braves for bonuses, incentives, and $25,000.[97]

Few players in baseball history have experienced frequent, dramatic changes like Evers. After rising up from a low-paying, blue-collar job to stardom, pennants, and World Series championships, in 1910, his career plummeted. He suffered bankruptcy; a severe, nearly career-ending physical injury; and then, despondency. On the verge of a complete comeback, he drove his car into a trolley, leading to the death of his friend and a second experience of profound sorrow. Dropping out of baseball as he faced psychological depression for a second time, he pulled through, rising once again to become a successful player-manager, only to be unceremoniously fired after one and a half seasons. Then, beginning in 1914, he serendipitously found himself—even in the era of tight-fisted, reserve clause–supporting owners—as baseball's only free agent. When the Braves offered him $25,000, he knew he could bring stability to his career. Married since 1908, and the father of two small children, Evers seized the chance to rebuild his life.[98]

BOSTON

When Evers reached Boston, he arrived in a city exploding with change. Bostonians had constructed dams, drained marshes, and filled in bays. They had built striking buildings: a Renaissance-style symphony hall (1900); a Greek Revival museum of fine arts (1909); and the modern concrete and steel Fenway Park (1912). They were absorbing thousands of immigrants from Southern Europe and Eastern Europe. The city's population of 670,000 exceeded by 50,000 the population nearly 100 years later, in 2010. And these new immigrants altered a social fabric that had only recently been transformed by Irish immigrants.[99] The Irish had exited their homeland in mass numbers—37,000 in 1847—because of the potato famine and had migrated to cities in the northern United States. They had settled in East Boston, cleaning yards, mopping up stables, and loading ships as they barely survived in the wooden shacks of Boston's cholera-infested slums.[100] The landlords of these ramshackle dwellings, the Oldcomer Bostonians, the Puritan and Pilgrim descendants, adapted slowly and reluctantly to the newcomers, Irish Catholic laborers who, according to Noel Ignatiev in his brilliant book *How the Irish Became White*, struggled fiercely to achieve acceptance.[101]

During the Civil War, Boston's Irish gained respectability by fighting in the Union army—sometimes as substitute conscripts—and then laboring in armories, factories, and shipyards. After the war, they built such municipal buildings as City Hospital and hauled gravel to fill in Back Bay. Some Irish immigrants found jobs that provided subsistence beyond their wages back home in Ireland, but few found opportunities to move to the top rung of the economic ladder, occupied by bankers and corporate board members who belonged to Boston's Anglo-Saxon elite.

By the 1870s, the Irish had found an alternate way upward, and they successfully channeled their energies into politics. Local businessmen—grocers, saloon owners, and funeral directors—who served a wide variety of customers, might achieve political office and serve as a ward "boss," providing services to Irish American families in return for their votes. The boss might provide assistance to a family low on coal or find a job for a newcomer, all within the political machine: "Once a local boss took over, his ward was divided into precincts, each with a captain in charge. Each captain supervised perhaps a dozen lieutenants who, in turn, supervised workers assigned to specific streets." Citizens then upheld their end of the bargain on voting day. If the machine ran smoothly, an effective boss could turn out the electorate with "machine-like precision."[102]

In Boston's West End, Martin Lomasney, "The Mahatma," emerged in the 1880s as a powerful political boss, so revered that, according to Doris Kearns Goodwin, West Enders revered him as a "god." Lomasney succinctly phrased his theory of politics, saying, "The great mass of people are interested in only three things—food, clothing, and shelter. A politician in a district such as mine sees to it that his people get these things. If he does, then he doesn't have to worry about their loyalty."[103] In the North End, when the local ward boss died, he was replaced by the bright, active, 29-year-old son of Irish immigrants: John F. Fitzgerald. Across the harbor in the East End, a 30-year-old owner of a liquor importing business, Patrick J. Kennedy, ruled as political boss.[104]

At the turn of the twentieth century, the traditional rulers of Boston, Yankee Protestants, not only witnessed the Irish Catholics acquiring political power, they also observed new waves of immigrants from Southern Europe and Eastern Europe, with cultures sharply different from Anglo-Saxon Protestantism, and with languages and traditions that appeared much more difficult to assimilate with than that of the Irish. Massachusetts experienced a transformation in the first decade of the century, when nearly 150,000 Italians, 80,000 Poles, and 25,000 Lithuanians entered the state, settling in urban areas. Overwhelmed by massive droughts in southern Italy, while attracted by American businesses that offered industrial jobs, Italians settled eastern U.S. cities; in Boston, they headed toward the North End and East Boston neighborhoods. Working at construction sites, at granite quarries on the railroads, or in the neighborhoods as cobblers, leather workers, or grocery owners, Italians formed their own institutions, including social clubs, benevolent societies, and churches. At church, they solemnly honored the feast of the Madonna delle Grazie, and they colorfully celebrated festivals in honor of St. Rocco, St. Joseph, and St. Anthony.[105]

EVERS ARRIVES IN BOSTON

Evers would open the season at South End Grounds, a ballpark in close proximity to Boston's Anglo and Irish residents. South End Grounds stood in industrial Boston, across from the New York, New Haven, and Hartford Railroad grounds. Smoke poured out of the nearby rail yards. The Hartford Railroad ran parallel to the third-base line, a roundhouse stood just beyond the outfield seats, and large warehouses bordered the park. The facility stood directly across from the Huntington Grounds, home of the Red Sox until 1912. Roxbury's Irish could walk to the park, while other Bostonians could travel to South End Grounds via electric trolley. The South End Park, in its nineteenth-century form, loomed as a "fairytale, with covered viewing stands, turrets, and intricate ornamentation," but after it burnt to the ground in 1894, ball club owner Arthur Soden, who was underinsured, recovered insufficient funds; he was unable to rebuild the park to its legendary, Camelot-like status. Also known as the Walpole Street Grounds, the aging, rickety South End Park, rebuilt three times and now in its final phase, held about 11,000 spectators.[106]

The city of Boston celebrated the acquisition of Evers, who many felt might be able to lead the Braves back up in the division standings, at least to a point of respectability. Baseball observers like John McGraw anticipated that Evers would guide a solid group of younger players to an improved record. Evers, anointed captain by Braves manager George Stallings, was a ripe 32 years old. Most of the team ranged from 20 to 25 years of age. In early May, the Boston fans arranged a welcoming game for Evers. Fans in the Deadball Era often set up gift-bearing events for their stars during pregame ceremonies. The *Boston Globe* announced a Johnny Evers welcoming tribute. In the spring of 1914, John F. "Honey Fitz" Fitzgerald, who had left the mayor's post a few months earlier, encouraged Boston fans, in particular the Royal Rooters, to show up at the South End Grounds on Tuesday, May 5. Fitzgerald called upon Boston fans to "give a welcome to Johnny Evers that will make the little fellow feel that we all appreciate his skills as a ballplayer and the traits that mark him a gentleman."[107] Yet, Boston fans never found the opportunity to greet their new player. A driving New England rain caused the game to be postponed, and the Braves soon left on a four-week road trip.

EARLY OPTIMISM DIMS

Despite the optimism generated by the arrival of Evers, the Braves' first few games provided fans with few reasons for hope. When the Braves inaugurated the season on April 14, at Ebbets Field, in Brooklyn, they suffered misfortune. On Opening Day, Braves shortstop Walter "Rabbit" Maranville left the team to attend to his ill brother, and third baseman Charlie Deal strained a ligament in his leg, only to be replaced by the sore-armed Oscar Dugey, whose cheery outlook masked his frailty: "My arm is not very good, but I will try to get them over somehow."[108] But neither Dugey nor his teammates could stop the Brooklyn team, a sixth-place finisher in 1913. The first four batters in the Braves' lineup could not hit safely all day, and the Braves surrendered, 8–2. Manager Stallings could offer "no alibis for defeat," but he suggested to reporters that his players lacked experience, saying that on his "kid team . . . barring Evers, not a player was more than 25."[109]

In the second game, the Braves demonstrated a model for incompetence: Evers popped up with the bases loaded, eliminating the team's one chance to score. A *Boston Globe* writer concluded, "In a nutshell, the Braves did not bat, they did not field, they did not throw well, and the pitching of Mr. Rudolph of the Bronx was weak at critical stages of the conflict." The Braves lost, 5–0.[110]

The Braves failed repeatedly, losing their third consecutive game to the Philadelphia Phillies. Finding new ways to lose, the Braves transformed well-hit balls into a series of "good outs." In the third game of the season, the Braves' batters made contact with the ball, but as a *Boston Globe* reporter noted, "usually straight into the hands of some waiting fielder." Unable to hit the ball safely off of the Phillies' Cy Marshall, players blasted the ball, "sailing at either an infielder or a man in the outer works with the precision of a bullet from a sharpshooter's rifle." Braves pitcher Hub Perdue, for whom the team held high expectations, held Philadelphia to one run in the first inning, but he met his undoing in an unexpected manner—through his success as a batter. With two out and outfielder Larry Gilbert on first and catcher Hank Gowdy on second, Perdue, normally a weak hitter, smashed a ball into left-center field, scoring both runners. But Perdue loped into third base, worn out and gasping for air. Maranville followed Perdue to the plate, and on the very next pitch, he grounded out to short. Perdue's "laborious dash around the bases" proved costly, and in the next inning, "When he walked out to the middle of the diamond, he was puffing and panting and seemed tired out." He lost command of his pitches, and the Phillies soon "batted his offerings around without mercy."[111]

FACING THE ORIOLES' RUTH

After losing to the Phillies and two earlier games to the Brooklyn Robins (later the Dodgers), a team that had endured 10 straight losing seasons, the Braves next went down to defeat to the minor league Baltimore Orioles. On April 19, the Orioles, members of the International League, played the Braves in an exhibition game, and for the first three innings, the Orioles sent up their new pitching "recruit," George Herman Ruth. The veteran Orioles players had, only weeks earlier, christened the talented pitcher "Babe" because of his immature, innocent-looking demeanor. Babe had signed his first contract in the winter of 1914, with Orioles owner-manager Jack Dunn. Dunn earned money as an owner by acquiring young talent like Ruth, showcasing him, and then selling him to the highest bidder. Ruth, who had pitched well against teams that included the Philadelphia Athletics during spring training, once again showed off his talent. He struck out two, walked two, and allowed two runs, contributing to the minor league Orioles' 3–2 defeat of the Braves.[112]

During the exhibition game against the Orioles and five road games against the Phillies and Dodgers, the last-place, 1–4 Braves could not muster an offense. Despite hitting the ball smartly during spring training, in the first five regular-season games, the Braves batted .216, collecting only 36 hits in 167 at bats. They scored 10 runs to their opponents' 24.[113] Trying to "open their batting eyes a little wider," the Braves returned to the South End Grounds of Boston and took extra batting practice during the morning before the April 24 home opener. Yet, their pathetic batting continued. They suffered a 1–8 defeat in the opener, and after an April 25, 0–4 loss to Brooklyn, a *Boston Globe* reporter lamented:

> They did not hit a lick yesterday, nor have they been hitting since the session opened—and not very consistently previous to that. One hit, when it was needed in four of the six games that have been lost so far, would undoubtedly have meant just the difference between a defeat and a victory for the team. But the Braves failed to produce the hit, and hence their record stands six games lost and two won.[114]

Despite the Braves' unrelenting misfortune, Braves' reporters kept an upbeat frame of mind. Boston writer Melville Webb Jr., widely recognized for his in-depth knowledge of sports—especially Harvard football—surmised that the Braves would raise themselves out of the cellar. The team, he commented, "is not likely to stay there long if Stallings has drawn the right bead on the caliber of his outfit."[115]

OUTFIELDERS CAN'T HIT; PITCHERS CAN'T THROW

The Braves faced challenges on every front, and players, especially the outfielders, continued their wretched hitting. Giants manager John McGraw, who wrote a regular column on the National League, saw the Braves' "outfield as the weakest department, none of the trio being able to come through with wallops." Stallings, he notes, was "turning things upside down" to find new outfielders. Joe Connolly was batting .259, but center fielder Leslie Mann was batting .147 and right fielder Tommy Griffith .106. Wilson Collins, a part-time center fielder who played seven games, had an average of .222. When the outfielders' batting averages began to heat up, the team improved just marginally, and by the end of May, after 26 games, the team batting rested at .225, with an average of three runs per game (significantly less than the 3.44 Deadball Era averages). By June, McGraw judged the Braves to be a nonfactor in the pennant race.[116]

The Braves pitchers did not atone for the wretchedness of the team's hitters. On May 1, the Braves dropped to 2–8 after falling to the Giants, 11–2. This time feeble hitting was complemented by Dick Crutcher's pathetic pitching. "Stallings started with Crutcher in the box, and the first four men to face the Boston pitcher delivered two doubles and two singles. George 'Lefty' Tyler took over in the third, only to fare worse."[117] The following day, the Phillies visited Boston and won, 6–2, hitting three homers and four doubles against the Braves, even making two homers back-to-back in the first inning off Hub Perdue.[118] The home run totals in these games were staggering for 1914. The champion Cubs hit a total of 12 home runs in 1908; in the Deadball Era, Frank "Home Run" Baker led the American League in homers four times, with 12 home runs as his best in any season.[119]

And even when the Braves pitched well and limited another team's sluggers, they panicked, lost confidence, and tossed that one pitch that brought on defeat. On May 9, Lefty Tyler pitched brilliantly against the Giants, holding them to no runs for six innings, but in the seventh, with two out and the bases loaded, Tyler turned "peevish" and "exasperated" when umpire Cy Rigler called close pitches "balls." Losing his composure, his control, and "his former speed and accuracy," Tyler got knocked out of the box with a two-run, game-winning double by the Giants' John "Chief" Meyers.[120]

The level of pitching spiraled downward in part because of the Braves' inept fielding. Against Brooklyn two weeks into the season, the Braves' best fielder, Rabbit Maranville, mishandled a crucial although easy ground ball. With the bases loaded in the sixth, Maranville, probably distracted by Jake Daubert running from second to third, let a ball pass between his legs into left field, allowing two runs.[121]

NEAR WINS

On May 7, against the Giants, the Braves seemed close to victory, with a lead in the eighth, but they fumbled away the game when Maranville stabbed a hot grounder from Giants outfielder George Burns but stumbled. Burns reached first safely, and Red Murray crossed the plate with the tying run. A *Boston Globe* reporter described the next crucial blunder in the field, using imaginative language typical of 1914 sportswriters:

> But that was not all of the misfortunes of the Braves. [Art] Fletcher hit a low liner to center and [Leslie] Mann came galloping in to intercept the leather. He prepared to take the ball on the short bound and hold the runners on their bases. But Mann did not make allowances for the perversity of the flying baseball. He set his lunch-hooks south-southeast-half-south, and the depraved ball bounded west-southwest-half-west, eluding his grapplers by seven inches. The ball rolled to the fence in center. Mr. Fletcher rolled to third, and Mr. Burns rolled home with the winning run.[122]

The reporter also noted with metaphorical humor how the Braves could put themselves in such a humiliating position: "But just when it appeared that victory was about to drop like a ripe peach into the laps of the Braves, the frost of defeat withered the fruit, and the Gaffneyites found themselves still more firmly anchored in the subterranean recesses."[123]

Writers often used Native American terms for a team named the Braves: A defeat on May 8 earned a clever, but derogatory, remark: "Implacable fate, leering malevolently at the hapless Braves again buffeted them and sent them hapless to their teepees today. . . . Fate, the conscienceless jade, has apparently selected the seventh and eighth innings in which to humiliate and discourage the tribe of Stallings."[124]

Twenty-nine games into the season, John McGraw, in one of his weekly commentaries on National League teams, seemed perplexed by Boston's poor showing. He had met with Stallings, a "good friend of [his]," after a couple of Giants games and noted that Stallings was "all broken up," yet "not discouraged." Stallings declared mournfully, "I haven't been getting any pitching or any hitting. You can't win ball games when the other teams are making a million runs off your pitching and your players are not hitting a lick." McGraw saw in the Braves a team that could make the "National League strong in the Hub [that] year," because it was "fundamentally a much better club than Stallings finished with in fifth place last season." Stallings remained optimistic even after the Giants swept a recent series, saying, "We will finish better than we did last season. That club of mine is bound to get going."[125]

In early May, a *New York Times* reporter could write about the last-place Braves with total arrogance. The *Times* pointed out in a wry, acidly worded commentary that the Braves had no chance against a team like the Giants: "The New York Giants do not mind Brooklyn winning a game once in a while at the Polo Grounds, but when the Boston Braves assume that they can do the same thing, it is not only presumptuous but decidedly very bold." On May 7, the Braves, "without a word of warning, became very selfish and piled up a big lead." But the Giants, down 6–3 in the eighth, scored on Crutcher and Rudolph, administering a "smart lashing," a 7–6 New York victory. The *Times* concluded that the Braves had resumed their appropriate, subservient position: "Hereafter perhaps the Braves will behave themselves."[126]

Even the lowly Brooklyn Robins, a team that, according to the *Boston Globe*, "had been pummeled by every team in the Western circuit and had returned to Flatbush only to be used as doormats by the Giants," even this Brooklyn team, offered a stiff challenge to the Braves.[127] On June 1, after the Robins (called Dodgers or Trolley Dodgers by fans) had defeated the Braves, 6–2 and 4–2, the *New York Times* wrote about how the Dodgers' manager must feel: "Wilbert Robinson's ideas of success and pleasure, no doubt, is an endless succession of doubleheaders between the Dodgers and George Stall-ings's Braves." The Brooklyn Dodgers might lose to the Giants, but at least they could pass along the "humiliation they had suffered" to the Braves.[128] On June 2, the Braves played the Dodgers in a second doubleheader, and Brooklyn fans "saw Boston win a game, which is something to brag about: The first game of yesterday's doubleheader is the eleventh game the Boston team has won this year, and is naturally something of an epoch in the season for them."[129]

EVERS BANISHED

The Boston team found new ways of falling to defeat, and Evers created new antics that produced frequent ejections. In a May 26 away game against the St. Louis Cardinals, Evers began disputing ball and strike calls with his um-pire nemesis, Cy Rigler. In the third inning, Evers, according to the *Boston Globe*, "slipped him the endearing term of 'fathead,' and afterward besieged Rigler to know why he was being banished."[130] Three weeks later, in a home game against the Cardinals, Evers released his furies even more dramati-cally when confronting umpire Mal Eason. In the eighth inning, the Braves were leading, 3–2, when left fielder "Cozy" Dolan led off with a single to right and, on the next pitch, tried to steal second. Bert Whaling, the Braves' backup catcher, fired to Evers at second, who blocked the base with his wiry 125-pound frame, tagged Dolan, and then circled around the base with a heavy limp. When umpire Eason pronounced Dolan safe, Evers complained furiously, noting that Dolan's spike had cut through the sole of his shoe, bruising his foot. For Evers, the slashed shoe and bruised foot provided absolute and undeniable proof that he had stood between Dolan and the bag. The "Little Trojan" took off his shoe, pointed to the bruise, and then waved the shoe in Eason's face. Eason looked away from Evers and admonished him to just keep playing and "hurry up." "I won't hurry up," retorted Evers, "I have been spiked." Eason then tossed the defiant second baseman from the game, who, according to reporter J. C. O'Leary, "did not hurry up about it."[131]

Evers's feistiness signified the state of the Braves. Despite pathetic fielding, pitching, and hitting, and although they lost close games, strange games that seemed winnable, *Boston Globe* reporters wrote of the team's "gameness." The Braves' gameness offered Stallings a glimpse of hope. On May 4, the Phillies banged 15 hits for 10 runs against the Braves. Pitcher Dick Rudolph, although beaten, stood tall: "He was pounded to a pulp and was wild as a hawk, but he never lost his head, so came off with flying colors." Rudolph pitched high and inside to the Phillies, provoking accusations of attempted "beanings," but Rudolph earned the accolade "'game' pitcher," a description that he and other Braves received throughout the year. "Game" suggested a combination of toughness and persistence; it implied a high-spirited, determined outlook. Despite the unceasing losses, writers for the *Boston Globe* tried to be positive. When, on May 19, the umpire lost track of the count at a crucial moment in the eighth inning, helping the Braves lose to the Pirates, and dropping their record to 4–18, the paper reported that the "Braves were earnestly in the game from start to finish."[132]

In the midst of their misery, the Braves more than likely underestimated a talent who might have put them on the right track. On May 20, struggling to find game-winning pitching, Stallings turned to Adolfo Luque, a Cuban, the first Latin American pitcher to achieve success in the major leagues in the years before World War II. Luque had pitched for the Braves in the preseason and was now being asked to pitch against the Pittsburgh Pirates. With the advantage of hindsight it is easy to see how the Braves misjudged a great talent. Luque pitched into the ninth for a five-hitter against the Pirates but lost, 4–1, largely because of the defensive ineptness: Rabbit Maranville, the Braves' star infielder, committed four errors.[133] In 1914, Luque would return to the International League, and the "Pride of Havana" would later earn nearly 200 victories in the majors, including a Giants' victory in the 1933 World Series.[134]

The Braves' ineptitude continued, and the team fell further in the standings. On May 26, second baseman Miller Huggins of St. Louis employed the rarely used "hidden ball trick" as another maneuver to help defeat the Braves. In the seventh inning, with outfielder Jim Murray on first base, Boston's Jack Martin hit a grounder to Huggins at second and reached first on a fielder's choice. Huggins casually hung on to the ball, not returning it to the pitcher and simply tucking it under his arm. He had spotted an inattentive Martin.

As soon as Martin took a lead off first, Huggins tossed it to first baseman "Dots" Miller for an out. Martin's mental lapse arrived at a pivotal moment in the game and stifled a Braves attempt to rally: They lost again, 4–2.[135] On May 29, the Braves outhit the Phillies, 8–3, but lost, 3–1. Bill James issued walks that allowed Philadelphia base runners to score. The Braves put men into scoring position and then failed to drive them home.[136] The Braves clearly understood all manners of losing.

EARLY JUNE

By June 1, the team record stood at 10–24, a .294 winning percentage (see table 2.1). With 119 games to play, the odds of the Braves reaching the World Series rested at an astonishing 10,000 to 1. No team before 1914 (and no team since) had ever overcome such probabilities.[137] Because of eight rainouts in early spring, five of them in Boston, the team was forced to play doubleheaders on May 30, June 1, and June 2. The Braves lost four out of six games. The first week of June, when they finished 2–6, only compounded their misery. Then the Braves saw progress.

In the next few weeks of June, they took series from the Cubs and Pirates, and they played even with the Cardinals and Giants, but they faltered in the last week of June, stumbling at 3–4 and then falling into a five-game losing streak.[138] On July 4, the Braves hit another low point, losing to the Brooklyn Robins (Dodgers), 7–5, in an 11-inning game, and then 4–3 after having gained a 3–0 lead in the first inning. Both games, near victories for the Braves, proved especially painful. In the first game, the Braves rallied in the ninth, earning three runs to tie the score—yet they fell to defeat in extra innings. In the second game, the Dodgers scored the winning run in the ninth because of a series of Braves' mishaps. The Dodgers' first baseman, Jake Daubert, reached first and stole second, but the Braves' catcher, Hank Gowdy, overthrew second, sending the ball into center. Braves center fielder Josh Devore muffed the ball, and Daubert sprinted toward home. Devore fired a bullet to Gowdy, who, in a brutal collision with Daubert—the runner was knocked unconscious—dropped the ball.[139]

On July 5, Evers and the Braves stood 15 games behind the Giants; the odds of coming back to playoff contention remained close to impossible. Evers had faced agonizing trials before: a career-threatening injury, loss of his personal fortune, his firing as manager, and the death of a friend. He had climbed up from the depths of personal sorrow. And just when he seemed on the rebound—a lucrative new contract with a promising team whose fans had embraced him—Evers, who had played on 11-straight winning Chicago Cubs teams, found himself in baseball hell.

Table 2.1. National League Standings at the Close of Play, June 1, 1914

Team	Games	Wins	Losses	Ties	Winning Percentage	Games Behind	Runs Scored	Runs Allowed
New York Giants	33	22	11	0	0.667	—	158	127
Cincinnati Reds	42	26	15	1	0.634	—	181	127
Pittsburgh Pirates	38	21	15	2	0.583	2.5	143	112
Brooklyn Robins	34	16	18	0	0.471	6.5	129	144
Chicago Cubs	43	19	22	2	0.463	7.0	159	166
St. Louis Cardinals	45	19	24	2	0.442	8.0	150	164
Philadelphia Phillies	34	15	19	0	0.441	7.5	139	171
Boston Braves	35	10	24	1	0.294	12.5	96	144

Source: http://www.retrosheet.org.

· 3 ·

The Rabbit Springs Forward

$\mathcal{F}$or a team that seemed to be on the upswing in 1913, for a team that left spring training with a future brighter than most, and for a team for which baseball authorities had predicted inevitable success, the first two months of the season proved especially painful. Yet, statements from the time show that the Braves' leaders, manager George Stallings and captain Johnny Evers, remained resolute, enduring criticism from the media and resisting any attempts by teammates to blame one another. It was especially challenging to stay positive because the deficits of April and May were so massive that even when the Braves strung together a few victories, as they did in June, they still lingered in last place.

Walter "Rabbit" Maranville later recalled the first major road trip in May: "The impression we left was very bad considering we were a big-league ball club." After the first western trip, the press labeled them "misfits, country buttered ball tossers, and what not"; however, throughout the losing, Stallings continued to reassure them, saying, "Stick in there; we will show them."[1] The Braves began June playing as they had all spring, dropping six of their first eight games, but they won five in a row, beating Cincinnati and Pittsburgh and earning a 16–13 record for the month. The team then plummeted again, losing the first five games in July, and at that point, few baseball fans predicted success.[2]

UNCOOPERATIVE WEATHER

Rainy, cold weather had compounded the Braves' miseries throughout the spring: They rescheduled eight rained out games, and even in July, the New

England cold chipped away at what might have been a pleasant summer baseball experience. *Boston Globe* reporter J. C. O'Leary suffered through a bleak July 1 doubleheader against the Philadelphia Phillies:

> The low temperature was accentuated by the east wind, which blew at half a gale, and there was nothing in the work of the Braves to distract one's mind from the fact that it was a cold day. . . . Sitting through a doubleheader in such weather as yesterday is no pastime, but doing it and at the same time seeing both games is a positive hardship.[3]

For O'Leary, the only solace for both the Braves' disappointing play and the wretched weather was the games' remarkable brevity. Baseball games in the early twenty-first century can consume nearly three hours. In the Deadball Era—minus TV advertisements, frequent pitching changes, and batters tugging at their baseball gloves between pitches—games lasted two hours or less.[4] The first game of the doubleheader, O'Leary noted, took less time than any all season—one hour and 45 minutes. The second game flashed through baseball history in even less time—one hour and 35 minutes. Fans shivered through two losses: 7–2 and 5–0. "It was so cold," O'Leary wrote, "that the players had to hustle or freeze."[5]

Back in May—despite the losing and the cold—Stallings proclaimed, "Give me another month and we'll be in first place." Journalists in earshot coughed politely and then discussed whether such ranting deserved print.[6] The Braves' manager had forecast his team's prospects with dreadful inaccuracy: The Braves had performed miserably. Stallings undoubtedly offered these wild predictions because of his unyielding, hard-as-granite temperament. "Stallings never gave up," wrote Braves historian Harold Kaese. "He raved and raged like a maniac sliding up and down the bench, bouncing his nervous foot furiously and fining his players recklessly. He insisted that the Braves follow one principle, 'Players had to show up at the park every day in condition to play.'"[7] Kaese observed that Stallings remained hopeful. The Braves historian noted "The Braves lost games but they never lost the spirit of winning.[8] This principle meant that whether the Braves suffered a close loss or near annihilation, Stallings still demanded that his team members perform to the best of their abilities on every play. Perhaps it was his intuitive understanding of ideas rooted in baseball statistics: concepts like good players will eventually produce good averages on both defense and offense; good pitchers will ultimately earn victories; and, yes, a good team will inevitably win. Stallings's on-the-field commander, Johnny Evers, also pushed relentlessly forward. Evers continued to prod the team nervously and incessantly, "saucing them on the field." Evers and Stallings relentlessly scolded the young Braves players, in part because the two leaders still believed that their players would ultimately fall under the influence of baseball karma. As Stallings noted,

"I've never seen such luck. But don't think we're a tail-end team. It will take us a month to get back in shape, but then we're going to be hard to beat."[9]

SUMMER DOLDRUMS

On consecutive days, June 30 and July 1, the Braves lost three out of four, including a doubleheader to the Phillies. They lost a single game to the Brooklyn Robins on July 3, and a doubleheader to Brooklyn on July 4.[10] July 4 was a typical day for the Braves. Maranville made two errors in the first game and three in the second. "There were costly fumbles, bases on balls, wild pitches, and hit batsmen galore, and the work of the Braves on the bases was the poorest the Braves players have ever shown."[11] Boston's National League team served as vulnerable prey for its opponents.

On July 4, starter Bill James allowed 17 Brooklyn hits in the first game. Despite the barrage of Robins hits (the Robins were later rechristened the Brooklyn Dodgers), Boston, down only 4–1 in the ninth, tied the score, but the team lost in ways characteristic of the Braves: James was picked off first base, and the newly acquired George "Possum" Whitted made an error in the bottom of the ninth.[12] The day before the Braves lost in typical fashion, with pitchers Dick Crutcher and Paul Strand giving up six runs. The Braves, down three runs in the seventh, battled back only to come up short. Yet, they remained feisty as ever. Joe Connolly and coach Fred Mitchell were tossed out of the first July 4th game, and in the second game after "Lefty" Tyler hit (accidentally, according to reports) shortstop Ollie O'Mara in the back of the neck, both teams swarmed onto the field. Evers, eventually shoved away from the action, and Brooklyn's Kid Elberfield were sent to the bench.[13] Still, the Braves lost three out of five to the mediocre (31–35) Brooklyn team. After clambering up the standings in June, the Braves now appeared as a permanent fixture in the National League basement (see table 3.1).

The dim view from the basement only darkened, when, on July 7, the Braves left Brooklyn and took the rails westward to Chicago, stopping at Buffalo to play an exhibition game against the minor league Buffalo Bisons. Major-league teams, filling every possible date on the schedule, added minor-league games on their "off" days. Professional teams played these games to broaden their fan base and for another source of revenue. Even though they played regulars, including Johnny Evers and Hank Gowdy, the Braves experienced the definitive humiliation: a 10–2 thrashing.[14] This one game intensified the profound, interminable misery of the Boston Braves. The Braves had suffered losing seasons for 14 years. Now, in July, after losing three out of five to lowly Brooklyn, they languished

Table 3.1. National League Standings at the Close of Play, July 4, 1914

Team	Games	Wins	Losses	Ties	Winning Percentage	Games Behind	Runs Scored	Runs Allowed
New York Giants	64	40	24	0	0.625	—	303	249
Chicago Cubs	73	39	32	2	0.549	4.5	310	295
St. Louis Cardinals	74	37	35	2	0.514	7.0	274	261
Cincinnati Reds	71	34	36	1	0.486	9.0	266	265
Brooklyn Robins	64	31	33	0	0.484	9.0	256	270
Pittsburgh Pirates	67	31	34	2	0.477	9.5	216	223
Philadelphia Phillies	64	30	34	0	0.469	10.0	284	301
Boston Braves	67	26	40	1	0.394	15.0	238	283

Source: http://www.retrosheet.org.

in last place, 15 games behind the first-place Giants. The Buffalo game brought unacceptable shame and degradation to last-place Boston. Two Braves pitchers, Gene Cocreham and the usually solid Paul Strand (2.44 ERA in 1914) allowed the Bisons 11 hits, and the Braves, who fumbled the ball away three times, faced John Verbout, a career minor-league pitcher. They mustered only three hits.[15] Years later, Hank Gowdy remembered the game as the turning point in the season, a loss so painful that it intensified the unyielding, combative spirit of the Braves.[16] Evers later claimed that, although with some exaggeration, "We lost to a soap-company team. That's how bad we were."[17]

About the time that the Braves staggered into baseball hell, their counterparts across town, the Boston Red Sox, were fighting for the pennant. They sought to bolster their chances by adding to their roster a boyish-looking young talent: Babe Ruth. The Braves rarely measured up to the corresponding American League team, inhabitants of the magnificent iron and concrete Fenway Park. By July 4, the Red Sox, who had faced the same severe weather as the Braves, looked strong, with a 39–33 record. Up until this point in the season, and up until July 9, 1914, the Boston Red Sox baseball club had achieved the highest levels of success. The Red Sox burst into the twentieth century with the winningest pitcher of all time (511 games), a pitcher who had already won 286 games before his 192 as a Red Sox: Cy Young. They had also acquired Tris Speaker in 1907. Speaker, one of the greatest batters of all time, who averaged .337 in his nine years as a Red Sox (.345 lifetime), executed breathtaking catches in center field that made Boston fans swoon. In 1911, the Red Sox signed the great fireballer, "Smoky Joe" Wood, who won 34 games in 1912. The Red Sox (whose team names "The Americans" and then "The Pilgrims" graced the Boston American League uniforms until 1906) had earned three pennant-winning seasons: 1903, 1904, and 1912. In the first World Series in 1903, the Boston Americans defeated the Pittsburgh Pirates in eight games. In 1912, the Red Sox eliminated the John McGraw–led Giants in seven games.[18] By 1914, the Red Sox strutted onto the baseball stage as a proud, proven franchise.

CY, TRIS, AND "SMOKY JOE"

In 1901, Denton "Cy" Young, who, as a young pitcher, blew fastballs by batters in the manner of a cyclone, joined the Boston Americans. Young, reputed to be a reserved country boy, once rushed into the stands to challenge a heckler who had questioned his tenacity. In 1900, Frank Robison, the owner of his previous team, the St. Louis Browns, had questioned his skills and announced that after 11 years and 286 victories, Young "was all washed up." When he signed with Boston, Young appeared to Robison and others as shifting toward the downside of his career. Yet, even after 10 years of pitching, Cy Young, according to Pittsburgh Pirates superstar Honus Wagner, could throw even faster than Walter Johnson, who earned the reputation as being one of baseball's fastest, if not the fastest, pitcher.

But by the time of the Boston trade in 1901, even Young knew that he would have to vary his pitches as he grew older, so he learned how to improve his pitching. He understood that at a less-than-svelte 34, he had better adapt. He mastered two curveballs, one overhand and sharply breaking, and the other sidearmed and looping. He learned to throw his pitches with unmatched precision. Only a few months after the "all washed up" affront, he led the American League in wins (33), ERA (1.62), and strikeouts (158)—baseball's Triple Crown in pitching. In that same season, he threw five shutouts, including the American League's first perfect game, and in a feat incomprehensible in modern times, he walked only 37 batters in 371 and a third innings. The apparently ineffective pitcher showed enough determination to win nearly 200 games for Boston[19] (see table 3.2).

Young mentored and nurtured the Boston Red Sox star position player Tris Speaker. Speaker, branded "Spoke" and "The Grey Eagle" by Boston fans, desperately needed Young's assistance because Speaker fared miserably in his early years as a professional ballplayer. A failed minor-league pitcher, he hit well enough for the Texas League's Houston team to earn a Boston offer in 1907, yet his average for seven games was a pitiful .158. Rejected by the Red Sox and other major-league clubs, including John McGraw's Giants, he paid his own way to Boston's 1908 spring training in Little Rock, Arkansas. Not overwhelmed by Speaker's prowess, the Red Sox front office sold his contract to Little Rock of the Southern League. Proceeds from the sale paid the rent for Boston's spring training field. Boston later bought back his contract, yet he hit only .224 in 31 games in 1909. In the same year, Young helped Speaker hone his unpolished, although potentially brilliant, fielding skills. Reflecting on his rookie year, Speaker commented that Young "[u]sed to hit me flies to sharpen my abilities to judge in advance the direction and distance of an outfield ball."[20]

Speaker learned the position so thoroughly that he developed into an absolutely spectacular fielder. And while he earned fame as the best fielding center fielder in his time, he also won accolades for his baserunning and hitting. In 1912, his MVP (called the Chalmers Award) World Series championship season, he hit .383, with three hit streaks of 20 or more games. As a

Table 3.2. Cy Young Pitching Statistics

Year	Age	Team	Lg.	W	L	ERA	GS	CG	SHO	SV	IP	H	R	ER	HR	BB	SO	WHIP	SO/BB
1890	23	CLV	NL	9	7	3.47	16	16	0	0	147.2	145	87	57	6	30	39	1.185	1.30
1891	24	CLV	NL	27	22	2.85	46	43	0	2	423.2	431	244	134	4	140	147	1.348	1.05
1892	25	CLV	NL	36	12	1.93	49	48	9	0	453.0	363	158	97	8	118	168	1.062	1.42
1893	26	CLV	NL	34	16	3.36	46	42	1	1	422.2	442	230	158	10	103	102	1.289	0.99
1894	27	CLV	NL	26	21	3.94	47	44	2	1	408.2	488	265	179	19	106	108	1.454	1.02
1895	28	CLV	NL	35	15	3.26	40	36	4	0	369.2	363	177	134	10	75	121	1.185	1.61
1896	29	CLV	NL	28	15	3.24	46	42	5	3	414.1	477	214	149	7	62	140	1.301	2.26
1897	30	CLV	NL	21	19	3.78	38	35	2	0	335.2	391	189	141	7	49	88	1.311	1.80
1898	31	CLV	NL	25	13	2.53	41	40	1	0	377.2	387	167	106	6	41	101	1.133	2.46
1899	32	STL	NL	26	16	2.58	42	40	4	1	369.1	368	173	106	10	44	111	1.116	2.52
1900	33	STL	NL	19	19	3.00	35	32	4	0	321.1	337	144	107	7	36	115	1.161	3.19
1901	34	BOS	AL	33	10	1.62	41	38	5	0	371.1	324	112	67	6	37	158	0.972	4.27
1902	35	BOS	AL	32	11	2.15	43	41	3	0	384.2	350	136	92	6	53	160	1.048	3.02
1903	36	BOS	AL	28	9	2.08	35	34	7	2	341.2	294	115	79	6	37	176	0.969	4.76
1904	37	BOS	AL	26	16	1.97	41	40	10	1	380.0	327	104	83	6	29	200	0.937	6.90
1905	38	BOS	AL	18	19	1.82	33	31	4	0	320.2	248	99	65	3	30	210	0.867	7.00
1906	39	BOS	AL	13	21	3.19	34	28	0	2	287.2	288	137	102	3	25	140	1.088	5.60
1907	40	BOS	AL	21	15	1.99	37	33	6	2	343.1	286	101	76	3	51	147	0.982	2.88
1908	41	BOS	AL	21	11	1.26	33	30	3	2	299.0	230	68	42	1	37	150	0.893	4.05
1909	42	CLE	AL	19	15	2.26	34	30	3	0	294.1	267	110	74	4	59	109	1.108	1.85
1910	43	CLE	AL	7	10	2.53	20	14	1	0	163.1	149	62	46	0	27	58	1.078	2.15
1911	44	TOT	MLB	7	9	3.78	18	12	2	0	126.1	137	75	53	6	28	55	1.306	1.96
1911	44	CLE	AL	3	4	3.88	7	4	0	0	46.1	54	28	20	2	13	20	1.446	1.54
1911	44	BSN	NL	4	5	3.71	11	8	2	0	80.0	83	47	33	4	15	35	1.225	2.33
22 Years				511	316	2.63	815	749	76	17	7,356.0	7,092	3,167	2,147	138	1,217	2,803	1.130	2.30
162-Game Avg.				20	12	2.63	32	30	3	1	291	280	125	85	5	48	111	1.130	2.30
CLV (9 years)				241	135	3.10	369	346	24	7	3,353.0	3,487	1,731	1,155	77	724	1,014	1.256	1.40
BOS (8 years)				192	112	2.00	297	275	38	9	2,728.1	2,347	872	606	34	299	1,341	0.970	4.48
CLE (3 years)				29	29	2.50	61	48	4	0	504.0	470	200	140	6	99	187	1.129	1.89
STL (2 years)				45	35	2.78	77	72	8	1	690.2	705	317	213	17	80	226	1.137	2.83
BSN (1 year)				4	5	3.71	11	8	2	0	80.0	83	47	33	4	15	35	1.225	2.33
NL (12 years)				290	175	3.06	457	426	34	8	4,123.2	4,275	2,095	1,401	98	819	1,275	1.235	1.56
AL (11 years)				221	141	2.08	358	323	42	9	3,232.1	2,817	1,072	746	40	398	1,528	0.995	3.84

Source: http://www.baseball-reference.com.

fielder, he acquired a seemingly effortless, fluid motion. The illustrious early twentieth-century sportswriter Grantland Rice, commenting on Tris Speaker and Napoleon Lajoie, observed that they "neither wasted a motion or gave you any sign of extra effort. . . . They had the same elements that made a Bobby Jones or the Four Horsemen of Notre Dame—the smoothness of a summer wind."[21] And when the Deadball Era fan gazed out on the playing field to view the Red Sox fielders, the six-foot, 193-pound Texan—he had actually been a cowpuncher—was the most conspicuous of all players. (See table 3.3.)

Speaker played, by most baseball standards, out of position. Moving in from center field, he looked like a fifth infielder. He could catch anything and led the American League in putouts, and from his special position in short center field, he would rob batters of singles, throw out base runners attempting to stretch a hit, and, most unusually, perform unassisted double plays. He would snare a low line drive and then step on the bag just in front of a hapless base runner. Pitchers appreciated his talents. As teammate "Smoky Joe" Wood once noted, "At the crack of the bat he'd be off with his back to the infield, and then he'd turn and glance over his shoulder at the last minute and catch the ball so easy it looked like there was nothing to it, nothing at all."[22]

Wood and Speaker, teammates and the best of friends, brought fame to Boston in the 1912 season: Speaker for his MVP season and Wood for a remarkable season that included an unparalleled 16 straight wins. Wood won 57 games between 1911 and 1912. The son of a University of Pennsylvania lawyer, Wood later served as the school's varsity baseball coach for 15 years. (See table 3.4.)

As a player, Smoky Joe roughhoused and cursed his way to notoriety. Tussling with Speaker at a hotel in the spring of 1909, he injured his foot so severely that he could not pitch until June. Few players escaped Wood's vitriol. As respected journalist Hugh Fullerton noted, "He talked out of the corner of his mouth and used language that would have made a steeple horse jockey blush. He challenged all opponents and dilated upon their pedigrees."[23] He could scorch rival teams with both his language and his fastball. The great fastball pitcher Walter Johnson of the Senators once quipped, "Can I throw harder than Joe Wood? Listen, mister, no man alive can throw harder than Joe Wood."[24] On September 6, 1912, Johnson faced off against Wood in one of baseball's legendary games. Wood, who had won 13 consecutive games and who was closing in on Johnson's record of 16, defeated the great Washington pitcher, 1–0, in front of 35,000 riotous fans in Fenway Park.[25]

Table 3.3. Tris Speaker Batting Statistics

Year	Age	Team	Lg.	G	PA	AB	R	H	HR	RBI	SB	BB	SO	BA	OBP	SLG	OPS	TB	SH
1907	19	BOS	AL	7	20	19	0	3	0	1	0	1	4	.158	.200	.158	.358	3	0
1908	20	BOS	AL	31	125	116	12	26	0	9	3	4	8	.224	.262	.276	.538	32	3
1909	21	BOS	AL	143	606	544	73	168	7	77	35	38	53	.309	.362	.443	.805	241	17
1910	22	BOS	AL	141	608	538	92	183	7	65	35	52	38	.340	.404	.468	.873	252	12
1911	23	BOS	AL	141	589	500	88	167	8	70	25	59	35	.334	.418	.502	.920	251	17
1912	24	BOS	AL	153	675	580	136	222	10	90	52	82	36	.383	.464	.567	1.031	329	7
1913	25	BOS	AL	141	608	520	94	189	3	71	46	65	22	.363	.441	.533	.974	277	16
1914	26	BOS	AL	158	668	571	101	193	4	90	42	77	25	.338	.423	.503	.926	287	13
1915	27	BOS	AL	150	652	547	108	176	0	69	29	81	14	.322	.416	.411	.827	225	17
1916	28	CLE	AL	151	646	546	102	211	2	79	35	82	20	.386	.470	.502	.972	274	15
1917	29	CLE	AL	142	614	523	90	184	2	60	30	67	14	.352	.432	.486	.918	254	15
1918	30	CLE	AL	127	553	471	73	150	0	61	27	64	9	.318	.403	.435	.839	205	11
1919	31	CLE	AL	134	591	494	83	146	2	63	19	73	12	.296	.395	.433	.828	214	20
1920	32	CLE	AL	150	674	552	137	214	8	107	10	97	13	.388	.483	.562	1.045	310	20
1921	33	CLE	AL	132	588	506	107	183	3	75	2	68	12	.362	.439	.538	.977	272	12
1922	34	CLE	AL	131	518	426	85	161	11	71	8	77	11	.378	.474	.606	1.080	258	12
1923	35	CLE	AL	150	695	574	133	218	17	130	8	93	15	.380	.469	.610	1.079	350	22
1924	36	CLE	AL	135	575	486	94	167	9	65	8	72	13	.344	.432	.510	.943	248	13
1925	37	CLE	AL	117	518	429	79	167	12	87	5	70	12	.389	.479	.578	1.057	248	15
1926	38	CLE	AL	150	661	539	96	164	7	88	6	94	15	.304	.408	.469	.877	253	28
1927	39	WSH	AL	141	596	523	71	171	2	73	9	55	8	.327	.395	.444	.839	232	15
1928	40	PHA	AL	64	212	191	28	51	3	30	5	10	5	.267	.310	.450	.761	86	9
22 Years				2,789	11,992	10,195	1,882	3,514	117	1,531	436	1,381	394	.345	.428	.500	.928	5,101	309
162-Game Avg.				162	697	592	109	204	7	89	25	80	23	.345	.428	.500	.928	296	18
CLE (11 years)				1,519	6,633	5,546	1,079	1,965	73	886	155	857	146	.354	.444	.520	.965	2,886	183
BOS (9 years)				1,065	4,551	3,935	704	1,327	39	542	267	459	235	.337	.414	.482	.896	1,897	102
WSH (1 year)				141	596	523	71	171	2	73	9	55	8	.327	.395	.444	.839	232	15
PHA (1 year)				64	212	191	28	51	3	30	5	10	5	.267	.310	.450	.761	86	9

Source: http://www.baseball-reference.com.

Table 3.4. "Smoky Joe" Wood Pitching Statistics

Year	Age	Team	Lg.	W	L	ERA	GS	CG	SHO	SV	IP	H	R	ER	HR	BB	SO	WHIP	SO/BB
1908	18	BOS	AL	1	1	2.38	2	1	1	0	22.2	14	12	6	0	16	11	1.324	0.69
1909	19	BOS	AL	11	7	2.18	19	13	4	0	160.2	121	51	39	1	43	88	1.021	2.05
1910	20	BOS	AL	12	13	1.69	17	14	3	0	196.2	155	81	37	3	56	145	1.073	2.59
1911	21	BOS	AL	23	17	2.02	33	25	5	3	275.2	226	113	62	2	76	231	1.096	3.04
1912	22	BOS	AL	34	5	1.91	38	35	10	1	344.0	267	104	73	2	82	258	1.015	3.15
1913	23	BOS	AL	11	5	2.29	18	12	1	2	145.2	120	54	37	0	61	123	1.243	2.02
1914	24	BOS	AL	10	3	2.62	14	11	1	0	113.1	94	38	33	1	34	67	1.129	1.97
1915	25	BOS	AL	15	5	1.49	16	10	3	2	157.1	120	32	26	1	44	63	1.042	1.43
1917	27	CLE	AL	0	0	3.45	1	0	0	1	15.2	17	7	6	0	7	2	1.532	0.29
1919	29	CLE	AL	0	0	0.00	0	0	0	0	0.2	0	0	0	0	0	0	0.000	0.00
1920	30	CLE	AL	0	0	22.50	0	0	0	0	2.0	4	5	5	0	2	1	3.000	0.50
11 Years				117	57	2.03	158	121	28	10	1,434.1	1,138	497	324	10	421	989	1.087	2.35
162-Game Avg.				21	10	2.03	28	21	5	2	255	202	88	58	2	75	176	1.087	2.35
BOS (8 years)				117	56	1.99	157	121	28	8	1,416.0	1,117	485	313	10	412	986	1.080	2.39
CLE (3 years)				0	1	5.40	1	0	0	2	18.1	21	12	11	0	9	3	1.636	0.33

Source: http://www.baseball-reference.com.

FENWAY

In 1912, the world champion Red Sox played ball in a brand new, state-of-the-art stadium, Fenway Park. A year earlier, Boston owner General Charles Taylor had bought the Red Sox for his son, team president John I. Taylor. John had rechristened the old Boston Pilgrims the "Boston Red Sox," and with the lease for the old Huntington Avenue field about to expire, sought to build a new ballpark. The Taylors, astute players in the Boston real estate market, saw potential in the undervalued lands in the neighborhood, a former swamp at Landsdowne and Ipswich, an eight-acre property called the Dana Lands. The Taylors had witnessed the old, hazardous, wooden stadiums with insufficient seating. The Braves' old park, South End Grounds II, an arresting, double-deck park with medieval-style turrets, had burned to the ground in 1894. The Taylors also recognized that the newest concrete and steel stadiums, namely Shibe Park in Philadelphia and Forbes Field in Pittsburgh, were safe venues that could hold thousands of fans. Builders started construction just as the 1911 Red Sox season came to a close and assembled the new ballpark before the spring of 1912. The Taylors built an architectural Mona Lisa, a singular ballpark.[26]

Fenway, renovated and altered dramatically since its opening, sparkled with its " unique dimensions and properties," as Roger Angell describes in his *Once More around the Park*, troubling fielders and entertaining fans with "variously angled blocks and planes and nooks and corners of the outfield fences."[27] With its brick and concrete grandstand, and dimensions of 320 feet in left, 488 feet in center, and less than 314 feet in right, and with its green landscape, the ballpark graciously invited the modern, Progressive Era baseball fan.[28]

The Red Sox team, inhabitants of a remarkable concrete and steel park, heirs to the legacy of superstar pitcher Cy Young, and possessors of two celebrity players in Smoky Joe Wood and Tris Speaker, contrasted strikingly with the lowly Braves. The Braves, who occupied a cramped, run-down, old, wooden stadium, could not boast of past superstars. They had acquired a celebrity ballplayer in Johnny Evers, but even with Evers anchoring the infield and directing teammates across the diamond, the Braves hovered in last place at mid-season. The Red Sox organization advanced toward the baseball summit, and as one baseball historian notes, "they were on their way to creating the American League's first brief dynasty—winning the World Series four times in seven-year span, from 1912 to 1918."[29] Boston's ever-singing, sometimes marching, and always-boisterous fan club, the Royal Rooters, originally enthusiasts for the Braves, now cheered on the Red Sox.

BABE RUTH

The Red Sox empire contrasted sharply with the lowly Braves community, and, in July 1914, just as the Braves season reached its nadir, the Red Sox acquired from the minor league Baltimore Orioles a fascinating young pitching talent, Babe Ruth. Ruth's early life reads like the text of a Charles Dickens novel. Roaming the alleys and wharves of Baltimore harbor, the roguish, thieving, tobacco-chewing seven-year-old received from a judge the label "incorrigible."

Placed in St. Mary's Industrial Home, Ruth met Brother Mathias, his lifelong mentor, baseball instructor, and surrogate father. Ruth later reflected on Mathias, saying, "He was the father I needed and the greatest man I've ever known."[30] Mathias played Ruth in the infield (as a left-handed third baseman), in the outfield, and as pitcher, and he then allowed him to play for a semipro team on weekends. After witnessing Ruth strike out 22 batters in a St. Mary's game, Jack Dunn, owner of the Orioles, signed him to a contract in the spring of 1914. Ruth excelled, pitching well against the Braves, and even defeating the Philadelphia A's, the year's previous World Series champions, in a complete game. Dunn, needing cash for his financially strapped Orioles, received a generous offer from Red Sox latest owner Joseph Lannin and sold him to the Red Sox.[31]

In July 1914, only 19 years old and only five months out of St. Mary's, Ruth, definitely a "Babe," was called on to uphold the Boston Red Sox tradition. He was a July call-up whose talent might take the team to a pennant. His first outing was a categorical success, a "quality start" by modern standards: a seven-inning, 4–3 victory against Cleveland. Holding the Cleveland Naps to five hits in six innings, he allowed three runs during a tough seventh inning. On July 12, the *Boston Globe* applauded his first game: "Ruth leads Red Sox to victory: Southpaw displays high class in game against Cleveland." Fans scrutinized "Ruth, the giant left-hander, who proved a natural ballplayer and went through his act like a veteran of many wars. He has a natural delivery, fine control, and a curve ball that bothers batsmen, but has room for improvement and will undoubtedly become a fine pitcher."[32]

Boston fans cheered on their Red Sox as pennant contenders as the team moved into third place, one game behind the Tigers, on July 17.[33] The Red Sox played so proficiently that the team could afford to send Ruth down to the minor leagues. Bill Carrigan, the manager of the Red Sox , pitched Ruth for only 10 innings in six weeks, and when the Providence Grays, a minor-league team owned by Joseph Lannin, needed a pitcher for the International League pennant race, he transferred Ruth to the minors.[34]

THE BRAVES' TRACE OF OPTIMISM

While the proud Red Sox, content in their gleaming new stadium, battled for the pennant, the Braves could look from their lowly station with a trace of optimism because of recently acquired talent. On June 28, Stallings traded Hub Perdue to the Cardinals for George "Possum" Whitted and Ted Cather. These new acquisitions, although journeymen by most baseball standards, brought hope to the struggling franchise. In spring training, Perdue's star had shone brilliantly, and the young pitcher was one of the main reasons for Boston's early cheery outlook. In 1913, he earned a 16–13 record, with a 3.26 ERA, yet, up until late June 1914, he had floundered with a 2–5 record and 5.82 ERA.[35]

The five-foot, eight-inch Whitted, who played outfield and third base, offered the team much more passion than talent: He had played only 20 games for St. Louis, batting .129, with just 31 at bats. Whitted, who, in 1918, wrote a *Baseball Magazine* article, "Making Good in the Majors: How a Ball Player May Improve Himself by Hard Work and Perseverance," mastered the outfield by chasing "miles and miles" of fly balls and improved his batsmanship by grasping the nuances of hitting the curve. Under the tutelage of Stallings and Evers, he pushed his average up to .261.[36] Ted Cather, another right-handed-hitting outfielder, had hit .273 in 39 games for the Cardinals. Cather found reassurance in his new environment and hit a career best .297 in 50 games for the Braves (in a year when the league average was .251).[37]

On July 2, Stallings traded backup shortstop Jack Martin to the Philadelphia Phillies for Josh Devore, a five-foot, six-inch left-handed-hitting outfielder, only one inch taller than Rabbit Maranville. "The Seelyville Speed Demon" had stolen 61 bases as a leadoff hitter for the pennant-winning 1911 Giants. Traded from New York to Cincinnati to Philadelphia in 1913, and although showing limited duty as a Phillie in 1914, he had hit .302 before the trade.[38] Always optimistic, the Braves management saw the new acquisitions as a chance for improvement.

And hopes rose higher because of the hitting success of two other outfielders: Larry Gilbert and Joe (Joey) Connolly. Gilbert, a rookie out of Milwaukee in the American Association, had batted .282 as a minor leaguer. Until July 3, 1914, he had been batting .293. Connolly, the left-handed power hitter, was surpassing his 1913 effort, when, despite a season-ending broken ankle, he had led the Braves in runs and RBIs. Well into the 1914 season, after 50 games, he was batting .301. Perhaps because of Connolly and Gilbert, or perhaps because of the new acquisitions, the Boston media displayed glimmers of optimism. And even with the Braves 16 games out, the *Boston Globe* praised the Braves' outfield, hoping that the team might at least crawl out of the cellar.[39]

After the July 7 debacle with Buffalo, the Braves won eight of 11, at one point sweeping a three-game series with the Cincinnati Reds. On July 19, the third game of the series, the Braves were down by two in the ninth, but they scored three runs to win. This victory pulled the team out of the basement, as they passed seventh-place Pittsburgh in the standings. The cap-tossing, shouting players celebrated like World Series champions. "They cheered like college boys. They almost smothered Stallings." Stallings, in turn, encouraged his players: "Now we'll catch New York. We're playing 30 percent better than anyone in the league. They won't be able to stop us."[40]

After the Braves swept Cincinnati, Stallings witnessed an astonishing resurgence among his pitchers. In the third week of July, and then starting again at the end of the month, the Braves scorched National League teams with two six-game win streaks, when pitchers held the opposition to an average of less than one run per game. In a five-game series against the Pirates, they threw four shutouts. Up until mid-July, Braves pitchers had thrown two shutouts. Starting on July 17, they held opponents scoreless 17 times: The pitching was nothing less than miraculous.[41]

MIRACULOUS SPITBALLS

The Braves owe their incredible winning streak to pitchers successfully throwing the Deadball Era's trademark pitch: the spitball. During the Deadball Era, pitchers fired a filthy, scuffed, and irregularly shaped baseball, a baseball that might endure an entire game. Sam Crawford of the Tigers recalled, "We'd play a whole game with one ball, if it stayed in the park. Lopsided, and black, and full of tobacco juice and licorice stains."[42] If a pitcher added moisture to this slightly softened, mud-colored ball, the ball would sail toward the plate, darting down at the last moment, much like a split-finger fastball in the modern era, and the puzzled batter might sock a single or double, but rarely a home run. Home runs would flourish in the 1920s, once the umpires began to replenish the ball supply on a regular basis, and once the spitball was outlawed.[43]

The spitball offered the most confounding pitch to batters of the Deadball Era. The origins of the spitball are as mystifying as the pitch itself. Who, after all, would want to take credit for the spitball? But records suggest that spitball pitchers as far back as the 1860s were deceiving batters. A player for the Brooklyn Eckfords observed Baltimore's Bobby Matthews, who pitched in 1868. Matthews would massage the ball and leave a portion of the ball untouched. After dampening the untouched part, he would hurl the ball toward the plate, and "[t]he ball not only would take a decided outcurve at times, but other times would drop and curve."[44] By 1910, pitchers were abusing the ball in new and creative ways, each outdoing the other. In the words of baseball analyst Rob Neyer, "They slathered every manner of slippery substance on the ball, and also competed with each other to come up with new ways of scuffling and discoloring it."[45] Spitball masters the likes of Ed Walsh of the Cubs would raise their gloves in front of their faces on every pitch so that the batter could not detect whether the ball had been moistened. Walsh, using a fastball motion, threw the pitch so that it went "down and away, straight down, and down and in."[46] Cleveland's Stanley Coveleski could throw the spitter "down, out, or down and out," with great control. His ploy was to go to the ball with his mouth on every pitch, faking it when necessary. "But I'd always have them looking for it."[47]

Dick Rudolph of the Braves followed the same general approach. Rudolph generally threw four pitches: fastball, curve, and slow ball or change, adding the spitball to his repertoire just to keep the batter guessing.[48] "I used the spit more as a blind, but the batter can never tell when I'm bluffing and when I am actually going to cut loose with a spit ball," said Rudolph. Judged to be a "wise pitcher," Rudolph knew that his pitch had not reached the quality of a Coveleski spitball: "The best you could say for it was that it was wet," observed his catcher, Hank Gowdy.[49] F. C. Lane, born in 1885, and later editor of *Baseball Magazine* in 1912, gained fame as one of baseball's first sabermetricians. An exemplar of progressive, scientific baseball, he understood how Rudolph upset the timing of a batter: "What Rudolph does do, however," Lane wrote in a 1919 installment of *Baseball Magazine*, "is to bluff at throwing the spitter, and this is just as bad as actually using the twister, as far as batting is concerned."[50]

Rudolph showed pinpoint control with his other pitches, including a deceptive, sweeping curveball. He achieved mastery in part because, as Braves coach Fred Mitchell pointed out, "He could almost read a batter's mind." Mitchell would sit with Rudolph on the bench as the short, slight pitcher accurately predicted a batter's next move.[51] Rudolph could unexpectedly toss a changeup (or, as he called it, the "slow ball"), surprising the batter, the catcher, and even himself:

> Half the time, when I wind up, I don't know myself that I am going to throw a slow ball. Oftentimes the catcher will signal for a fastball. I will intend to give him a fastball. But the batter will shift his feet or change his position, or give some indication at the last minute, that it would be a good stunt to feed him a slow ball. And so I will give him one.[52]

Now, in the summer of 1914, Rudolph's "study of the profession" yielded success: He won 12 games in a row.[53]

Teammate Lefty Tyler also baffled batters in the late summer of 1914. Tyler, according to sportswriter Tom Meany, was "untouchable, when he had to be, which was most of the time." Somehow Tyler managed to win 1–0 games—10 in his career—tossing his slow ball or changeup, fastball, and curveball from the cross-fire delivery. Tyler would move over to the left side of the rubber, swing his foot toward first instead of toward the plate, and then throw sidearm. This unconventional pitching motion (now an outlawed practice) afforded him an extra moment to hide the ball. Batters often suffer when they face left-handed pitchers, and they experienced absolute agony when facing Tyler. In 1914, he earned a 16–13 record, with a 2.69 ERA, and at one point, he helped the team battle to the top with 23 consecutive scoreless innings.[54]

Bill James, the Braves' six-foot, three-inch righty, began his ascent to pitching stardom in July 1914. Like Tyler, he threw a slow ball, or changeup, and, like Rudolph, he tossed the spitter, two pitches he acquired while pitching in 1912 for Seattle in the Northwestern League. By 1914, "Seattle Bill" had emerged as an unhittable spitball master. Beginning on July 9, the 22-year-old reeled off a spectacular record—19–1, with a 1.51 ERA. If James had not lost a 12-inning game, 3–2, in Pittsburgh, on August 22, he would have secured 20 straight victories, a major-league record. Although posting a 7–6 record up until July 9, James put together a second half so remarkable that he finished 26–7. He earned the league's best winning percentage, at .788, and his innings pitched, with 322, his strikeouts, with 156, and his ERA placed him in the league's top five. John J. Ward, of *Baseball Magazine*, lauded his skills: "[T]he further acquisition of experience should make him one of the best all-around pitchers in history."[55]

A RABBIT AT SHORTSTOP

In July, the Braves surged upward, largely because of their pitching, but also because of their young, agile shortstop the impish, energetic, bold, eccentric, and always talented Walter "Rabbit" Maranville. Even if fans thought that the Braves' pitchers would falter, even if fans cast doubt on George Stallings's highly optimistic predictions, they were certain of the never-say-die attitude of their shortstop, Rabbit Maranville.[56] While some baseball writers have claimed that he received his moniker because of his long, pointy ears, Maranville, according to his own account, earned the nickname Rabbit from an exuberant seven-year-old, who, after seeing him in a minor-league game, giggled, "You hop and bound like one." Maranville approved of the label because there was a more disparaging alternative: "They'd been calling me Stumpy until then."[57]

Rabbit played baseball with the exuberance of a young child, snaring the ball with acrobatic fielding, and teasing coaches, players, fans, and even umpires with entertaining belt-high basket catches. Willie Mays transformed the basket catch into a national phenomenon in the 1950s, but Maranville popularized the feat in 1914. Rabbit would extend his unwebbed, "pancake" baseball glove and snag routine fly balls at the last second, just after the ball grazed his uniform. He turned his catches into a fan favorite, earning the label "vest-pocket catch" for what even he labeled "peculiar."[58] Not all players appreciated the entertainment value, but Cubs left fielder Jimmie Sheckard recognized the underlying skill beneath the vest-pocket snare: "I'll bet you he don't drop three fly balls in his career, no matter how long or short he may be in the game." Sheckard then explained, "Notice the Kid is perfectly still, directly under the ball, and in no way is there any vibration to make the ball bounce out of his glove."[59] A trick play for some grew into Maranville's standard practice.

At five feet, five inches tall and 155 pounds (he claimed that he was 126 pounds in 1912, his rookie season), Rabbit was an undersized player, who, next to Braves first baseman Butch Schmidt, who stood at six feet, one inch tall and weighed in at 200 pounds, appeared to be the size of a child. When he first arrived at training, the Braves trainers, perhaps as part of a hazing ritual, gave him the uniform of a player equal in size to Schmidt, "Big Ed" Donnelly. Without complaining, Maranville received Big Ed's uniform, which took more than a few rolls of the pants so that he could make himself "presentable."[60] For one moment in his career, Rabbit Maranville appeared less than confident. Even though Rabbit was diminutive by 1914 baseball standards, manager George Stallings saw his value:

> He came into the league under a handicap—his build. He was too small to be a big leaguer in the opinion of critics. I told him he was just what I wanted: a small fellow for short. All he had to do was to run to his left or right, or come in, and size never handicapped speed in going after the ball.[61]

RABBIT BEING RABBIT

In 1914, few fans, players, or journalists expected that Maranville would ever receive an honor as one of baseball's best, namely enshrinement as a Hall of Famer. Maranville earned as much fame for his level of play as for his lighthearted pranking. He mimicked other players and played invisible pepper, a pregame drill where a batter rapidly hits the ball to nearby infielders. He achieved great notoriety when he handed out a spare set of eyeglasses to apparently nearsighted umpires. Baseball historian Harold Seymour recalled

seeing Maranville at Ebbets Field in Brooklyn. Seymour, the batboy, appreciated Maranville's novel way of arguing a low-ball strike: "[D]ropping to his
knees and making a few practice swipes with his bat." Seymour also witnessed
one of Maranville's mischievous attacks on the umpires. As a teammate was
arguing with an umpire, Maranville, crawling on all fours behind the official,
and then grinning, playfully encouraged his fellow player to gently shove the
ump head over heels. He was known to crawl through an umpire's legs and
occasionally sit down on base runners as they slid into second.[62] While on a
summer road trip, he brought with him the strangest of companions, a pet
monkey, whom his teammates claimed looked more attractive than Rabbit.
Taking a shortcut, he once swam the Charles River, and he was well known
for a stunt in which he "dove fully clothed into the fountain outside of the
club's St. Louis hotel and emerged soaking wet with a goldfish clenched between his grinning teeth."[63]

Probably because he so often sought amusement and pleasure, Maranville, too, fell victim to pranksters . During the 1914 pennant race, he suffered at the hands of Germany Schaefer, who, like Maranville, had achieved
a reputation as a high-spirited, fun-loving showman. Once, as a rain shower
hit the ballpark, Schaefer showed up at the plate wearing a raincoat and rubber boots. A second baseman for the Detroit Tigers, Schaefer gained celebrity
status in 1905, when he stepped to the plate in the ninth inning with two out,
the Tigers down by one, and the game-winning run on first. Schaefer boldly
proclaimed that he would belt a homer into the left-field bleachers. After he
smashed the game winner as predicted, he slid into each base, shouting to
the crowd as if he were in a horse race: "Schaefer leads at the half." He slid
dramatically into home, jumped up, removed his cap, and announced to the
crowd, "Ladies and gentlemen, this concludes this afternoon's performance. I
thank you for your kind attention."[64]

As the pennant race intensified, and as Boston edged up to New York,
the Giants' manager, John McGraw, a friend of Schaefer, apparently encouraged Schaefer to prank Maranville. Schaefer sought out Maranville when
the Braves, just a half game behind the Giants, were playing an away game
in Philadelphia. Schaefer wined and dined Maranville, introduced him to
an engaging lady friend, and he sent them out partying for the night. When
Maranville arrived back at the hotel around 10 the next morning, his roommate revealed the truth: "You big sucker, that's one of McGraw's pet tricks,
and to think that you fell for that Germany Schaefer and girl act. Get to bed;
you have been framed very nicely." Maranville went to the ballpark late that
day and "half asleep." Although the exhausted Maranville made three errors,
and even though he was blurry eyed, he managed three hits and four RBIs in
an 8–3 victory.[65]

FEISTINESS

But as one player noted, despite his antics, Maranville "was a likable SOB." Players and coaches valued the infielder, in part of because of his sense of humor, often self-deprecatory. He brought a fresh perspective to his diminutive size by saying "that he was just right, that everyone else was tall."[66] During spring training in 1913, he was absolutely single minded en route to his winning the starting position for shortstop over Art Bues, Stallings's nephew. "Listen," asserted Maranville, "I think I can beat out your nephew. What I want to know is how many cousins and uncles do you have behind him?" Stallings could only laugh at Maranville's use of humor in the diplomatic maneuvering that was part of player selection. The Braves' manager appreciated Maranville's feistiness, and Maranville won and kept the job.[67]

Maranville's ceaseless mischief highlights his 24-year baseball career. Baseball fans know of his pranks because in 1953, a year before his death, Rabbit penned an autobiographical account filled with colorful tales. Within the collective memory of baseball fans, these lively anecdotes, many of which were promoted by Rabbit himself, have superseded his talents. Maranville's baseball skills, moreover, were unusual for a Hall of Famer. His .258 lifetime batting average, for instance, remains one of the lowest for any position player in the Hall of Fame, but, in 1914, Stallings often placed the lean shortstop in the cleanup spot, and the MVP runner-up (to Evers) knocked in 78 runs, leading the team. During his career, he hit an astonishing 21 of his 28 home runs inside the park, along with 177 triples, 19th in baseball history.[68] His defense at shortstop was not just thrilling, but efficient. In his lengthy career, he led the league in putouts six times and double plays five times.[69] The *Baseball Page* ranks him as the 22nd best shortstop in baseball history, ahead of Luis Aparicio and Phil Rizzuto,[70] and in the *New Bill James Historical Baseball Abstract*, Bill James ranks him 10th in "career value" amongst shortstops.[71] Maranville biographer Bob Carroll contends that Boston's Evers–Maranville second-to-short duo surpassed Chicago's Evers-to-Tinker (-to-Chance) combination. "Maranville is the greatest player to enter baseball since Ty Cobb arrived," Braves manager Stallings once said.[72]

Stallings could tend toward the hyperbolic. No one can compare to Ty Cobb. Cobb, after all, batted over .300 for 23 years, with a lifetime average of .367. Yet, Maranville experienced a long, successful baseball career, and working with his keystone partner Johnny Evers, he spurred the Braves on throughout July 1914.

Like many career ballplayers of the time, Maranville found his roots in the immigrant working class in the United States. The son of an Irish mother and French father who worked as a policeman, Maranville apprenticed to be a pipe fitter but found baseball as a means of moving up the economic ladder.[73] Historian Steven A. Riess places Maranville and teammate Johnny Evers into a broader pattern, writing, "Baseball was probably more valuable as a source of vertical social mobility for the Irish than for any other ethnic group."[74] Grantland Rice thought of Rabbit at that point in his career, his early years in Boston, as the "link between the old days and the new in baseball":

> He broke in with the hard-bitten crew in Boston and wasn't exactly a sissy, reveling in the atmosphere in which he found himself. For years he was a turbulent figure on the field, fighting enemy ballplayers and umpires—and even the players on his own team—when he found it necessary.[75]

It was this great, immeasurable, combative mind-set of Deadball Era players that gave Maranville his special quality.

The July 7 loss to minor league Buffalo traumatized Maranville and the Braves. After losing to the Buffalo International League team, 10–2, the Braves boarded the train for Chicago, where Stallings glared at players, formed his best Theodore Roosevelt machismo posture, and roared, "Baa! You couldn't even beat a bunch of females," and slammed the door to his stateroom.[76] Maranville, angered yet inspired, jabbed at Evers. "Can you play better ball than you have been playing?" When Evers responded, "I think I can," the two infielders joined together to cross-examine everyone on the team, pushing them to play harder. Driven by these tough, wiry infielders, the Rabbit and "The Crab," the Braves, from July 8 until July 11, won three out of four in Chicago. Just before their next series against the Cardinals, the St. Louis newspapers announced, "Cardinals Will Be in First Place When Lowly Braves Leave Town." But the Braves took two out of three from St. Louis, four out of five from Pittsburgh, and then 16 out of the next 19. "From misfits we became the talk of the baseball world," wrote Rabbit.[77]

ASCENDING SLOWLY

Turning points in a baseball season are difficult to determine. Hundreds of variables influence a season; momentum slows, speeds, and shifts as each batter approaches the plate. Historians, like baseball fans, mistakenly dream up crucial moments, events that are not understood by the participants themselves as pivotal (U.S. citizens, north and south, did not see Gettysburg as crucial in 1863). Yet, in this case, players like Maranville judged the Braves' defeat at the hands of the minor-league team in Buffalo as a decisive moment during the Braves' 1914 season, and just after the Buffalo debacle, the team's level of play rose sharply.

However, most baseball observers at the time believed that the Braves had displayed only incremental improvement, and that the two perennial powers of the National League, the Cubs and the Giants, would battle for the pennant. By July 13, John McGraw, writing in his biweekly evaluation of the National League, sensed that the pennant race was at a turning point: he saw the Cubs steadily gaining on the Giants: "It is disheartening to watch a rival slowly creep up." On July 13, the Cubs, who had just split a two-game series with the Giants, were six games over .500, just three and a half games behind the Giants. McGraw judged lowly Boston as "improving . . . finally beginning to hit." Better hitting, he observed, "is what Stallings has been crying for all year." And while Boston might battle from game to game, at best they would crawl out of the cellar: "I don't think Boston will come home in last place."[78]

The Braves defied all baseball pundits, and by the third week in July, they had moved up in the standings, past both Pittsburgh and Brooklyn. "Coming into their own again . . . With sterling stuff," the *Boston Globe* reported. The Braves, on July 20, put together a formula for their new winning: Stallings's craftiness, stellar pitching, and Evers's resolve. Tyler, the Braves' left-handed pitcher, four-hit the Pirates for a 1–0 victory. Even the great Honus Wagner, the eight-time National League batting champion, failed to get a hit. Stallings had slyly manipulated the rules of the Deadball Era to his advantage. Announcing the lineup, even the pitcher, at the last second, Stallings penned left-handers Josh Devore and Joe Connolly into the starting lineup, but as soon as he saw Pirates' left-handed pitcher, Wilbur Cooper, emerge from behind the grandstand, he recalled his list and substituted Oscar Dugey and Ted Cather, two right-handed-hitting outfielders. Dugey managed two of the Braves' six hits.[79] Stallings's stealth lineup helped bring a victory.

During the game against the Pirates, Evers performed in his usual tempestuous manner and engaged in a "debate" with umpire Bill Hart. Evers asserted that Pirates first baseman Ed Konetchy had run 10 feet off the base path, and Hart claimed that he had not seen the apparent blunder. Evers retorted tartly, "but that's what you are in the game for, to see everything."[80] Evers, temperamental throughout July, was "banished" on July 8, during a Cubs game, for arguing a call against Maranville. He channeled his rage into brilliance on the ball field, and during an eight-game span, until July 18, while the Braves journeyed on a "western" road trip, he fielded 98 out of 100 chances, while hitting .402.[81] Maranville recalled his play with Evers throughout this time as a "charm." Any batter who hit toward the middle of the infield sent the ball into "Death Valley."[82] Fans worshiped Evers's "fighting spirit," identifying with his "continuous arguments against umpires as to rules." They judged his double-play partner, Rabbit Maranville, as equally determined. Deadball Era fans were enthusiastic. They flung hundreds of seat cushions onto the field to show their approval, tossed hundreds of cigars onto the field to celebrate a home run, and stridently chanted in unison a call that countered the umpire's call.[83] The fans, often labeled "cranks" or "bugs," cheered for "The Crab" and "Rabbit" at every opportunity.

ASCENDING SHARPLY

Before they left on July 7 for the trip "west"—in 1914, Chicago and Cincinnati were in the western realm of professional baseball—the Braves were 28–40, with a winning percentage of .412 (the same as the year before). During the road trip, they won 12 of 16 games; observers witnessed the Braves playing a new, successful brand of baseball. *Boston Globe* sportswriter Melville Webb broke down the western trip, analyzing the batting data from every angle. In 1914, he viewed baseball through numbers, carefully observing fielding averages and batting averages for every series. Batters managed to hit just .247 during the trip, and they batted just .181 in a sweep of the Pirates. Yet, despite meager batting averages, the Braves played successful "small ball," stealing 24 bases and, most impressive, hitting 26 sacrifices. More than anything else, it was pitching prowess that produced victory. On the trip west, their pitchers managed to shut Pittsburgh out four times in five games. Rudolph and James pitched one shutout each, and Tyler pitched shutouts in both the first and last games of the series.[84]

In the last three weeks of July, as the Braves captured series from Chicago, Cincinnati, and Pittsburgh, they moved up to another level of baseball esteem, rising from fifth place to fourth place in the standings and reaching the "first division." Each league, American and National, included eight teams, only the best of which was eligible for the World Series. But the top four teams of each league earned the distinction of being in the first division, an honor in the Deadball Era baseball world. Braves manager George Stallings often mentioned this achievement, and *Boston Globe* reporters expressed a healthy respect for first-division teams. And on July 21, when the Braves passed St. Louis to move into the first division, the Boston press celebrated. The Braves won in a typical fashion: unhittable pitching and a heavy dose of Maranville: "The Braves' Dick Rudolph mastered the Pirates lineup, shutting them out, 6–0," the *Globe* reported, "Maranville was all over the infield, and nothing got past him. He outshone his distinguished rival Hans [Honus] Wagner."[85] On July 24, *Globe* cartoonist Wallace Goldsmith drew a picture of a headdress-wearing Indian, knife between the teeth, scalp clenched in hand. He is bursting through a giant map of the west, soaring over raucous Boston fans, and shouting out, "Ugh! Bust um heap wide open! Cheering Boston fans proclaim, 'You're in First Division, Kid!'"[86] The Braves, at .500 by August 1, finished a stunning 18–10 in July.[87] (See table 3.5.)

Table 3.5. National League Standings at the Close of Play, August 1, 1914

Team	Games	Wins	Losses	Ties	Winning Percentage	Games Behind	Runs Scored	Runs Allowed
New York Giants	88	52	36	0	0.591	—	404	340
Chicago Cubs	96	52	42	2	0.553	3.0	421	406
St. Louis Cardinals	98	51	45	2	0.531	5.0	375	367
Boston Braves	91	45	45	1	0.500	8.0	337	350
Cincinnati Reds	94	45	48	1	0.484	9.5	360	370
Philadelphia Phillies	91	42	49	0	0.462	11.5	402	424
Brooklyn Robins	88	39	49	0	0.443	13.0	362	369
Pittsburgh Pirates	92	39	51	2	0.433	14.0	283	318

Source: http://www.retrosheet.org.

RECKLESSNESS

In the midst of the pennant race, during the first week of August, Maranville and some of the Braves players broke all the training rules, consuming alcohol and almost inadvertently harming the team. Hank Gowdy, invited by a wine importer to dinner at his home in Hyde Park, Massachusetts, brought along a host of Braves, including Bert Whaling, Gene Cocreham, Butch Schmidt, Bill James, Josh Devore, and Rabbit Maranville.[88] The players, who were originally looking forward to a delicious spread and amusing baseball banter, shifted their intentions after Gowdy proposed to homeowner Harry Levine, "Harry, let's have a drink." Maranville, aware of his tendency to overimbibe, had limited himself to beer, despite offerings of scotch, bourbon, wine, and champagne, but when Gowdy called him out as a sissy and claimed that "champagne was the best drink of them all," Maranville acquired a taste for the beverage: "The first two glasses didn't taste so good. The next ones did, but I forgot to count. I remember shooting out imaginary lights on the way home."[89] At the time, home was a boardinghouse near the ballpark on Massachusetts Avenue that came with rent of seven dollars per week.[90] The possibility of turning the season around, and perhaps achieving a pennant, faded when teammates called him out to drink, challenging his manhood. Maranville was part of a culture that demonstrated masculinity, not just through athletic prowess, but also via alcohol consumption.[91]

Maranville awoke the next morning in misery, suffering from dehydration. "My mouth was as dry as if I had just come across the Sahara desert. I got started on that water and must have drunk a gallon when stars started shooting out of my head and my head was going around like a dynamo."[92] Next he contemplated whether he could even play the next day, as he queried his drinking buddy, Butch Schmidt, "Do you think we can make it?"[93] The two knew that they "got to make it." They went out to the ballpark, tried to "sweat this stuff out of us" and then disguised their hangover from Stallings: "We ate some [corned] beef for dinner and it made us most sick."[94] Stallings, shrewd enough to understand reality, offered medical advice: a bath and a couple hours of sleep before the game. Gowdy and the other scotch- and champagne-drinking players had advised Maranville not to drink water—some kind of Progressive Era urban legend to cure hangovers.[95]

By the time the game started, Maranville was suffering from the ills of dehydration: "I was so thirsty that I was spitting cotton, or so it felt that way to me."[96] He was disoriented, but his innate baseball skills broke through. In the 10th inning, with the Braves up to bat, Maranville's thirst so overwhelmed him that he was swallowing water from a canister when he was supposed to be batting.

When teammates screamed that he was supposed to be at the plate, he yelled, "Up where?"

"Go up there and hit one, Rabbit," urged outfielder Joe Connolly, as he handed Maranville an oversized bat.

"Hit who? I'll fight anyone here," Rabbit answered.

Directed to the plate, Maranville received a query from the umpire, who asked, "Where have you been?"

Rabbit, hungover, confused, and impertinent, responded, "None of your business; all you have to do is umpire."

The umpire, patient as ever, said, "Don't get too close to the plate, Rabbit; you are liable to get hurt."

"Tell that pitcher out there to throw the ball," Maranville responded.

"Strike one," said the umpire.

Rabbit retorted, "What do you mean strike; he never threw the ball."

"Yes he did," said the umpire.

"He won't throw any more by me," Rabbit declared.

The pitcher started his windup, and Rabbit started to swing at his motion. When bat and ball met, the ball sailed over the left-field fence. Rabbit was still standing at home plate when Gowdy rushed up and said, "Run Rabbit; you made a home run, and the game is over."

Rabbit, still bewildered, muttered, "Run from whom?" Gowdy pushed him toward first, and he stumbled around the diamond, proud that he managed to touch each base.

Rabbit later claimed, "I never did see the ball I hit." The pitcher, Babe Adams, also later lamented, "I know darn well you never did." He had seen Maranville's talents at work in earlier innings, when he hit two singles and stole two bases.[97]

Maranville's personal recklessness influenced in his baseball life in numerous ways. And during the 1914 pennant chase, he played without abandon, sacrificing himself for the good of the team. Up against Pittsburgh, and just a few games out of first place, the Braves once again faced Babe Adams, twelve days after the home run episode. Adams had earned accolades as one of the greatest control pitchers in baseball history—1.27 walks per game during a 17-year career. Adams's control was so spectacular that on July 17, he had pitched against the Giants for 21 innings without walking a man (and yet lost, 3–1).[98]

According to Maranville, the dark-featured, round-faced pitcher held the Braves scoreless for seven innings, and Maranville, having whiffed at Adams's precisely thrown curves and fastballs, conferred with Stallings, seeking other possibilities for reaching base. Stallings reminded Maranville of three of John McGraw's players—Fred Snodgrass, Buck Herzog, and Art Fletcher—

who all were regularly awarded first base because they managed to get hit by a pitch.[99] Stallings advised him, "They were all choke hitters like yourself. You know how they would stick out their arms, get their sleeves hit, and go to first base." But Maranville protested that he, unlike his Giants counterparts, did not have long sleeves. "Get on there somehow," ordered Stallings. Maranville dutifully marched to the plate and stuck out his arm for the next two pitches. Adams missed the plate and his arm as the umpire, to Maranville's surprise, yelled "Ball one," followed by "Ball two." Rabbit extended his arm out further on the next pitch, only to be hit squarely on the forehead. Knocked unconscious for a few minutes, he still managed to drag himself to first and help the Braves win, 4–2, taking two out of three from the Pirates.[100] "Getting ahead in the game" is how Maranville labeled this incident, and it was the kind of play that his teammates found inspiring. "I don't know whether he infected the team or the team infected him, but it got to the point where we believed we could win every game, and he got to the point where he believed he could make every play," said Johnny Evers.[101]

PEACE AND WAR

In July 1914, while Maranville and his teammates were engaged in mischief, and while the Braves were scrapping their way out of last place, Americans learned of the assassination of Archduke Francis Ferdinand and the subsequent diplomatic maneuverings of the European powers. Few observers of these events, American or European, anticipated the calamitous events that would follow. Throughout 1914, first as European tensions rose, and later as European societies rushed into humanity's first total war and slaughtered one another by the thousands, Americans perceived themselves as a peace-loving, baseball-playing country.

Satirist William A. Phelon, writing for *Baseball Magazine* months before the war, showed a far better understanding of world politics than any politician or statesman of the time. Phelon imagined a set of scenes in which Charles Murphy, the owner of the Chicago Cubs, encountered European world leaders. Murphy actually traveled to Europe in the winter of 1914. In a comical, pseudo-dialogue six months before World War I broke out, Phelon has Murphy meeting President Poincaré of France and telling the French leader that the greatest living ballplayer is Napoleon Lajoie; Murphy then gets a kiss on both cheeks. When, a week later, he meets Kaiser Wilhelm, Murphy asserts "real quick" that the most talented American ballplayer is clearly Honus Wagner (German descent). "Never saw a man so pleased, grateful," responds Murphy, who then contemplates the kaiser's potential ability as a baseball magnate. As he drew his caricature of Charles Murphy, Phelon offered up a permanent peace solution for Europe: American baseball:

> Europe is in regular ferment—a seething condition of interior unrest—and the only remedy, both in my opinion and that of other great statesmen, is baseball. Give them baseball and there will be no more wars. The rules of the game alone, now that there are so many of them, would keep the European nations busy for fifty years translating, learning, and applying them. What causes war? Too much surplus time, too much surplus energy. If a nation gets all wrapped up in baseball, it will spend its surplus time following the game, and its surplus energy following the umpires![102]

In the spring of 1914, just as 19-year-old Babe Ruth was pitching his way to the major leagues, a 19-year-old Bosnian Serb, Gavrilo Princip, a self-avowed radical anarchist terrorist, was scheming to assassinate Archduke Francis Ferdinand, heir to the throne of the Austro-Hungarian Empire. In May, Princip attended target practice in a Belgrade park; his inaccuracy prompted jeers from his fellow radicals. Born in 1894, in a town ravaged by the Balkan Wars, Princip coordinated his assassination plot with the Serbian Black Hand, a secret military society dedicated to forming a southern Slav nation independent of the Ottoman and Austro-Hungarian Empires, two longtime dominant powers. When the archduke attended Austrian military exercises in Sarajevo, Bosnia, Princip, assisted by the Black Hand and aided by a set of tragicomic circumstances—the archduke's driver took a wrong turn—found himself face-to-face, or at point-blank range, with the next emperor and his wife, Sophia. As every high school student learns, Princip's assassination of the archduke sparked a series of military and diplomatic maneuvers—still debated today—that enflamed Europe and launched the world into World War I.

The archduke had wanted to avoid war with the Serbs, and yet his assassination led to a set of violent acts perpetrated by Austrians against Serbs, and then to the great inferno of World War I. After the burial of Francis Ferdinand on July 4, 1914, the Austrian military leaders deliberated and then designed an attack on Serbia; on July 5, the Austrians received unqualified German support, the infamous "blank check." In the weeks that followed, as Princip and other Serbians were tried, Austria knowingly formulated an ultimatum so strenuous that Serbia could not possibly comply. Still, at this point, a general war did not appear inevitable, and Kaiser Wilhelm traveled on his annual North Sea cruise. And on July 14, 1914, U.S. president Woodrow Wilson paid for his own admission to a baseball game and watched the Detroit Tigers defeat the Washington Senators, 2–0. As the Austrians, Germans, British, French, and Russian governments negotiated, postured, and ordered troops to "premobilize," European powers—despite communications between cousins Kaiser William and Tsar Nicholas, in the notorious "Willy-Nicky telegrams"—headed down a seemingly unavoidable route to war. Austria declared war on Serbia on July 28, and Russia initiated its mobilization on July 30. On August 1, Germany declared war on Russia. France then mobilized, and, by August 3, Germany had declared war on France.[103]

American newspapers ran front-page stories covering these events. In Oregon, for instance, the small-town *Medford Mail Tribune* carried the following headline on August 1: "Germany Declares War on Russia."[104] And as war broke out, sports enthusiasts in the United States still followed baseball with passionate interest, and as war news intensified, Americans, intuitively grateful they were not at war, even more greatly appreciated their peaceful, leisurely, idyllic national pastime. American baseball fans, especially those in Boston, valued the Braves' climb to the top.

· 4 ·

August Madness

𝒥n early August, Europeans gathered at newspaper offices and telegraph posts, and when they heard of the war declarations, many broke out into the streets, bursting into song, parading, and waving flags. Jubilant, sometimes hysterical crowds filled the squares and boulevards of Vienna, Berlin, St. Petersburg, and London. Reflecting this patriotic fervor, English poet Rupert Brooke soon wrote "Soldier," one of five sonnets collectively called *1914*. "If I should die, think only this of me: That there's some corner of a foreign field, That is forever England." Both Brooke's passionate love of country and the joyful, celebratory citizens who filled European streets represented the ardent nationalism of all European countries, a "spirit of 1914."[1]

Not all Europeans welcomed the euphoric, flag-waving crowds. Citizens in rural areas, working-class Socialists, and minorities in both Russia and the Austro-Hungarian Empire approached war somberly, fearful of the near future. They distanced themselves from the "August Madness." European leaders, nevertheless, immediately began to mobilize millions of soldiers and citizens to engage in the first global war, the first total war. European imperial powers drew their soldiers into this world war from Australia, India, and Africa. Combatants battled in Europe, the Middle East, Africa, and the Pacific. And for the first time in history, the war was all-encompassing: Governments drew on every available resource to support millions of soldiers and sailors. The war transformed the hearts and minds of nearly all participants. Nearly 70 million soldiers participated, 8.5 million of them died, and approximately 6 million civilians lost their lives.[2]

Why the war? Its origins are still cloudy, yet European leaders quite clearly directed the events that enflamed Europe and the world. It is also now evident that World War I, or the Great War, transformed the world, and that it influenced World War II and events beyond. As Hew Strachan in 2003 concluded: "This is of course the biggest paradox in our understanding of the war. On the one hand it [World War I] was an unnecessary war fought in a manner that defied common sense, but on the other it was the war that shaped the world in which we still live."[3]

In August and September, just as Americans were observing the Braves' surge to catch the first-place Giants, they read of the war and saw how the new, modern warriors were killing tens of thousands and decimating the European landscape. Much of World War I was fought in the trenches, but when the war broke out in August, highly mobile troops cut through the terrain in Belgium, France, and East Prussia. In August, the Germans would form an army of 3.8 million, the French 3.8 million, and the Russians 3 million. As massive armies attacked with modern firepower, human destruction reached unprecedented levels. At the Battle of the Frontiers, fought in August of 1914, both the Germans and the French suffered more than 250,000 casualties.[4]

The Germans, ignoring Belgium's international legal status as a neutral country, and avoiding France's heavily fortified eastern border, hoped to attack swiftly through their small neighbor, sweep down through France, and seize Paris, even before the Russians had fully mobilized in the east. Following the general script of this strategic plan, the Schieffen Plan, the Germans brought their siege guns and attacked the Belgians' reinforced concrete forts. The grandest siege gun, Big Bertha, exemplified the new modern war tactics: the howitzer could launch a 2,100-pound shell as far as nine miles.

By August 12, the Germans had begun launching shells, and Belgian defenders, trapped in their forts, if not crushed and burned, choked to death on concrete dust. By August 16, the Germans had destroyed all key Belgian forts, but the Belgians offered unexpected and fierce resistance. The German command, fearful of retaliation, terrified by what they perceived to be snipers, or *francs-tireurs*, and in need of a rapid, successful attack, instructed soldiers to act without mercy. Germans torched the town of Tamines and massacred hundreds of civilians; they ravaged the city of Leuven, burning a medieval library.[5]

These were real war crimes, sometimes reported in a straightforward fashion, but often conveyed in a stylized tabloid manner of perverse tortures and execution; for instance, it was alleged that nuns were being tied to church bells and were then crushed as the bells began to toll. About 6,500 civilians, French and Belgian, were killed in the first month of the war (180,000 Belgian refugees fled to England). The Belgian government issued reports about the atrocities, and Louis Raemakers's poignant cartoons found their way to Britain and the United States. Americans read of the vast European armies battling over territory in Prussia, Belgium, and France.[6] The British propaganda machine seized on these incidents, and the atrocities were heavily reported in 1915, and investigated by the Bryce Commission in the same year. Yet, even in the summer of 1914, the brutality of the war was evident. In late August, the Germans crushed the Russians in the decisive Battle of Tannenberg, later described vividly in Aleksandr Solzhenitsyn's *August 1914*.[7]

THE BRAVES' RISE TRUMPS WAR NEWS

But Boston fans experienced solace as the National League team contested for the pennant. "News of the European war becomes of almost secondary importance, in Boston at least," read the August 11, 1914 installment of the *Boston Globe*, "because of the shift yesterday in the standing of the National League clubs that landed the Boston Braves in second place." The Braves, who had been in last place on July 18, had soared to the top at a remarkable rate. "From Cellar to Attic in 23 Days," read the sports headline.[8] On the front page of the August 15 edition of the *Boston Globe* appeared major stories about Belgian resistance, patriotic attitudes of the British, the French forces in Vosges, and speculation on Turkey entering the war. Juxtaposed next to the war news at the top of the paper a large, striking picture of the Braves' Bill James, with an article entitled "Giants Again Shrivel to Pigmy Size before Braves' Withering Fire." By August 15, the Braves had won 27 games out of their last 33. The *Globe* praised the turnaround: "Newspapers in other cities that ridiculed the Braves a few weeks ago are now praising them."[9]

How the Braves managed to climb to the top so rapidly is a complex tale. One ingredient of the success, what writers intuitively viewed as the Braves' "fight," involved the regular use of sacrifice hits. In the Deadball Era, managers employed the hit-and-run, stealing, and sacrifices—not magnificent Ruthian home runs. Managers like John McGraw, while following the Deadball Era, or small-ball approach, stressed stolen bases. George Stallings, on the other hand, emphasized the sacrifice hit. The team regularly turned games around with sacrifice bunts, the Braves' offensive weapon of choice in 1914. By the end of the season, the Braves boasted three of the top sacrifice hitters in the National League: Johnny Evers, third, with 31; Rabbit Maranville, second, with 27; and Butch Schmidt, the hefty, power-hitting, middle-of-the-lineup first baseman, with 10. While the Braves were second in runs scored, third in on-base percentage, and third in home runs (35), they led the league in sacrifices, far outdistancing any other team. Their 221 sacrifice hits soared above the next best team, the Chicago Cubs, who had only 191. The Braves also led the league by a small margin in RBIs; they excelled at knocking in runs, especially after they had sacrificed them into scoring position.[10] The quality so often associated with the Braves, "fight," often came in the form of the sacrifice hit, and the individual yielding for the greater good of the team best represented the Braves' determination to win.

When Stallings evaluated his team's success, he praised its fighting spirit, a youthful spirit that embraced each victory, while ignoring a series of defeats. The team—even the experienced Evers—played like exuberant adolescents, unmindful of the pain of defeat. The position players averaged 26.5 years of age, an entire year younger than the rest of the National League. In the midst of the comeback, Stallings expressed a realistic, although fighting, optimism: "I never cross my bridges before I come to them. I do not know where Boston is going to finish. But I can promise my team will fight to the end. The other clubs will know that they have been through a fight, not where Boston may finish."[11] While always pleased that he had a "fighting, hustling" club, Stallings concluded, "The best thing about the club is that it does not know it is defeated." The 1914 Braves seemed much like the "Miracle Mets" of 1969, a team that Roger Angell so accurately describes: "Their immense good fortune was to find themselves together at the same moment of sudden maturity, combined skills, and high spirits. Perhaps they won because they didn't want this ended. Perhaps they won because they were unbored."[12]

PITCHING IS KEY

The Braves succeeded because of their unyielding determination; their superb small-ball tactics; and the exceptional leadership of Maranville, Stallings, and Evers. But they triumphed in August 1914, largely because of brilliant pitching. The three "boxmen," a term for pitcher used since the nineteenth century—Bill James, Dick Rudolph, and "Lefty" Tyler—shut down the opposition with regularity, keeping the other teams to two or three hits and even fewer runs. On August 3, Tyler beat the Cardinals, 1–0, on a three-hitter; Rudolph and James pitched two- and four-hitters on August 4 and 5, respectively, against Pittsburgh. The Braves' pitchers, backed by their "usual brilliant fielding exhibition," shut out the Pirates twice. Toward the end of July and beginning of August, the three hurlers never lost when they stepped onto the mound.[13] By the end of the season, Tyler, James, and Rudolph averaged 310 innings each (Justin Verlander, in his 2011 Cy Young Award–winning year, pitched 251 innings), placing fifth, sixth, and seventh, respectively, in the National League in strikeouts. Tyler allowed opposing batters to average .249, as he tallied a 1.28 WHIP, winning 16 games; James, while winning 26 games, let batters hit .225, as he earned a 1.14 WHIP; and the batting average against

Rudolph was .238, as he established a phenomenal 1.04 WHIP, and he, too, won 26 games.[14]

On August 1, the *Boston Globe* reported on Rudolph's pitching prowess from the previous day. The Braves were battling the Cardinals in a four-game series from July 30 to August 3. Against the St. Louis Cardinals, "Dick had the visitors fooled up to their eyes." Rudolph pitched a "masterful" two-hitter against his old teammate Hub Perdue, retiring batter after batter (with one play a questionable call at first after a brilliant Maranville defensive feat), and even when Cardinals outfielder Lee Magee moved around to third on three errors, Rudolph stopped the bleeding with two groundouts. The Braves, after hitting three sacrifices and six hits, managed to scrape by with a 2–0 victory. Rudolph's success against St. Louis explained the Braves' trajectory: timely hitting, a few sacrifices, and dominating pitching. The Braves, who had won four in a row, 11 of their last 13, spiraled upward, not only in the standings, drawing the attention and energy of Boston fans. The Braves' popularity in Boston soared, but the South End Grounds, uncomfortable and confining, restricted attendance. In a most gracious gesture, Boston Red Sox owner Joseph Lannin invited the Braves to move to Fenway Park.[15]

On the first Saturday of August, the Braves, having won five out of their last six games, entered Fenway Park and were greeted by 20,000 exultant fans, the largest crowd to attend a National League game in Boston. The Braves added a new ingredient to their success: thousands of wildly enthusiastic fans. Most were Boston natives, but oftentimes significant pockets of fans represented a player's hometown. And on August 1, a couple thousand fans arrived from Springfield, Massachusetts, and Windsor Locks, Connecticut, to root for local heroes Walter "Rabbit" Maranville and Leslie Mann, respectively. The national pastime, although played on a national scale, had a provincial character: hometown Americans rooted for the local hero in the major leagues. The fans who had traveled to Fenway Park, like the ones from Windsor Locks and Springfield, held a personal investment in victory and helped bring the crowd to a fever pitch.

ECSTATIC FANS

The Braves sent out emerging ace Bill James, who held the Cardinals scoreless until the eighth. When the Braves, scoreless for six innings, finally tallied three runs in the seventh on a hit by Joe Connolly and a sacrifice fly by Rabbit, fans "went into a tumult of ecstasy and cheered and yelled continuously for five minutes." But the Cardinals fought back to tie the score, shocking the overconfident Braves fans. In the 10th inning, Stallings sent in a couple of pinch hitters, including the righty George "Possum" Whitted, to battle against the talented lefty "Slim" Sallee. With two outs, Whitted drove in the winning run. Fan excitement moved up another notch. "The game was over, but the fans were in no hurry to leave and remained to cheer. One would think from the enthusiasm manifested that a world championship had been won."[16]

Whitted had batted in Johnny Evers for the winning run. Evers, who seemed to face unceasing harsh trials—even in the midst of a win streak— now suffered from both a strained neck and shoulder pain; he had missed the second St. Louis game on Friday, July 31. According to *Boston Globe* writer J. C. O'Leary, Evers's pain was caused by pleurisy, an inflammation of the lining around the lungs. Yet, Evers persisted: He played on Saturday in the Fenway Park game, and on Monday, August 3, the final game of the series, the infielder turned in three sensational plays that helped Lefty Tyler hold St. Louis to no runs on three hits. Fans could see Evers "noticeably wince" during one throw. And Evers, despite the pain, knocked in a thrilling ninth-inning game winner. Tyler opened up the ninth with a single, and Josh Devore sacrificed him to second. Evers, always a tough, annoying batter, hit a foul inches to the right of first base, and then another inches to the left of third base. On the third attempt, he blasted a high chopper over the pitcher's mound; second baseman Art Butler knew he had to make a "lightning one-handed play" to throw out the hustling Evers, but he rushed the throw, snapping it over the first baseman's head. The Braves had secured four games in a row against the Cardinals, a highly competitive team that a week earlier, in third place, five games behind the Giants, had been talking pennant.[17]

Evers and the Braves pitchers carved a path forward, preserving the team's win streak. Now, Honus Wagner, who, on June 9, had collected his 3,000th hit, and the Pittsburgh Pirates were visiting the Braves.[18] Dick Rudolph tossed his second two-hit shutout in five days. And one of the hits, this time a Wagner liner to diving right fielder Josh Devore, was disputed. The umpire called Wagner out, and then, as Devore appeared to let go of the ball, safe. But it was Evers who starred for the team once again. Evers completed, as sportswriter O'Leary noted with a small degree of hyperbole, "One of the greatest plays ever seen." Pittsburgh's fleet, base-thieving Max Carey smashed a bounder to the back of second. With the ball five feet behind the bag, and with Carey steaming down to first, Evers "caught the ball—and this apparently was premeditated—in such a way that his arm extended so that he could make a throw to first without any backward motion. While still in the air, he let the ball go, and it was on its way to first before his feet touched the ground." When Evers threw out the speedy Carey with his barehanded toss, the crowd cheered wildly. And although Evers's three base hits did not contribute to the score, the Braves, manufacturing a run with Charlie Deal's sacrifice bunt, earned a 1–0 victory.[19]

A PINNACLE AND A SETBACK

As the Braves reached their pinnacle, team captain Johnny Evers, the veteran who had battled bankruptcy, suffered a traumatizing car accident, and endured depression, now faced the greatest of personal losses: the death of a child. On August 6, Evers and the Braves won, 5–4, over the Pirates, their ninth win in a row. During the game, Evers learned that his three-year-old daughter, Nellie, had been stricken with scarlet fever. Nellie's five-year-old brother Jack had previously contracted the disease and had been isolated in the Evers's home in Troy, but Nellie, given special permission to break the quarantine, acquired scarlet fever herself. Jack survived, but Nellie passed away before Evers could return home. Scarlet fever, a common disease that often affected children younger than 10, had no antibiotic treatment in 1914. The disease struck fast: The time between the infection and the onset of symptoms was short. The trauma of Nellie's death strained Evers's family life. His wife Helen and son Jack left the family home, and his wife soon filed for separation.[20] In anger and despair, she blamed Johnny, saying, "Where were you? You were never around."[21]

Personal traumas that touched national figures like Evers were not always highly publicized. Bostonians did not read about Evers's marital problems. Yet, Boston fans had learned of Nellie Evers's illness and death, and they supported Johnny in their own quiet ways, perhaps a personal note, and also through cheering fervently in the stands. The public record leaves little evidence about this event. Newspapers chose to be generally silent (rumors circulated that Evers had wanted to cease playing for the 1914 season). Evers's primary biographer, Gil Bogen, has provided the few records that exist on the event. Still, this hyperactive, overly sensitive ballplayer unquestionably suffered deeply from this loss. On August 6, the Boston papers noted his anxiety: "Johnny Evers had much to worry him during the game. He received word early in the day that his little daughter Helen was very ill with scarlet fever."[22] Evers left the team on August 7, and the Braves, undoubtedly distracted and concerned, lost, 5–1. According to the *Boston Globe*, they played "without the services of Johnny Evers, whose baby died early yesterday morning, before he reached his home in Troy. The whole team was somewhat upset and did not play its usual game."[23]

BRAVES NOW PENNANT WORTHY

On August 10, Bill James shut down the Cincinnati Reds, 3–1, holding them to six hits, including "two infield scratches, a lucky double, and one fair by inches only."[24] Three and a half weeks earlier, Boston had lagged behind, in last place, 11 and a half games behind the New York Giants. Now the Braves found themselves in second place, six and a half games behind New York. After August 13 and 14, the Braves grew even more confident as they earned two victories from the "popularly dreaded Giants." On August 15, the Braves, behind Tyler, beat the Giants' Christy Mathewson. In the bottom of the 10th inning, the Giants loaded the bases with no outs, but Tyler halted the rally and preserved a 2–0 Braves victory. These victories affirmed that the Braves had moved beyond the win streak phase and stood prepared to fight for the pennant. From July 17 until August 17, they played 27 games, losing only four (one tie).[25] Crushing National League opponents from mid-July to mid-August partially proved to the baseball world that the Braves could contend; sweeping the Giants offered irrefutable evidence that the Braves could triumph over any of the first-division teams.

And now the Braves were vigorously pursuing the champions from New York, the formidable team led by Christy Mathewson and John McGraw that had secured pennants in 1904, 1905, 1911, 1912, and 1913, as well as a World Series in 1905. McGraw ultimately won 10 pennants and three World Series. Mathewson, the most illustrious athlete of his time, had averaged nearly 28 wins per season for 10 years, winning 37 games in 1908.[26] This tandem of celebrity manager and superstar pitcher, probably the most popular sports figures of the time, loomed over the young Braves, new to the national stage. The Giants' powerhouse included not only the dominant Mathewson, but a rotation that included Rube Marquard and Jeff Tesreau. These pitchers received the support of first-rate position players: George Burns (not the comedian), Fred Merkle, Fred Snodgrass, and Art Devlin, all players who, following McGraw's tactics, could bunt, sacrifice, hit-and-run, and, above all, steal bases, to advance around the diamond.

A FIERY MCGRAW

The Braves and Stallings challenged John J. McGraw, the short, sturdy, fiery manager whom Grantland Rice described as "[o]ne of the greatest natural leaders any sport has ever known. Baseball to him was more than a game. It was a religion and a war combined. . . . Few can understand how he gave his very soul to the game he loved so well."[27] This most controversial of Deadball Era managers is still studied in the twenty-first century. As Frank Deford notes, McGraw acted as a "pugnacious little boss who would become the model for the classic American coach—a male version of the whore with a heart of gold—the tough, flinty so-and-so who was field-smart, a man's man his players came to love despite themselves."[28] McGraw earned two widely known nicknames: "Muggsy," a label that explained itself with one quick look at the man, and "Little Napoleon," a title that branded him as a clever strategist and shrewd judge of baseball talent.

The son of Irish immigrant John William McGraw, who arrived in the United States in 1850, during one of the most devastating years of the potato famine, John Joseph McGraw, was born on April 7, 1873, the second oldest of nine children. The elder McGraw hardworking, sober, and well educated, found it difficult to buy basic necessities for his growing family. Despite 12 years of schooling, he failed to find a teaching position; after having served with the Union during the Civil War, he found maintenance work on the Elmira, Cortland, and Northern Railroad. For the McGraws, the "main ingredients of their lives were toil and denial: managing week by week to have food on the table and enough clothing to protect against the region's harsh winter."[29]

Despite improvements in public health, diseases, similar to the one that had killed Johnny Evers's daughter, ravaged communities in the late nineteenth century. Disease compounded the McGraw's want, and in the winter of 1884–1885, a diphtheria epidemic swept through his hometown of Truxton, New York, closing schools and forcing families to bar their doors. His mother, weakened after giving birth to her eighth child, died within five days. A week later, McGraw and his siblings watched powerlessly as his older stepsister Anna coughed, wheezed, and took in her last breath. By the end of January 1885, three more of McGraw's siblings had succumbed to disease. His father had always treated his children with severity, and after the trauma of 1884–1885, the widower, expecting more from young John, lost patience with the 12-year-old, particularly when the young man showed his ceaseless passion for baseball by inadvertently throwing balls through windowpanes. The father once beat young John for swinging a stick at a rock; the boy simply wanted to sharpen his batting skills. One evening, nearly five months after the diphtheria epidemic, the father flew into a violent fury when he learned that John had smashed yet another window. He seized John, hurling him against the wall, flogging him and beating him in the face.[30]

DEDICATED TO BASEBALL

McGraw, unable to endure the sufferings any longer, ran away from home, worked at a small hotel, and dedicated himself to learning the game of the baseball. The learning curve seemed sharp, but the hard working former altar boy invested his hours memorizing and studying the annual *Spalding*

Base Ball Guides. Ready to demonstrate his baseball wisdom to the world, he triumphed over both teammates and opponents in any disputed call. The teenager proved himself in local games as a pitcher by a tossing a remarkable, unhittable looping curveball. He soon pleaded with Albert Kenney, owner of a local boardinghouse and professional baseball team, to allow him to join his Olean club as an infielder. Not even 17 when he joined the Olean baseball team of the New York–Pennsylvania State League, McGraw initiated his career with a pitiful performance at third base and reacted anxiously to his first grounder: "For the life of me, I could not run to get it. It seemed like an age before I had the ball in my hands, and then, as I looked over to first, it seemed like the longest throw I had to make. The first baseman was the tallest in the league, but I threw the ball high overhead." That afternoon, McGraw blundered seven more times, usually throwing over the first baseman's head. Released after Olean's sixth consecutive loss, McGraw found his way to the team in Wellsville, New York, where he brought his infield play up to a passable level—with fewer wild throws—and he hit for a strong .365 average.[31]

His career ascended higher when teammate Albert Lawson, a baseball promoter, organized a team of American All-Stars and invited McGraw to join a baseball touring group to Cuba. Playing exhibitions against local teams, his opponents affectionately called him *El Mono Amarillo*, the "yellow monkey," acknowledging both his yellow uniform and high-spiritedness.[32] Heading north into Florida during baseball's spring training, McGraw's team challenged the Cleveland Spiders, a club known for such standouts as "Patsy" Tebeau, Clarence "Cupid" Childs, and a rookie pitcher, who, whipping fastballs like a cyclone, had already earned the name "Cy" Young. After McGraw played errorless baseball and smashed three doubles in five plate appearances, telegraph reports sent to northern newspapers and baseball weeklies sparked national attention. The son of an Irish immigrant was now listening to offers from established professional baseball teams.[33]

BALTIMORE WELCOMES MCGRAW

McGraw, the Irish scrapper from Truxton, soon joined a group of brash, boisterous baseball combatants: the often triumphant and always infamous 1890s Baltimore Orioles. McGraw drove the Baltimore Orioles to three first-place and three second-place finishes, including two Temple Cup victories, the 1890s World Championship Series. In 1894, Orioles player-manager Ned Hanlon assembled the classic small-ball team: McGraw, as a third baseman, joined five-foot, four-inch "Wee Willie" Keeler, the on-base percentage king of the 1890s. Keeler earned fame as a bunter, a hit-and-run expert, and the inventor of the "Baltimore Chop," a smash hit that bounded so high he could scamper safely into first before the infielder's throw. McGraw, as the team's leadoff hitter, would slap an infield single or walk to reach first and then dash to third when Keeler artfully poked the ball through the infield.[34]

The Baltimore team fought for victory by any deceitful means necessary. McGraw was known for stealthily holding the opposing player's belt as the player attempted to run between bases (and crafty players who wanted to score learned to unbuckle their belts). Orioles groundskeeper Tom Murphy hardened the area just in front of home plate so that the Orioles could get an extra high bounce when they exercised the notorious Baltimore Chop. Murphy altered foul lines and transformed the first-base line into a slight decline, assisting the speedy Orioles, and he allowed the grass to grow high in right field, where Wee Willie Keeler could stash extra baseballs to replace those that rolled by him.[35] Keeler displayed great skills and averaged .345 during a 19-year career, because, as he put it, "I hit 'em where they ain't."[36] Accurate and timely hitting earned plaudits from opponents; Baltimore's other tactics, however, drew reproach. Tim Murinane, the distinguished Boston sportswriter, decried the Orioles' tactics as the "dirtiest ever seen in this country." He listed the Baltimore team's offenses: "[D]iving into the first baseman long after he has caught the ball, throwing masks in front of the runners at home plate, catching them by the clothes at third base, and interfering with the catcher were only a few tricks performed by these young men from the South."[37]

Certainly other teams, not just the Orioles, unleashed a fighting spirit, and 1890s baseball, uncivilized by twentieth-century standards, still found itself in the formative stages: Pitchers threw 50 feet to a plate that measured a foot wide, players wore a covering for a glove, and only one umpire called balls and strikes. Fighting was common. Fans threw bottles and debris at players, players slugged umpires, and teammates beat up opposing players. The hot-tempered McGraw fought off any slight with both fists and invective, eventually earning the nickname "Muggsy." McGraw disdained the label, and any player who dared to shout out "Muggsy" only earned a fistfight. Of course, the more frequently McGraw displayed his loathing of the name, the more players cried, "Muggsy."[38]

"IT'S TRUXTON AGAINST THE WORLD"

The origins of the slur "Muggsy," despite varying accounts in baseball books, found its roots in McGraw's past, a past that he desperately fought to overcome. Baltimore, McGraw's real hometown (he chose to be buried there), had functioned as the political turf for John "Muggsy" McGraw, a ruffian ward boss, rumored to be manager McGraw's father. McGraw wanted to cut loose from this imagined past.[39] What would drive a man to wrestle with his own teammates? Why would McGraw instinctively smash a ball into the mouth of Cleveland's tough guy, Pat Tebeau, and then spit on him?[40] What would cause a man to scrap in fistfight after fistfight—and lose in nearly every battle? As the legendary Hall of Fame umpire Bill Klem noted, "It is highly doubtful McGraw ever won a fistfight. And it is highly doubtful that he ever ducked one." It was this profound need to break from the hardship of his hometown of Truxton that drove McGraw, suggests Deford. According to Deford, McGraw, as he attained success in his career, regularly cared for a pet dog, usually a Boston bull terrier, always named "Truxton." McGraw would "sit down with his dog and partake of the same breakfast: orange juice, scrambled eggs, bacon, toast, and coffee. He would feed his dog a little bit of bacon, and then this is the refrain John J. McGraw would scream out: 'It's Truxton against the world!'"[41]

At the turn of the twentieth century, McGraw brought his combative mind-set to his job managing the Orioles, and then later, the New York Giants. After the Orioles experienced a wholesale restructuring in 1899, with manager Ned Hanlon and such stars as Willie Keeler forming a new team in Brooklyn, McGraw signed on as a 25-year-old player-manager for the Orioles. He then began to intensify his antiumpire broadsides. McGraw's outbursts yielded a steady revenue stream to National League president Nick Young. Young recalled, "Every other day or so—perhaps not quite so often but pretty near it—I received a five dollar note wrapped up in a business-like letter reading, 'Dear Mr. Young, Inclosed please find $5. Which I pay for the privilege of calling Umpire So-and-so a stiff.'"[42]

But, when, in 1901, the Orioles entered the new American League, a league designed by President Ban Johnson to promote a civilized, profamily game, McGraw failed to live up to the new, refined, genteel standards. In the American League's first year, Johnson depended on the Orioles, and Johnson wined and dined McGraw, signing him on as a member. Yet, McGraw's antiauthoritarian behavior conflicted with the cultured, Victorian tenor of the new league, and after umpire Jim Haskell ejected McGraw on May 7, 1901, and after McGraw battled with umpire Joe Cantillon later in the month, Johnson suspended McGraw for five days. Johnson decreed, "Mr. McGraw will not even watch the games from the bench for five days. I ordered him kept away from the grounds as a penalty for using foul and profane language on the diamond."[43] But the cursing, taunting, and even brawling continued throughout that season, and in August, Johnson banned McGraw's top pitcher, "Iron Man" Joe McGinnity, who, as Giants fans swarmed onto the field, stomped on umpire Tommy Connolly's feet—after having twice spat in his face. At that point, McGraw began negotiating with Andrew Freedman of the National League's New York Giants and secured an $11,000 managerial contract, the highest in baseball at that time.[44]

MATHEWSON AND MCGRAW

As the Giants manager, McGraw was able to draw away former Orioles, including McGinnity. He also built the foundation of his team with a new, young, handsome, Bucknell College–educated pitcher, Christy Mathewson. Deford writes that "Mathewson was golden, tall, and handsome, kind and educated, our beau ideal, the first all-American boy to emerge from the field of play."[45] Mathewson's talent in the first 15 years of the new century proved simply incomparable. It was superstar caliber: "373 victories, tied for the highest in National League history, and 37 wins in 1908, a modern professional record; in four seasons, he won 30 or more games. Five times he led the league with the lowest ERA, with a lifetime average of 2.13."[46] Batters stood in awe of Mathewson, knowing that he had mastered a variety of pitches, that he exercised pinpoint control, that he had a precise memory of each pitch he had thrown, and that he might just toss his noted "fade-away," a pitch that broke in on right-handers and away from left-handers (the equivalent of the screwball).[47] Perhaps in a slight decline in 1914 (his ERA reached 3.00), Mathewson still threw more than 300 innings, earning 24 victories.[48]

Mathewson achieved national repute for both his ability and great stature. The first truly national baseball hero, he served as a model for popular fictional characters: Gilbert Patten's Frank Merriwell, and then later Howard Garis's "Baseball Joe." Joe Matson, or "Baseball Joe," a character of talent and integrity, appeared in 14 boys' sports novels produced by Edward Stratemeyer, the creator of Tom Swift, Nancy Drew, and the Hardy Boys.[49] According to one observer, Mathewson "talks like a Harvard graduate, looks like an actor, acts like a businessman, and impresses you as an all-around gentleman."[50] Fans appreciated his athletic talent, intelligence, exceptional good looks, and religious devotion—he never played on Sundays; and major-league players recognized Mathewson as a Renaissance man, a college-educated professional who read William James and Victor Hugo while traveling on the road. As teammate Fred Snodgrass once recollected, "Matty could do everything well. He was checker champion of half a dozen states. He'd play several opponents simultaneously and beat them all—a good billiards player, a pretty fair golfer, and a terrific poker player."[51]

McGraw and Mathewson, who took lead roles for this grand New York production, appeared as an odd couple. While McGraw, from Deford's perspective, had gained a reputation as "hardscrabble shanty Irish, a pugnacious little boss," Mathewson, on the other hand, achieved fame as the virile, blond-haired, blue-eyed, college-educated gentleman.[52] McGraw embodied the tough immigrant's son, the battler who had brawled his way to fame and fortune; Mathewson, the tall, graceful, naturally gifted pitcher, exemplified "muscular Christianity," a popular Anglo-American ideal that advanced physical vitality, Christian values, and manhood. "Muscular Christianity," a reaction to the perceived effeminate, sentimental church ceremonies of the late nineteenth century, drew the support of such organizations as the YMCA and prominent citizens the likes of Theodore Roosevelt. This new masculinity promoted the notion that Jesus Christ offered a role model, not just as a moral exemplar, but also as a physically fit man's man. Mathewson, the robust, world champion, gentleman athlete, attained such a reputation as a respected gentleman that when umpires—and there were only two on each playing field in 1914—failed to get a clear view of a controversial call, they glanced over to Mathewson to receive a fair and honest judgment.[53]

Mathewson and McGraw, although so dissimilar in style, forged such a durable bond that they joined forces on the baseball field for 16 years. Off the field they were devoted friends, and the two men and their spouses shared an apartment in the Upper West Side of New York City. The two men, eight years apart in age, like older brother and younger brother, held common values. Both reveled in their role as public figures. Although Mathewson shielded himself from overbearing crowds and often pulled down the blinds in railway cars, he performed vaudeville one year and accepted endorsements for razors, sweaters, Coca-Cola, and even pipe tobacco.[54]

Although McGraw experienced "nerves" when on the stage, in 1913, he also took to the vaudeville stage for a successful 15-week stint. Both men enjoyed the good life, which their endorsements and high salaries had produced, and both men were fiercely competitive, game-playing gamblers, capable of coarse language. Mathewson, despite his golden-boy reputation, fought, argued, and even swore: "He could command enough four-letter words to hold his own in locker room repartee."[55] McGraw spoke with a tongue that, according to reporter John Sheridan, "would burn holes in nickel twelve inches thick."[56] In one season, 1905, his verbal tirades pushed umpires into tossing McGraw out of games 13 times, still a season record in 2014.[57] In 1906, the Chicago Cubs' Harry Steinfeldt, at the request of National League president Harry Pulliam, documented the exact words that McGraw shouted at umpire James Johnstone: "a damn dirty, cock-eating bastard, and a low-lived son-of-a-bitch of a yellow cur hound."[58]

While the two men enjoyed the rough-and-tumble of the baseball world, they found intellectual pursuits beyond sports. Mathewson, as a college freshman at Bucknell, played baseball and football, joined the band, the glee club, the dramatic society, and Latin Philosophical, served as class president, and earned a 96 percent in analytic chemistry, 96 percent in German, 94 percent in Tacitus, and 93 percent in Horace.[59] As a 19-year-old, McGraw, despite his basic, elementary education, negotiated a deal with St. Bonaventure College (called Allegany at the time), where, during the off-season, he would swap college courses for baseball coaching. McGraw found his part-time coursework challenging: "I find wrestling with books much harder than I find wrestling with umpires." Still, he persisted in his studies for three years, achieving honor roll in Latin, geometry, and rhetoric. McGraw never fulfilled his degree requirements; however, in the opinion of biographer Charles C. Alexander, "He'd learned how to behave in the company of educated people, how to organize his thoughts and express himself clearly; in short, he'd learned a great deal besides baseball."[60]

FOR THE LOVE OF BASEBALL

What brought McGraw and Mathewson beyond their common background and values was a profound affection for baseball: its strategy, tactics, and, above all else, pitching. Describing the experience in the New York City apartment, McGraw's wife Blanche noted, "Jane [Mathewson's wife] and I led normal lives. We fed the men and left them alone to talk baseball."[61] McGraw, a former pitcher, appreciated Mathewson's thinking approach to baseball and, early in his career, offered tips on how to improve his changeup. McGraw saw Mathewson as a like-minded baseball man and complimented him because he "mastered the science of the game from the pitcher's standpoint."[62] Mathewson and McGraw, like typical progressives, and much like the Braves' Johnny Evers, approached pitching in a rational, systematic manner. In McGraw's book on baseball, *Scientific Baseball*, he included a chapter by Mathewson, where the pitcher broke down each element of pitching: types of pitches (fastball, slow ball or changeup, curve, spitball, and fadeaway), the physiology of a good pitcher, the grip of the ball, arm movement, arm angles, the position of the feet, the snapping of the wrist, speed of delivery, and control of pitches.[63]

McGraw built a baseball management strategy based on superb pitching, stellar defense, and dynamic baserunning, and McGraw would execute the strategy carefully and thoroughly. The apprentice ballplayer learned to master McGraw's teachings; the experienced player unquestionably followed his orders. Rube Marquard, one of his star pitchers, summed up the player's view of "Little Napoleon": "He loved his players, and his players loved him. Of course, he wouldn't stand for any nonsense. You had to live up to the rules and regulations of the New York Giants, and when he laid down the law, you better abide by it."[64] Marquard passed along the story of the powerful Giants outfielder Red Murray failing to abide by McGraw's rules. With one out and a man on second, and the score tied in the ninth inning against the Pirates, McGraw ordered Murray to bunt, but Murray, eyeing his favorite pitch, a high fastball, slammed a game-winning home run over the left-field fence. In the locker room after the game, as Murray cheerily burst into song, McGraw offered no congratulations; instead, he issued a stern rebuke and a $100 fine. Murray had failed to follow orders.[65] And as star outfielder Fred Snodgrass remembered, McGraw's players needed a thick skin:

> And sometimes Mr. McGraw would bawl the dickens out of me, as he did everybody else. Any *mental* error, any failure to think, and McGraw would be all over you. And I do believe he had the most vicious tongue of anyone who ever lived. Absolutely! Sometimes that wasn't easy to take, you know.[66]

Snodgrass, however, questioned McGraw's public persona; he knew that the dictatorial "Little Napoleon" image revealed a half-truth. McGraw, he contended, "allowed initiative to his men." While McGraw demanded that each player know the art and science of baseball, the Giants "stole when we thought we had the jump and when the situation demanded it. We played hit-and-run when we felt that was called for." McGraw, despite his reputation as the fierce, gunpowder-eating, blood-drinking manager, knew and understood his players.[67]

By 1914, John "Muggsy" McGraw and his star player, Christy "Big Six" Mathewson, both much more nuanced than their public personas, had proven themselves as high achievers, leaders of one of baseball's greatest teams. McGraw had assembled a group of first-rate players who complemented Mathewson's abilities, and who adapted well to McGraw's strategy and tactics. First, he acquired topflight pitchers, including Jeff Tesreau. The six-foot, two-inch, 225-pound spitball specialist put up stellar numbers in 1914, winning 26 games; he started 41, pitching 322 innings, with a 2.37 ERA. Left-handed pitcher Rube Marquard, who had learned the fadeaway from his traveling roommate Mathewson, struggled to a 12–22 record in 1914, despite compiling a solid 3.06 ERA and a 1.15 WHIP. Marquard, who praised McGraw as the "finest and grandest man I ever met," displayed the toughness that the manager so admired, but Marquard's season took a turn for the worse after he gained a 3–1 victory against Pittsburgh on July 17, a game in which he and Babe Adams both threw a remarkable and exhausting 21 innings.[68]

STRONG AT ALL POSITIONS

McGraw put together a stellar cast of position players, including Fred Merkle, who, according to *Baseball Magazine*, was the "most finished fielder in the league." Merkle, known for his "bonehead" mental error that changed the 1908 season, was, in the view of one teammate, the "smartest man on the club," and he could shrewdly steal third despite lacking in speed.[69] Fred Snodgrass, known for his 1912 World Series "muff" (Snodgrass had dropped a routine fly ball in the 10th inning of the deciding game of the 1912 World Series), showed spectacular speed in center field and was flanked by an even fleeter outfielder, George Burns, *Baseball Magazine*'s 1914 National League All-American left fielder.[70] Catcher Jack Meyers, a member of California's Cahuilla tribe, and like other Native American ballplayers of the time tagged "Chief," hit .286 in 1914, just below his outstanding .291 lifetime average. Meyers, a former student at Dartmouth, read Plato and visited art museums on his off days.[71] Larry Doyle, a .290 lifetime hitter, the team captain, and second baseman, embodied the ideals of a John McGraw position player: "hustling, aggressive . . . full of nerve, grit, and courage." Doyle, who showed surprising power for a Deadball Era second baseman, fulfilled McGraw's last requirement: baseball intelligence. When an umpire ejected McGraw, and they did so early and often, Doyle served as his designated replacement.[72] This team had lived up to its name: "Giants." From 1911 until 1913, they rose above all other National League teams, and until August 1914, they had dominated the pennant race. (See tables 4.1 and 4.2.)

The powerful Giants, the victors in the last three National League pennant races, the team led by baseball's most notorious manager, John McGraw, obstructed the Braves' ascent. Yet, chasing the Giants for the pennant on August 13, the Braves had cut the Giants' lead to five and a half games. On August 14, the *Boston Globe*'s main sports story mentioned "Rudolph out-

Table 4.1. New York Giants Monthly Splits, 1914

Month	Games	Won	Lost	Winning Percentage
April	8	4	4	0.500
May	24	17	7	0.708
June	28	16	12	0.571
July	27	15	12	0.556
August	27	11	15	0.423
September	35	17	17	0.500
October	7	4	3	0.571

Source: http://www.baseball-almanac.com.

Table 4.2. New York Giants Team versus Team Splits, 1914

Opponent	Games	Won	Lost	Winning Percentage
Boston Braves	23	11	11	0.500
Brooklyn Robins	22	13	9	0.591
Chicago Cubs	22	13	9	0.591
Cincinnati Reds	22	13	9	0.591
Philadelphia Phillies	22	12	10	0.545
Pittsburgh Pirates	23	13	9	0.591
St. Louis Cardinals	22	9	13	0.409

Source: http://www.baseball-almanac.com.

pitching Marquard," and, indeed, Dick Rudolph, a Bronx native, impressed his fellow New Yorkers by holding the Giants to three runs. But the story of the day was, "Sacrifices Produce Key Runs." Joe Connolly, the Braves' best hitter, led off the sixth with a single; then Maranville knocked a sacrifice bunt down the first-base line. Giants pitcher Rube Marquard scooped up the ball, but after failing to touch the elusive Rabbit Maranville, wheeled and threw the ball over the head of the first baseman. Maranville held at first, and Connolly stopped safely at second. Butch Schmidt, the six-foot, one-inch, 200-pound Braves first baseman, laid down a perfect sacrifice bunt as Connolly and Maranville moved to second and third. The Braves' third baseman, Red Smith, popped a foul for the second out, but center fielder Leslie Mann smoked a single to left, and with two more runs, the Braves had a comfortable 4–0 lead.[73] As it had so many times before, the sacrifice bunt swung the game in the Braves' favor.

The Braves clawed at the Giants' lead in the standings, and, on August 15, the *Globe*'s front page shared an account of the Braves' victory, with headlines reading, "Germans Advance on Allies." On August 14, the Braves had played their "normal game": Their best pitcher, Bill James, although feeling ill, scattered six hits in nine innings; their top hitter, Joe Connolly, socked a double, a single, a home run, and, in the typical Braves manner, a sacrifice fly; their best fielder, Johnny Evers, executed a brilliant fielding play as he took a wide throw from catcher Hank Gowdy "with one hand, and in a lightning-like move, clapped the ball on [Art] Fletcher as the latter was going into second on an attempted steal." The emerging young star, catcher Hank Gowdy, called the right pitches and hit two "safe ones."[74]

Gowdy stepped up as the Braves' clutch hitter the following Saturday. The game attracted more than 33,000 New Yorkers to the Polo Grounds, where they cheered on the Giants and their pitching idol, Christy Mathewson. The Braves rarely challenged the crafty Mathewson, who limited the Braves to no runs in nine innings—the only threat was a Gowdy triple in the sixth. In the top of the 10th, Gowdy powered another triple, driving home Boston's new third baseman Red Smith from second. Gowdy then scored an insurance run as an unnerved Mathewson let loose a wild pitch. In the bottom of the 10th inning, the Giants loaded the bases with no outs, but Lefty Tyler induced a pop fly, struck out Red Murray, a pinch hitter for Mathewson, and made center fielder Bob Bescher ground out to Evers.[75] *Globe* writers, who tended to overuse the "Giants into Pygmies" metaphor, joked that the Giants, only three and a half games ahead of the Braves, were "reduced to the size of Lilliputians."[76]

GIANT KILLERS

Throughout August, the dominant Giants of Mathewson and McGraw fought off the bothersome, relentless Braves, often dubbed "Giant Killers" by the press. During that month, the Giants slowed down, going 11–15, with a six-game losing streak. Still, the Giants finished the month with a record of 63–50.

The Giants saw another pennant within their reach, but the Braves kept charging. Although stumbling against the Cubs, the Braves won series against the Reds, Pirates, Cardinals, and Phillies—all part of a 20-game road trip. Baseball analysts from the time noted the Braves' stunning success against the western teams, a 45–21 record, while 14–27 against eastern teams. On August 26, a few of the Braves, as high spirited as ever, brawled with the Chicago Cubs' infamous third baseman, Heinie Zimmerman. A highly talented, aggressive hitter who had nearly won the Triple Crown in 1912 (.372 average, 14 home runs, and 99 RBI), Zimmerman swung at Evers viciously as the second baseman tagged Zimmerman on a routine play. When Evers tagged him for a second time, "not so gently . . . by bringing the ball down rather sharply on Zimmerman's head, behind the ear," Zimmerman "throttled" Evers. *Globe* reporter J. C. O'Leary, drawing from World War I military terms, wrote that next, "Maranville got into the action like a torpedo boat attacking a battleship. He grabbed 'Zim' by the arms, and the latter made a swipe at him. The Rabbit came back and landed one on Zim's mouth, badly cutting his lip." Umpire Mal Eason reacted to the melee by ejecting Zimmerman, Evers, Maranville, and even the mediator of the free-for-all, Butch Schmidt. Losing three players from the heart of the order, three-quarters of their infield, cost the Braves dearly, and they went on to lose, 1–0.[77]

The Braves lost the next game, too, an extra-inning, 3–2 loss to the tough St. Louis Cardinals. The Cardinals, still battling for the pennant, moved past the Braves into second place, but the testy, fighting Braves only faltered, and after they learned that Evers and Maranville would only receive fines for their role in the Zimmerman fracas, the Braves returned to their winning ways, gaining victories in seven out of the next eight games.[78]

When, at the end of August, they won the second game of a double-header against St. Louis, with a four-run, ninth-inning comeback, O'Leary explained their success: "By fighting, fighting, fighting: fighting hard, fighting first, last, and all the time."[79] Sweeping the powerful Giants proved to the Braves and the baseball world that the win streak was not mere good fortune.

THE LABOR DAY PENNANT CRESCENDO

The pennant race reached a crescendo on Labor Day weekend: The Braves and Giants both held first place in the National League, and on Monday morning, September 7, Labor Day, the Braves faced the legendary Mathewson in the first game of a doubleheader at Fenway Park. Mathewson's status as a living legend usually shielded him from the verbal attacks that many teams regularly inflicted upon the starting pitcher. The Braves' youth, under the brash leadership of Evers and Stallings, pierced right through the Mathewson aura, and Braves players shouted, "You think you can stop us Mathewson? Not a chance?"[80] The Braves taunted "Big Six," even deriding him as "Milk Legs" for his knock-kneed gait. Mathewson, the coolheaded veteran, held the Braves to three runs for eight innings as the Giants took a 4–3 lead. But in the 10th, Josh Devore beat out an infield hit, and Herbie Moran, who three days before had been knocked unconscious by a pitch, walloped a ball into the overflow crowd at Fenway. The ground-rule double put Moran on second and Devore on third. With the crowd yelling—and now they cheered for Johnny Evers more than before—the Braves' captain smacked a liner into left that drove home the winning run.[81] The Fenway fans, 36,000 of them, morphed into an "outdoor asylum" and swarmed onto the field. Stallings, blocked by hundreds of well-wishers, could move off the field only with a help of a police escort.[82]

In the afternoon game, a second phase of fans poured in, this time, 40,000. With the Braves and Giants still one game apart, it was no surprise that both sides played aggressively, intimidating one another at every opportunity. In the sixth inning, the Giants scored four times, and Lefty Tyler threw high and inside twice, the second time grazing Fred Snodgrass, who, according to the *New York Times*, "twinkled his fingers at Tyler, forgetting to remove his thumb from the nose." The nearly riotous Boston fans "shrieked in anger," and Tyler, catering to the crowd, pantomimed Snodgrass's famous World Series muff. In the next inning, after Snodgrass fended off a fusillade of bottles in center field, Boston mayor James Michael Curley rushed onto the field, and "[l]aying aside his official dignity, he precipitated himself . . . upon Umpire Emslie, demanding that Snodgrass be fired from the game."[83] Emslie resisted Curley and the policeman, but McGraw, probably seeing that the game was firmly in control—the Giants were up by eight runs in the eighth—put Bob Bescher in as a replacement for Snodgrass.[84] The Giants went on to win, 10–1, and the two teams, tied for first place, then battled one another for the deciding game of the series the next day. On Tuesday, McGraw inserted the declining Rube Marquard as pitcher—Marquard had lost his last eight; Stallings slotted his new superstar, the spitballing Bill James. James tossed a three-hitter, securing an 8–3 victory and the Braves' grip on first place (see table 4.3).[85]

In retrospect, the Labor Day games seem like a turning point in the pennant race; however, throughout most of July and August, the Braves, because of their timely hitting, fighting mentality, and, above all else, phenomenal pitching, found themselves on an upward trajectory. The Giants, in turn, especially because of Marquard's poor showings, spiraled downward. Yet, the 1914 National League chase for the pennant sparked interest throughout the summer and fall. Fans sensed that after the Giants and Braves played through the September schedule, they would meet on September 30, for a final showdown. On September 16, the Braves stood only three and a half games ahead, and, on September 19, after the Giants had taken three from the Reds, the New Yorkers remained just three games back.

Giants players still acted shocked to see Boston as the frontrunner; earlier in the season, a few players had quietly rooted for the Braves, hoping to see the team progress, but "never expecting they would have a chance to win a flag." McGraw, in spite of the surge by the Braves, anticipated his fourth pennant in a row: "My club has not quit. . . . I have been through too many campaigns to believe that a small lead such as Boston holds at this state of the race will decide the outcome."[86] Nonetheless, the Braves charged onward, exuding as much confidence as McGraw. Owner Jim Gaffney decided on a celebratory "Johnny Evers Day," to be held on September 16, in a game against the Cardinals, well before the season's end, and even though the Braves were just three games ahead of New York. Organizers designed a day to congratulate the team captain for his baseball successes, indirectly offering solace for his recent troubles. On September 16, the Braves players, represented by George Stallings, presented Evers with a silver service. Evers played his best, with six putouts and five assists, and he helped on two double plays. He also scored one of the Braves' six runs, most dramatically in the eighth inning. With the game tied at three runs apiece, Evers singled and then perilously reached third on an error. As he reached home on a sacrifice fly, the band played "When Johnny Comes Marching Home." The crowd yelled "itself hoarse."[87]

Table 4.3. National League Standings at the Close of Play, September 8, 1914

Team	Games	Wins	Losses	Ties	Winning Percentage	Games Behind	Runs Scored	Runs Allowed
Boston Braves	124	69	53	2	0.566	—	475	442
New York Giants	123	68	54	1	0.557	1.0	545	454
Chicago Cubs	130	69	59	2	0.539	3.0	526	534
St. Louis Cardinals	132	67	62	3	0.519	5.5	479	464
Philadelphia Phillies	122	57	65	0	0.467	12.0	510	558
Pittsburgh Pirates	127	57	66	4	0.463	12.5	399	420
Cincinnati Reds	128	56	70	2	0.444	15.0	455	508
Brooklyn Robins	124	55	69	0	0.444	15.0	493	502

Source: http://www.retrosheet.org.

AHEAD NEAR THE FINISH

Soon the Braves tore off to the finish line, and, on September 21, as they defeated the Pirates, 6–5, the Giants lost to the Cubs, 5–0. Throughout the final phase of the season, Stallings showed unwavering support for his pitchers. On September 21, in the seventh inning, with one out and the go-ahead run on third, even after Dick Rudolph had allowed three hits, and even after Evers had pleaded with him, Stallings kept Rudolph on the mound, and the Braves beat the Pirates, 6–2. The next day, the Braves beat the Pirates for a second time, 8–2, and the Cubs again defeated the Giants, hammering Mathewson for five runs in the first inning.[88] The Braves' lead grew to five games.

At five games back, the Giants would have to play spectacularly well. *Globe* writers realized that with 19 games left, the Braves' lead was nearly insurmountable. If, for instance, the Braves slowed to a 12–7 record, the Giants would need to go 15–4 to catch them, a possible but demanding effort. The final blow to the Giants came on September 23, when their best pitcher, Jeff Tesreau, lost to the Cardinals, 2–1, and then Marquard lost his 13th straight game; for the first time all year, the Giants lost both games of a doubleheader.[89] The Braves split a doubleheader with the Reds, and the Giants dropped to six games back. The Giants played, according to Boston writer Melville Webb, the worst ball seen at the Polo Grounds in years; they "not only have 'cracked,' but seemed to have 'busted,' and beyond all possible repair."[90]

Long after the Braves clinched the pennant, they continued to fight relentlessly, showing the same feistiness and determination they had exhibited in July, when they had begun to scrap their way out of the basement. On the last day of the season, although 10 and a half games ahead of the Giants, Evers kept battling umpires. On that final playing day, Evers was thrown out of the game for "kicking over a decision." When umpire Bill Hart paused at length before calling Brooklyn third baseman Gus Getz safe, Evers threw his glove into the air and complained incessantly for an entire inning. Hart had no choice but to toss him.

The most trying part of the season finale was the Braves' loss of one of their best players because of aggressive baserunning. The Braves had picked up Brooklyn's Red Smith in early August. Smith had batted .245 for Brooklyn, but .314 for the Braves. He finished the year with a .395 slugging percentage, seven home runs, and 85 RBIs (sixth in the league). Despite being perceived as a relatively weak-fielding third basemen, he had played respectfully, earning a .937 fielding percentage, third for third baseman.[91] On the last day of the season, Smith broke his leg in the ninth inning of the first game of a doubleheader. Playing as hard as ever, he tried to stretch a single into a double. After sliding into second, he raised himself into a sitting posture and said to the Dodger second baseman, "I think that I have broke my leg." Cared for by a physician from the stands, and driven to the hospital in a touring car, Smith suffered a broken ankle, an injury that kept him out of the World Series.[92]

"GAMENESS"

Without Smith, the Braves lost one of their strongest bats, the player who followed the team's best power hitter, Butch Schmidt. Smith had played with a determination that had inspired his teammates. While the Braves and their fans appeared heartbroken, and although oddsmakers reduced the Braves' chances to win the World Series, Stallings and Evers expressed their usual resolution: "We will go right on and fight it out . . . the boys will go in and fight all the harder for his sake, as well for their own." Evers recognized the loss but claimed, "I don't believe the absence of Smith is going to make such a difference in the strength of the team as appears to be generally thought."[93] It was this "gameness," this blend of recklessness and grit, that had led to Smith's injury, but it was the same fierceness and tenacity that had pushed the team from last to first. Stallings and Evers maintained such a high level of confidence largely because they understood the remarkable quality of the Braves' comeback. The Braves, at a low point in July, were soaring high that August. By August 15, they had won 27 out of the last 33 games.

BATTLES IN EUROPE

Three weeks later, during the Giants–Braves Labor Day weekend series, just as the pennant had reached its turning point, the German army arrived just 30 miles outside of Paris, and British and French troops defended their positions at the Battle of the Marne. The world sensed a great turning point in history. Generals and soldiers alike grasped the meaning of this battle; as France's General Joseph Joffre asserted on September 5, "At the moment when the battle upon which hangs the fate of France is about to begin, all must remember that the time for looking back is past; every effort must be concentrated on attacking and throwing the enemy back. . . . Under present conditions no weakness can be tolerated."[94] The Great War had already reached incomprehensible proportions, with both the Germans and French suffering nearly a quarter of a million men missing, wounded, or killed.[95] The Battle of the Marne would decide whether the Germans would capture Paris, and, as we now know, and as eminent historian Barbara W. Tuchman observed, the battle "determined that the war would go on."[96]

If the Germans could seize the French capital, as they had in the culmination of the Franco-Prussian War in 1871, they could dominate Western Europe and, no doubt, rule colonies throughout the world. The Germans had annihilated the Russian Second Army just a week earlier at the Battle of Tannenberg. At the same time, the western German offensive had set the Belgians, French, and British reeling backward in an uncoordinated retreat. The two major allied commanders, Sir John French of the British Expeditionary Force, and French general Charles Lanzerac, cast blame upon one another for the chaotic pullback. But just as the Germans stood on the threshold of triumph, they faltered and ultimately failed. "Snatching defeat from the jaws of victory" is a cliché often associated with Helmuth von Moltke, German chief of staff at the Marne. How Moltke and his commanders decided on tactics, and how the Allied Powers formed a military response, is still unclear, yet we do know that the Germans swept down toward Paris—minus two corps that had been sent to the Eastern Front—and when German general Alexander von Kluck, leading the First Army, progressed to the east of Paris, he left his right flank exposed. Trying to swing back, Kluck separated his army from General Karl von Bulow's Second Army, and when the French and British diagnosed this flaw, the British Expeditionary Force moved into the gap. The Germans, beset by overextended supply lines and hampered by ineffective wireless communication, were forced to retreat.[97]

The September victory proved decisive for the Allied Powers. The British and French had formed a successful partnership. The French had new heroes: General Joffre was now celebrated as France's new Napoleon; General Ferdinand Foch earned glory for his battle tactics and his belief in the mystique of the will. Foch, who famously preached, "The will to conquer is the first condition of victory," had called for his troops to "Attack, attack," just when retreat appeared to be the most rational move.[98] The people of France could thank their most celebrated defenders, the 600 determined taxicab drivers who transported 6,000 troops during a crucial juncture of the battle. The heroic effort stunned the Germans: "The French élan," wrote Moltke, "just when it is on the point of being extinguished, flames up powerfully." Henri Bergson, the French philosopher who won the Nobel Prize in Literature in 1924, expressed wonder at the event: "Joan of Arc won the Battle of the Marne."[99] This unexpected occurrence, an Allied victory just when the Germans appeared triumphant, rightfully earned the title "Miracle of the Marne."

But in the Battle of the Marne, thousands perished, and, of course, this 1914 slaughter had no match in the United States. For Boston baseball fans, the pennant race, in fact, offered a respite from the headlines of the war. As the Braves won in September, as they surged by other contenders, newspapers gave manager George Stallings the title of "Miracle Man." The Braves now forged their own "miracle season." Journalists were now paying tribute to the Boston team as the "Miracle Braves."

Braves Warm Up: "Rabbit" Maranville, Hank Gowdy, Johnny Evers, Butch Schmidt, and Dick Rudolph.
The Rucker Archive

Johnny Evers, World Series, 1914.
George Grantham Bain Collection, Library of Congress

Rabbit Maranville Prepares for the World Series.
George Grantham Bain Collection, Library of Congress

Maranville Leaps.
The Rucker Archive

Giants Manager John McGraw and Cubs Player/Manager Johnny Evers, 1912.
George Grantham Bain Collection, Library of Congress

Fenway Park from First-Base Line, 1914.
George Grantham Bain Collection, Library of Congress

Fenway Park Game 3 World Series; October 12, 1914.
John F. Riley, Library of Congress

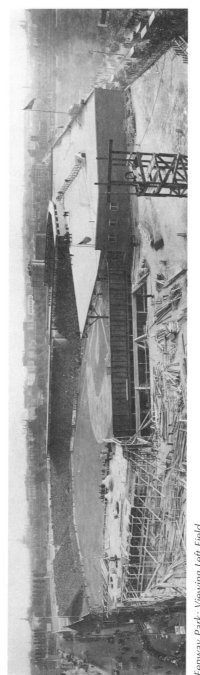

Fenway Park: Viewing Left Field
Courtesy Trustees of the Boston Public Library, Print Department

"Lefty" Tyler Winds Up.
George Grantham Bain Collection, Library of Congress

Bill James Warms Up, World Series, 1914.
George Grantham Bain Collection, Library of Congress

Dick Rudolph Warms Up, World Series, 1914.
George Grantham Bain Collection, Library of Congress

Dick Rudolph's Grip on the Ball.
George Grantham Bain Collection, Library of Congress

Bill James, Manager George Stallings, "Lefty" Tyler, Dick Rudolph, World Series, 1914.
George Grantham Bain Collection, Library of Congress

Connie Mack and Coach Ira Thomas, World Series, 1914.
George Grantham Bain Collection, Library of Congress

Eddie Collins with Connie Mack.
National Baseball Hall of Fame and Museum

First Baseman "Butch" Schmidt Swings a Powerful Bat, World Series, 1914.
George Grantham Bain Collection, Library of Congress

Johnny Evers and George Stallings, World Series, 1914.
George Grantham Bain Collection, Library of Congress

Eddie Plank, October 10, 1914; Shibe Park, Philadelphia, World Series, 1914.
George Grantham Bain Collection, Library of Congress

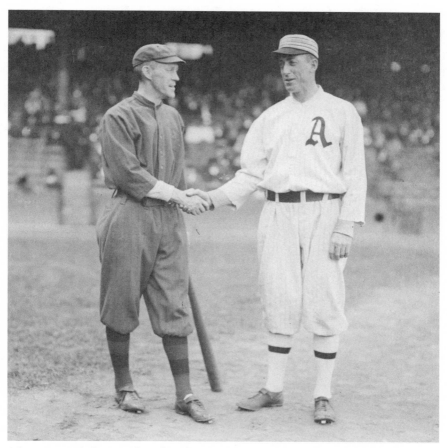

Johnny Evers Shakes Hands with Eddie Plank before Game 2, 1914 World Series.
George Grantham Bain Collection, Library of Congress

Evers Reviews the Rules Before Game 2 of the World Series.
The Rucker Archive

Evers steals second; World Series 1914.
The Rucker Archive

Hank Gowdy, Dick Rudolph, Joey Connolly, "Lefty" Tyler, Oscar Dugey; World Series, 1914.
George Grantham Bain Collection, Library of Congress

Hank Gowdy: A .545 Batter in the World Series.
George Grantham Bain Collection, Library of Congress

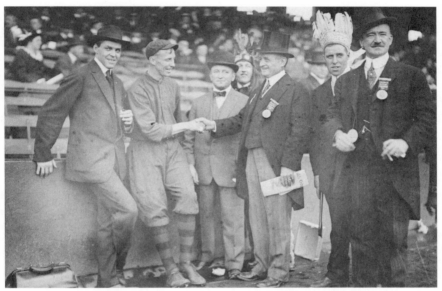

Hank Gowdy Congratulated by Former Boston Mayor "Honey Fitz" Fitzgerald.
George Grantham Bain Collection, Library of Congress

Watching World Series Game from Rooftops of Philadelphia, 1914 World Series.
George Grantham Bain Collection, Library of Congress

George Stallings in the Dugout, World Series, 1914.
The Rucker Archive

Philadelphia A's Team Photo, 1914.
National Baseball Hall of Fame and Museum

THE BRAVES CHAMPIONS 1914

Mgr. STALLINGS   Capt. EVERS   Pres. GAFFNEY
Top Row: JAMES, CATHERS, DEAL, DAVIS, COTTRELL, COCHREHAN, HESS, MANN, GOWDY, SCHMIDT, WHALING
Middle Row: WHITTED, DUGEY, TYLER, STRAND, DEVORE, GILBERT, SMITH and MORAN
Bottom Row: CONNOLLY, MITCHELL, JOHNNY CONNOLLY (Mascot), RUDOLPH, MARANVILLE, CRUTCHER, MARTIN, EVERS

Boston Braves 1914 Team Picture.
The Rucker Archive

TWO PIECES OF BUNTING.

Battlefields of a Different Kind
by Donnell, from the *St. Louis Globe-Democrat*

• 5 •

"The World Upside Down"

$\mathcal{A}$lthough the Braves overcame unprecedented adversity in their last-place-to-first-place rise from July through September, in October they faced the most imposing of challenges: one of the greatest teams in baseball, pennant winners and world champions in three of the previous four years—the mighty Philadelphia Athletics.

Dynastic rulers of the American League, the Philadelphia Athletics dominated in every dimension of the game: pitching, hitting, power, speed, and defense. Fortified by one of the greatest infields of all time, the Athletics' pitching arsenal of Albert "Chief" Bender, "Bullet Joe" Bush, Herb Pennock, Eddie Plank, Bob Shawkey, and Jack Coombs stood ready to gun down the expected feeble attack of the Boston club. "The $100,000 infield" featured Stuffy McInnis at first, Eddie Collins at second, Jack Barry at short, and Frank "Home Run" Baker at third. The Braves' team batting average rested at .251, with a .317 on-base percentage, while the A's sluggers led the majors in batting average, at .272, with an on-base percentage of .348. The A's remained unsurpassed in most of the key hitting categories, including RBIs (627), runs scored (749), runs scored per game (4.74), and on-base plus slugging percentage (.699). The A's, markedly swifter than the Braves, stole 231 bases, significantly more than the 139 of the Braves, who were last in the majors.[1] Oddsmakers rated the battle-tested, powerful champions from Philadelphia 10–4 winners over the inexperienced, vulnerable challengers from Boston.[2] And while George Stallings had demonstrated Wellington-like skills in his battles against "Little Napoleon," John McGraw, he would now encounter baseball's great dynastic ruler, a founding father of the modern game, and the most respected man in baseball: the Athletics' Connie Mack. (See tables 5.1 and 5.2.)

Stallings appreciated the talent of Mack's team and immediately tried to seize the high ground by meticulously preparing for his opponent. Stallings never hesitated in requesting the assistance of other teams. The Philadelphia Phillies' coach, Pat Moran, had scouted every offensive and defensive tendency of the Athletics during the last few weeks of the season. With a day off in New York on Sunday, October 4, the entire Braves team invested hours reviewing Moran's reports. Pitchers, catchers, coaches, and team captain Johnny Evers would be in tune with every A's offensive tendency; Stallings would recognize the A's defensive flaws.

The next day, Christy Mathewson reviewed with the Braves the strengths and weaknesses of the Athletics' batters, and John McGraw advised the best defensive tactics against Mack's team.[3] The A's players, in turn, saw no need to prepare. The A's perceived themselves as invincible world champs who would inevitably triumph over a lucky team from the weak National League. Mack had sent Al Bender to observe the Braves against Brooklyn in an October game; Bender, not recognizing the talent and desire of the young Boston team, instead went on a fishing trip.[4]

RALLYING THE PRESS

Stallings readied his team for the World Series not only by thoroughly scouting his opponent, but also by fiercely jabbing at the psyche of his counterpart, Connie Mack. Before the first game of the World Series, he undertook a wily psychological maneuver that allowed him to appear justifiably wronged and Mack uncharacteristically unsportsmanlike. In a noted incident, and there are multiple interpretations of this event, Stallings publicly scolded Mack regarding the use of the World Series practice field, indignantly claiming that Mack had kept the Braves from practicing on Shibe Field. It was a ploy that fired up the Braves, seeded doubt in the minds of Philadelphia fans, and rallied the national press to support the underdog Braves.[5]

Table 5.1.   Philadelphia Athletics Monthly Splits, 1914

Month	Games	Won	Lost	Winning Percentage
April	12	5	5	0.500
May	26	16	8	0.667
June	31	18	13	0.581
July	28	20	7	0.741
August	28	23	5	0.821
September	27	14	12	0.538
October	6	3	3	0.500

Source: http://www.baseball-almanac.com.

Table 5.2.   Philadelphia Athletics Team versus Team Splits, 1914

Opponent	Games	Won	Lost	Winning Percentage
Boston Red Sox	24	9	12	0.429
Chicago White Sox	22	17	5	0.773
Cleveland Naps	22	19	3	0.864
Detroit Tigers	22	12	9	0.571
New York Yankees	22	14	8	0.636
St. Louis Browns	23	15	7	0.682
Washington Senators	23	13	9	0.591

Source: http://www.baseball-almanac.com.

The Braves arrived in Philadelphia a few days before the incident, on Tuesday evening, October 6, well before Friday's first World Series matchup. As the National League pennant winner, the Braves planned to practice Wednesday morning at another National League stadium, the Phillies' Baker Bowl; in the afternoon, the Braves, already exceptionally well-informed observers, would view the Athletics playing against the Yankees in the regular-season finale. Before the A's–Yankees game, Stallings arrived at Mack's office and requested that Mack open up the A's Shibe Park for a Braves' practice on Thursday. Mack allowed Stallings to practice Thursday morning, but not from 2 p.m. to 3 p.m., when the A's had already been scheduled to practice.

Mack assumed that the practice schedule was in order, yet was shocked, miffed, and infuriated when, on Thursday morning, he read in the Philadelphia newspapers how Stallings had claimed that the Braves could not practice at Shibe Park. In Stallings's account, Mack had denied the Braves a chance to practice at Shibe, an unsportsmanlike gesture. On Thursday morning, Mack angrily called Stallings, and Stallings answered the phone in a public setting with reporters nearby. Stallings, in a loud voice, self-righteously proclaimed to Mack, and, more importantly, to nearby reporters, that he had been wronged.[6] Mack, absolutely livid, broke from his usual gentlemanly manner, as "one word led to another until [they] both spoke things [they] should not have said."[7] The following morning, Boston and Philadelphia sports headlines ran the Stallings version: "Braves Find Shibe Park Closed to Them for Practice. Mack Turns Down Braves." Reporters voiced doubts about Mack. The A's had played all year at Fenway, now the home stadium for the Braves. The Braves had never played at Shibe. Stallings had accomplished his goals: an unsettled, angry Connie Mack; a supportive press; and a Braves team that never did practice at Shibe, furious and determined to defeat the seemingly unprincipled A's.[8]

66 YEARS

Stallings had frayed Mack's nerves, questioning Mack on what he held so dearly: his integrity as a sportsman. Connie Mack, upright and honest, had rightfully earned the designation as baseball's great gentleman, the game's most respected figure. He had earned such respect amongst ballplayers that even Ty Cobb, the notorious, vitriolic, sometimes vicious, and always aggressive superstar, viewed Mack as the "supreme master of the diamond," and the "greatest manager our national game has known."[9] In recent years, Mack's reputation has been stained by his image as a gaunt, mildly confused octogenarian manager whose major contribution to baseball was simply his ability to endure. Yet, Mack's greatness extended far beyond his durability. Mack helped found the American League and, consequently, modern baseball. He contributed innovations to the game, and as a shrewd judge of talent, he constructed two of the greatest baseball teams of all time: the Athletics of 1910 to 1914 and 1929 to 1931.[10] The lean, six-foot, two-inch manager, always dressed in a suit, starched collar, and bowler hat. Habitually polite, composed, and quietly authoritative, Mack stood above his contemporaries as the great statesman of baseball.

Baseball writers and fans are absolutely on target in their praise of Mack for his lengthy tenure and, more importantly, his unyielding devotion to the game of baseball. Indeed, those inside baseball during his 66-year big-league career could not have envisioned Major League Baseball without him. Mack lived for 94 years, and when he died in 1956, his life had spanned more than half of our country's history. Born in the year that Abraham Lincoln issued the Emancipation Proclamation and Louisa May Alcott signed on as a nurse at a Union hospital, he died in the same year that Cold War Soviet leader Nikita Khrushchev denounced Stalin and Elvis Presley gyrated in front of millions on the *Ed Sullivan Show*. In his autobiography, Mack writes about how he won a pennant in 1902, the year before the Wright brothers powered their first airplane from Kitty Hawk, North Carolina. In the year of his death, only two years after he had retired from baseball, a B-52 Stratofortress dropped a 3.75-megaton hydrogen bomb on Bikini Atoll in the Pacific. As Mack reminisced in *My 66 Years in the Big Leagues*, sometimes he felt "as old as Methuselah. I was here before the telephone, before electric lights, the talking machine, the typewriter, the automobile, motion pictures, the airplane, and long before the radio. I came when railroads and the telegraph were new."[11]

Mack began playing baseball in the late nineteenth century, just as basic rules were being formed; when he left the sport in the mid-twentieth century, the modern game remained firmly in place. In the 1880s, when Mack launched his playing career, the game was so new that the definition of a walk remained unclear. It took a batter eight balls to earn a walk in 1881, seven in 1886, and four in 1889. By 1950, when he retired, the standard rules of play—walks, strikes, and key distances—stood unalterable (although the height of the mound changed in 1969). In 1890, the best ballparks held only 10,000 fans; in 1932, Mack would coach the A's in front of nearly 77,000 fans at Cleveland Municipal Stadium. During the course of his lifetime, fans began to watch night games; they later viewed contests on television. Ball clubs moved from eastern cities to the west. After Mack's retirement, even his beloved A's moved from Philadelphia to Kansas City (and eventually to Oakland).[12]

By 1914, Mack had already completed an 11-year playing career and coached the Athletics for 14 seasons (he was to complete 50 consecutive seasons for the same organization). While recent accounts of Mack highlight his longevity in the sport, he would be better remembered as an innovator and, as early journalists labeled him, the "Tall Tactician." His resourcefulness, a trait shared amongst many hardscrabble immigrant families in the nineteenth century in the United States, shone through time and again as he guided baseball into the modern era.

The son of Irish immigrants and a native of Brookfield, Massachusetts, Mack entered the world in December 1862, while his father, Mike, was training with the Union army as a member of the 51st Massachusetts Infantry. Christened Cornelius McGillicuddy, his name was soon altered to Connie Mack. Baseball folklore mistakenly claims that reporters reduced the length of his name when it proved impossible to squeeze it into the scorecard, but the McGillicuddys, like many Irish families, simply shortened their name.[13] Mack was molded by his mother, a woman who shared with her son the qualities of "optimism, patience, gentility, stoicism, dignity, faith, and antipathy to alcohol," and his father, a hard-working East Brookfield mill worker. Joining his father in the cotton mill during his summers away from school from at the age of 10, Mack endured 12-hour workdays, six days a week.[14]

EPIDEMIC

Lifting himself up out of harsh working-class surroundings, Mack confronted not only the grind of the cotton mill, but also the dangers of widespread disease. He faced family traumas similar to those of McGraw and Evers. He and his seven siblings grew into adulthood at a time when public health and epidemiology remained in its initial stages. When his town was stricken by a scarlet fever epidemic in 1871, he witnessed the death of two sisters, 13-year-old Nellie and tiny Mary: "My little sister, Mary Augusta, only a year old, died in my arms."[15] Connie and his older brother, Michael Jr., had carried the burden of family support, because their father, regularly burdened by severe ailments, could work part-time at best. William Hogan, Mack's best friend and the player whose connections first set up Mack as a minor leaguer, died of consumption during Mack's first season in the minors. Hogan's sister, Margaret, whom Mack married three years later, gave birth to three children, but she died in 1892, at the age of 26, from complications due to childbirth. Mack, having suffered an "overwhelming" loss, started his career as manager in 1894 as a widower with three children.[16]

Measuring a lanky six feet, one inch tall at the age of 15, Mack quit school to work as a general hand at the Green and Twitchell shoe factory in East Brookfield. Playing the nineteenth-century varieties of baseball—one o'cat, four o'cat, and roundball—during his breaks, and later joining local clubs, Mack eventually received an offer from a minor-league team, Meriden of the Connecticut League. Meriden's best pitcher, Hogan, had urged the Meriden coach, Albert Boardman, to audition Mack as a catcher. Immediately thereafter, Mack received a telegram offering him a tryout, and he announced his intentions to his family: "That's what I want to do, play ball." One day after receiving the offer, Mack gave notice to George Burt, the factory foreman. "I'm quitting Saturday night. I'm going to be a baseball player."[17] Despite Burt's urging him to stay on for at least another week, Mack firmly stated his intention to leave. Years later, when he would recount the story, Mack, always the upright gentleman, regretted that he had been "too rude."[18]

Mack, although straightforward and tough, avoided profanity, a common practice among managers and players who so often practiced "kicking." Mack expected his players to follow his example, and A's players rarely received a suspension. Mack, avoiding both fire-and-brimstone sermons and stern reprimands, drew players to his side with judiciousness and wit. According to biographer Ted Davis, Mack described his interactions with one of his star players:

> One day, when we didn't have much of a crowd and the park for some reason was surprisingly still, Stuffy McInnis, my old first baseman, called out "Jesus Christ!" I called him over to the bench and spoke to him about it.
> "Did I say that, Mr. Mack?" he said in surprise.
> "Only so loud that everyone in the grandstands and bleachers was waiting for you to pray. Don't do it again."[19]

PATIENCE

No one person could exist in the competitive environment of Major League Baseball for so long—a half century—and no one individual could endure the great failures Mack experienced—17 last-place teams between 1934 and 1950, and one of the worst teams in baseball history, the 1916 team, with 117 losses—without the kindest, gentlest of all human traits: patience. Patience, indeed, is the attribute of Mack that most regularly appears in his biographical sketches. The documented examples are countless. And this practice was an acquired habit; he was not instinctively patient.

Mack recalled acquiring his kind, accepting frame of mind when, in 1897, he experienced a baseball manager's epiphany as coach of the Milwaukee Brewers. Mack had often listened to players' "hot words" in postgame blaming sessions:

> Then one day something came up that made me real sore. I was so mad I knew I couldn't talk calmly so I waited around until all the players had dressed and gone home. Then I changed my clothes in the solitude of the clubhouse and was alone with my thoughts. I still was hot as I went home, but when I awoke the next morning, it was just another ball game we lost. It was a bonehead play, yes, but the ballplayers are human, and it was all part of baseball.[20]

And Mack lived up to his own standards of behavior, earning a reputation as a "calm, dignified individual, almost a father figure to his players."[21] He treated all players with respect, never rebuking them in public—even for the most grievous of baseball sins. If a player committed a wrong, Mack might wait a few days and then discuss the omission with him. His patience was rooted in a certain pragmatism, an understanding that players who did not match his standards of propriety could still bring games into the win column.[22] A friend, detailing the personal flaws of one of Mack's pitchers, lamented, "He is selfish, crude, vulgar, a perfect boor. Connie, why must you put up with a person like that?" Mack, with a calm, matter-of-fact disposition, replied, "What you say is true. But we pay that man to pitch. And you must concede that he pitches rather well."[23]

Early in his baseball career, Mack had helped to bring victories to the A's by cajoling, soothing, and sometimes merely tolerating baseball's problem child and brilliant pitcher, Rube Waddell. Waddell, who, in 1904, earned a spectacular 4:1 strikeout-to-walk ratio, who defeated Cy Young in a famous 20-inning game, and who threw both a nasty curveball and a blistering fastball, earned a reputation as an unpredictable juvenile. Waddell lost concentration when opponents held up shiny toys, he suffered an injury while roughhousing in the days before a World Series game, he once left the team to go fishing, and at one point he disappeared from the team for days while living in a saloon.[24] While Mack and others knew that Waddell suffered the burden of alcoholism, Waddell's chronic absences aggravated A's players and pushed Mack to the edge. "I went after him strong," Mack asserted.

> I was laying on the words thick and fast, and I saw a nasty look come into Rube's eyes. Quick as a flash it dawned on me that I had gone too far.

Breaking off in the middle of a scorching sentence, I reached out my hand and said, "Say Rube, I had you that time. At that time you thought I was in earnest." And do you know the great big fellow who was ready a few seconds earlier to throw me through the door actually broke down and cried.[25]

Mack had the ability to sway even the most problematic players to his side.

The never-smoking, rarely drinking, always-attend-mass-on-Sundays Connie Mack lifted baseball, a game rightfully held in disrepute in the late nineteenth century, to a level of respectability. The tall, gaunt manager wore a fitted suit, a tie with stickpin, a bowler or boater, and a high, starched collar; Mack embodied Victorian respectability, yet he was amiable, approachable, and attractive. As baseball historian Norman Macht describes him, "Off the field Connie Mack made a handsome appearance, his thin frame erect; his face a little fuller, with a deep crease down his cheeks when he smiled; heavy, dark, straight eyebrows over his pale blue eyes; curly black hair neatly combed."[26]

Mack, the noble, steadfast executive, stood in contrast to the rough-and-tumble industrial world of the late nineteenth-century United States. In the 1880s and 1890s, as he acquired expertise in baseball, Mack witnessed what he later he described as an "age of violence." In 1892, at the Homestead steel plant, 12 deaths resulted in a battle between hundreds of steelworkers and Carnegie Steel's Pinkerton detectives.[27] In his autobiography, Mack reflects on the time period—presidential assassinations of Lincoln, Garfield, and McKinley, the Wild West, and industrial violence—commenting, "Early baseball was characteristic of its times."[28]

According to Ken Burns and Geoffrey C. Ward, "Fans routinely cursed and threw things at officials, and sometimes rushed onto the field to pummel them. At Washington, they loosed vicious dogs on one. . . . Players attacked umpires, too, with curses, fists, bates, and spikes."[29] So unruly were the fans that, in the eyes of Mack, "An umpire had to be at least a middleweight boxer to hold his own on the diamond. Fistfights were common occurrences. Barrages of bottles and cans showered the field. Some games developed into a free-for-all battle."[30] And in 1901, when the "peacemaker," Ban Johnson, formed the American League, a league whose goal was to bestow civilization on umpires, fans, and players, Mack stood ready to sign on. Johnson, in turn, recognized that Mack would represent the new league as an exemplary manager.[31] In his long career, Mack was baited by others who hoped to agitate him, and as a baseball manager, he was often expected to furiously respond to verbal attacks. Yet, the A's manager, often exhibiting a keen wit, defused situations and shrewdly established himself as an even greater authority. In 1950, toward the end of Mack's career, first baseman Ferris Fain threw an errant toss. Instead of condemnation, he earned the following response from Mack: "Now, Ferris, you shouldn't have thrown that ball." Fain then snapped, "What did you want me to do with it? Stuff it in my pocket?" "Perhaps," answered Mack, "that would have been safer."[32]

TOUGHNESS WITH HUMOR

Mack's patience was built upon another of his prominent traits: toughness. As a player, he challenged management; as a manager, he held his ground with players. When he first reached the big leagues as a player for the Washington Senators, he demanded $800 for his work in the month of September, four times the monthly pay of $200 he had received in the minors.[33] And when he managed, any player—even the great ones—who broke the "Mack Rules of Baseball" conduct, suffered the consequences. In the 1890s, when an average manufacturing worker might earn a dollar a day, Mack fined suspended players $25 per day. In the early 1930s, during an away game, after the talented and fiery Mickey Cochrane slammed his catcher's mask down, Mack sent him packing to Philadelphia.[34] In 1935, when pitcher John Cascarella blew an apparently unbeatable lead, Mack directed the player off the field and "out of the stadium before the game is over."[35]

Mack's survival rested not only on the bedrocks of patience and toughness, but also on his sense of humor, wit, and irony. "Get them off there, James," he once urged Jimmy Dykes as he stepped up to the plate with the bases loaded. Dykes smashed the first pitch into a triple play. "Well, James," he stated matter-of-factly as he slapped the ever-present scorecard on his leg, "You got them off there, all right." In a game in the early 1930s, Max Bishop knocked a ball into the outfield that should have been a triple. When Bishop was tagged out at third, Mack wryly noted, "If you hit another triple, Max, please stop at second base."[36]

In 1902, Mack's sense of humor allowed him to parry the thrusts of longtime adversary John McGraw, whose rough, vitriolic style contrasted in every respect with the genteel manner of Mack. McGraw, the player-manager of the Baltimore Orioles, had earned two suspensions from American League president Ban Johnson. McGraw had retaliated against a player with a smash to the jaw; he had later threatened to spike an umpire. In the spring of 1902, McGraw, under suspension, began secret talks with the National League.[37] While in the midst of negotiations, he condemned Mack and his Athletics, saying, "Looks like the American League has a white elephant on its hands in Philadelphia."[38] Instead of lashing back at an apparent insult, Mack embraced the derogatory term. In the same way that the Democratic Party welcomed the donkey logo, Mack playfully accepted the white elephant image. At the time, Mack found himself in a position of strength. As a manager in the newly formed American League, he was taking in substantial gate receipts; fans certainly enjoyed watching his 1902 A's win the pennant. After the A's earned their championship, they could gaze upward to a white elephant banner that was hoisted over the ballpark. And, in 1905, when Mack and McGraw convened at home plate during the opening ceremonies for the World Series, McGraw, to the surprise of the crowd, broke into an Irish jig; Mack had just honored him with a handheld, carved white elephant.[39]

THE "TALL TACTICIAN"

Mack's integrity and wit were matched by his skill as a manager; he had deservedly earned the title the "Tall Tactician." Regarding Mack's great prowess as a manager, H. G. Salsinger of the *Detroit News* commented: "He directed players like a great orchestra conductor leads his musicians, except Mr. Mack used a scorecard instead of a baton."[40] Literally directing players with his scorecard, he helped the Athletics secure wins. "Positioning defense," wrote former Cardinal manager Whitey Herzog, "can be worth five or ten games a year."[41]

Ballplayers, including the notoriously headstrong Ty Cobb, admired Mack's directives. Cobb, who joined the A's for the final two years of his career after leaving the Detroit Tigers, recalled Mack's guiding him in the outfield: "I was out here in the outfield just after joining the A's, and a player came to bat that I had played against for several years. I looked toward the dugout, and Mr. Mack was cutting the air with that scorecard. He wanted me to move to the right." Not one to accept an order without question, Cobb hesitated: "I ought to know more about this batter than Connie Mack does. I must have shagged a hundred of his flies." Although he moved to his right, "Mr. Mack kept on waving. And I moved another dozen feet to the right. By this time Mr. Mack was halfway out of the dugout, signaling frantically. He didn't stop waving until I was ten more feet to the right."[42] Perfectly positioned, Cobb fielded the out.

Mack conceived his defense in the manner that Johnny Evers endorsed, an interconnected band tying together all players. Like Tony La Russa, he understood ". . . that the premium is on the stuff you do to get guys out—positioning and how you are going to pitch particular players. I want to be able to have a comfortable feeling . . . that who ever comes to bat, I have a general idea where the ball is supposed to go."[43] Mack understood the bonds among position players.[44] As a *Washington Post* writer noted, "He is known as the silent man of baseball, but his is an absolute monarch, as absolute as that of the czar of Russia and lots more friendly. . . . He is usually about three steps ahead of his opponents when it comes to that idea thing. . . . What he is, is a clairvoyant."[45] Mack guided his defense to yield outs, to produce results.

An energetic entrepreneur, Mack, in 1900, founded the Athletics baseball franchise as part of Ban Johnson's start-up organization, the American League. The new league drew teams from three sources: Johnson's Western League, a minor-league circuit he organized in the 1890s; cities that the National League had vacated; and the Atlantic Seaboard cities that could afford at least two professional teams: New York, Boston, and Philadelphia.[46] Johnson sent Mack to Philadelphia to lay the foundation for a new team, and Mack successfully negotiated with Ben Shibe, the industrial baron of baseball manufacturing. Shibe's company, A. J. Reach and Co., would produce the American League's baseballs. Both men, Shibe and Mack, had earned reputations of impeccable integrity, and they offered complementary skills to the new club. Shibe provided the capital; Mack offered experience as a player and manager. Shibe grasped the technicalities of business; Mack understood the subtleties of baseball. Shibe would help build the new stadium, Columbia Park; Mack would assemble ballplayers. Ban Johnson, an astute businessman himself, anticipated a successful partnership.[47]

"MR. MACK"

Connie Mack, baseball's courtly statesman, earned a profound, heartfelt respect from writers, players, fans, and umpires. Mack expected to be addressed as "Mr. Mack," and he, in turn, addressed his players as "Mister." If a player produced a clutch hit, or if a pitcher worked his way out of a bases-loaded, no-out jam, Mack would stand when the player returned, shake hands, and offer a warm, "Thank you." Stanley Coveleski, recalling his playing days with Mack, claimed, "He was a very considerate man. If you did something wrong, he'd never bawl you out on the bench or in the clubhouse. In the evening he'd ask you to take a walk with him, and on the way he'd tell you what you'd done wrong."[48]

Treating others respectfully also meant that a player should never act brashly or arrogantly, and Mack strove to model that behavior in front of his players. When, in the 1929 World Series, the Athletics engineered a late-inning comeback from an 8–0 deficit, Mack remained placid: "I just sat there, and when we won the game I walked off with hardly a word to the boys. It doesn't help any to appear to be too pleased before such an important series is won. Such an attitude might lead to overconfidence, and that's fatal."[49] Following Mack's unwritten rules for appropriate bench behavior, the Athletics limited obscenities, refrained from nasty comments, and kept the quietest dugout in baseball.[50]

Mack's demeanor slowly altered baseball decorum. "Connie Mack," asserted Rube Bressler, one of Mack's 1914 pitchers, "did more for baseball than any other living human being—by the example he set, his attitude, the way he handled himself and his players. . . . Over a period of years, others followed, and baseball became respectable. He was a true gentleman, in every sense of the word."[51]

As a catcher for the Washington Senators during the rough, boisterous baseball days of the late nineteenth century, Mack admitted, "We got away with a lot back in the days when we played with only one umpire." Avoiding blunt, profane verbal attacks on batters, Mack, as a catcher, opted for subtle, psychological blows. "Say, that's a nice little dip in your swing. Always wished I had one like that."[52] Keen to a player's appearance, habits, or a recent error, Mack, often chattering, would gently annoy batters. Wilbert Robinson, Mack's friend and the Brooklyn manager, asserted, "Don't let anyone kid you, that Connie Mack was some kind of a tin god behind the plate. He could do and say things that got under you more than the cuss words that other catchers used."[53]

As a player, he pushed the rules to the limit, ingeniously deceiving umpires and players. Before a late nineteenth-century rule change went into effect (Mack helped to inspire the change), a first or second strike foul tip earned the batter an out. Mack learned to slap his hands or click his tongue, stealthily imitating the sound of a foul tip, causing umpires to call batters out prematurely. Mack, one of the first catchers to move up directly behind the batter, often antagonized players by "tipping," or slightly touching a bat, forcing a player to miss as he swung.[54] "Don't ever say I was a great catchaw," he once told Bob Considine and a group of reporters, "but I was kind of tricky."[55]

Yet, time and time again, Mack proved to the baseball world his great integrity. And when Mack managed, umpires regarded him with such respect that they would welcome his explanation of a rule. According to writer Edwin Pope, during a World Series game a Giants player sprinted home well ahead of Philadelphia's throw, but he failed to touch the plate. Encouraged by his players to protest the no-call, Mack answered calmly, "He beat the throw, didn't he?"[56]

"THE $100,000 INFIELD"

Mack recruited players who demonstrated great integrity and, of course, who, like "the $100,000 infield," displayed remarkable talent. By 1910, Mack had stocked his team with core players, the seven or eight players who might deliver a championship season. The center fiber of this core, the group that would lead the team to four pennants and three World Series championships between 1910 and 1914, had received the title "the $100,000 infield." First baseman John "Stuffy" McInnis, second baseman Eddie Collins, shortstop Jack Barry, and, at third base, Frank "Home Run" Baker, stood at the top of the league both offensively and defensively, creating one of the elite infields in baseball history. Baseball writers commonly attest to the 1911 Athletics as one of the all-time greatest teams, ranking it near the 1927 Yankees. In 1911, the "$100,000 infield" led the league in defense and averaged .322 at the plate. By 1914, the A's infielders had secured three World Series championships, and they were still in their prime, only in their 20s: McInnis was 23, Collins and Barry were 27, and Baker was 28.[57] The 1914 A's loomed with near-Olympian proportions over the callow Braves.

Frank "Home Run" Baker appeared as a distinct threat, not merely because he had earned four consecutive home run titles, but mainly because as a "Mr. October" in 1911, he had slammed two consecutive World Series game-winning home runs against Rube Marquard and Christy Mathewson, the Giants' two premier pitchers. Baker's game winners provided him solace and redemption, because he had unfairly received the label of "soft" ever since August 1908, when he had complained that Ty Cobb, sliding into third, had spiked him, gashing his forearm. Although he had finished the game bandaged and wounded, Baker, at the time, had been misjudged as a yielding, spineless player. Pointing to a photo of Cobb sliding forcefully—yet legally—into third, the *Detroit Free Press* labeled Baker a "soft flesh darling." A tough, country boy from Maryland, he stoically endured this stigma for years.[58]

Baker eventually destroyed the misperception that he played "soft." John McGraw misperceived Baker in 1911, when, in Game One of the World Series, Fred Snodgrass, in attempt to steal third, slid, like Ty Cobb, full force into Baker—spikes high, slashing his forearm and knocking the ball loose. The Giants won that first game, but in the second game, with one man on and two outs in the sixth, the left-handed-hitting Baker, facing Giants left-handed ace Rube Marquard, knocked a game-breaking, two-run homer over the right-field fence. With the World Series tied, the Athletics faced the great Christy Mathewson, who held on to a 1–0 lead until the top of the ninth, when Baker smashed a game-tying home run into the right-field seats.[59] The eminent sportswriter Fred Lieb later reflected, "The Giants fans were aghast; a Baker home run off Marquard could happen, but not off Matty. I still can remember the awesome silence that followed the crash of Baker's bat."[60] As the game shifted into extra innings, Baker kept a rally moving with a pivotal hit and then blocked Snodgrass as he bolted toward third base, again with spikes flying high. Baker executed the play perfectly and, despite bandages on his forearm, went on to gather nine hits (.375 average) and five RBIs, driving Philadelphia to a 4–2 World Series victory. After Baker, the wounded warrior, hit two crucial home runs in two consecutive World Series games, a feat nearly miraculous in the Deadball Era, and after he led the A's to a championship, he gained new stature. From this point onward, the press viewed him as the mighty "Home Run" Baker.[61]

Columbia graduate Eddie Collins, self-confident in every respect, proved his extraordinary value in his breakout 1910 season, when he led the American League in steals, placed third in hits and RBIs, came in fourth in batting average, and stood at the top in most fielding categories. A passionate student of the game, like his Braves counterpart Johnny Evers, Collins wrote 10 articles for *American Magazine* that analyzed all angles of the sport (much to the chagrin of his teammates, he explained how opposing pitchers tipped off their pitches). And like Braves manager George Stallings, he was highly superstitious, wearing gum on his cap button until he had two strikes, at which point he would plug the gum in his mouth and begin chewing. His superstitious rituals coincided with great success on the playing field. As a .421 hitter in the 1913 World Series and a winner of the 1914 American League MVP (the Chalmers Award), Collins held high expectations for the 1914 World Series.[62]

John "Jack," or "Black Jack," Barry, like Mack, was the son of Irish immigrants from Connecticut. Barry, a spectacular fielder, had gained a reputation as a clutch hitter. Noting Barry's timeliness at the plate, Stony McClinn of the *Philadelphia Press* commented, "If Barry's batting average was only .119, and a hit was needed to win a game for the Athletics, it's a cinch that 99 percent of the fans would rather have Barry at bat than any other man on Mack's payroll."[63] The Detroit Tigers' manager, Hugh Jennings, once noted, "I'd rather have Barry than any .300 hitter in the business . . . in a pinch he hits better than anybody in our league outside of Cobb."[64] A first-rate bunter, Barry was so skillful that Mack would give him the green light to try a "double squeeze," a sensational play where runners on second and third took off even before Barry bunted the ball to third. The runner from second would round third, dash home, and slide into the plate as the catcher tagged the runner from third. Reserved, diligent, and hardworking, Barry anchored the A's infield, covering such a wide range that third baseman Baker could cover close to third, while second baseman Collins shaded to first. Equipped with a strong arm and sure hands, Barry, along with his keystone partner, Eddie Collins, engineered strategies to stop the widely used double steal.[65] Capable of spectacular double plays, Barry, according to Hugh Fullerton, was the "best in the game at taking throws, blocking the base, and holding runners close to second."[66]

Barry threw across the diamond to first baseman Stuffy McInnis, the youngest A's infielder. McInnis, a compactly built, five-foot, nine-inch, 162 pounder, artfully defended first base. He was so agile that he could manage the one-handed reach, a rare feat for the time, and so lithe that he could execute a ground-level split while reaching for a throw coming from across the infield. McInnis led the league in fielding percentage six times. His defensive statistics were at the top in double plays, putouts, and assists.[67] Earlier in his career, he had played shortstop so well that fans would cheer, "That's the stuff, kid, that's the stuff."[68] The boyish-looking Stuffy could scoop up hard-to-catch throws because of his unmatched flexibility and a technological innovation that he helped to pioneer: the claw-type first baseman's glove. McInnis, a lifetime .307 hitter, posted RBI numbers that regularly placed him at the top of the league. A contact hitter who could push players around the base paths, McInnis maintained an inconceivable strikeout record, striking out only 189 times in more than 7,300 at bats (Major League Baseball began following this stat in 1913).[69] As John McGraw noted after the 1913 World Series, "Baseball never had a first baseman in the class of McInnis."[70]

SPEED IN THE OUTFIELD AND
SKILL BEHIND THE PLATE

Mack recruited speedsters for the outfield, "men who could travel fast enough to burn their galoshes." In center field, he chose Amos Strunk, "The Flying Foot," the "Mercury of the American League," an outfielder who could track down fly balls that other center fielders could never reach. As baseball writer J. C. Koefed observed, "He moves with the speed you would exert should you accidentally touch a red hot range." Strunk contributed to his manager's fame through his key role in Mack's famous "double squeeze play." With Barry bunting, it was Strunk, standing on second, who could race from second to third, and then home. Strunk, who, in Mack's view, "made his job of playing center field look a lot easier than it really was," led the league in fielding percentage four times between 1912 and 1918. A patient, left-handed hitter, he placed in the top 10 in the American League for slugging three times between 1913 and 1916.[71]

In right field, Mack placed the left-handed-hitting Eddie Murphy. Murphy measured up to Mack's standard for speedy outfielders; in fact, he was so fast that in 1914, he stole 36 bases, 11 more than Strunk, "The Flying Foot." Murphy, a vibrant, blossoming star, batted .295 in 1913 as a 22-year-old; in 1914, he hit .272, with a .379 on-base percentage, sixth highest in the American League.[72]

Eight-year veteran Rube Oldring covered left field for the A's. Oldring, in the opinion of early twentieth-century baseball statistician Irwin Howe, was a "fast and reliable outfielder, good at laying down a bunt and . . . a fast and intelligent base runner." A cornerstone of Mack's championships, Oldring, in 1913, turned in a Series-changing defensive gem against the Giants, snaring Moose McCormick's sizzling liner to left field to prevent a runner at third base from tagging and scoring a run. Philadelphia fans later awarded him, as the team's most popular player, a new Cadillac. Yet, Oldring suffered from nagging injuries throughout much of the 1914 season and performed just below his normal level.[73]

The A's guarded home with one of the best, Wally Schang. The gregarious, switch-hitting, second-year player led American League catchers in five categories: batting average (.287), extra-base hits (22), home runs (3), slugging percentage (.404), and RBIs (45). Graceful, energetic, and highly skilled behind the plate, Schang, one of the "wonders of the year in 1913," had starred in the 1913 World Series, with a .357 batting average and a team-leading seven RBIs. A power hitter, Schang had, for most of his career, earned praise for his defensive work, but, in 1914, he struggled in the field, playing most of the year with a broken thumb on his throwing hand. Still, the young pro was one of the league's best, and the Braves' George Stallings first recognized his greatness, recruiting him for the Buffalo Bisons in 1912.[74] (See tables 5.3 and 5.4.)

PITCHING DEPTH

Mack's pitchers excelled in all respects. Four starting pitchers—Chief Bender, Ed Plank, Bob Shawkey, and Bullet Joe Bush—averaged 16 wins apiece; three starting pitchers—Herb Pennock, Weldon Wyckoff, and Rube Bressler—averaged 11 wins each. Few teams in baseball history have enjoyed such a rich and deep supply of starting pitching. The A's, after all, could call on seven starters who had won more than 10 games. These A's pitchers completed 87 games and saved 16 others, while compiling a team ERA of 2.78. They carried the team to absolute domination of the American League. Leading the league since June, the Athletics offered no chance to even such talented teams as the Boston Red Sox, winner of 91 games. Leaving the Red Sox eight and a half games behind, the 1914 A's celebrated victory 99 times.[75] (See tables 5.5 and 5.6.)

It was no great surprise that Mack would select Charles Albert "Chief" Bender for the first game. Bender, labeled "Chief" because of his Ojibwe (Chippewa) roots, had earned a 2.26 ERA and a 17–3 winning record, with a

Table 5.3. Philadelphia Athletics 1914 Season Batting Statistics

Pos.	Player	Age	G	PA	AB	R	H	HR	RBI	SB	BB	SO	BA	OBP	SLG	OPS	TB	SH
C	Wally Schang[b]	24	107	355	307	44	88	3	45	7	32	33	.287	.371	.404	.775	124	7
1B	Stuffy McInnis	23	149	628	576	74	181	1	95	25	19	27	.314	.341	.368	.709	212	29
2B	Eddie Collins[a]	27	152	659	526	122	181	2	85	58	97	31	.344	.452	.452	.904	238	28
SS	Jack Barry	27	140	555	467	57	113	0	42	22	53	34	.242	.324	.268	.592	125	31
3B	Home Run Baker[a]	28	150	637	570	84	182	9	89	19	53	37	.319	.380	.442	.822	252	8
OF	Rube Oldring	30	119	498	466	68	129	3	49	14	18	35	.277	.308	.371	.679	173	13
OF	Amos Strunk[a]	25	122	483	404	58	111	2	45	25	57	38	.275	.364	.342	.706	138	20
OF	Eddie Murphy[a]	22	148	684	573	101	156	3	43	36	87	46	.272	.379	.340	.720	195	10
OF	Jimmy Walsh	26	68	273	216	35	51	3	36	6	30	27	.236	.340	.384	.724	83	23
C	Jack Lapp[a]	29	69	241	199	22	46	0	19	1	31	14	.231	.338	.286	.624	57	10
OF	Tom Daley[a]	29	28	103	86	17	22	0	7	4	12	14	.256	.347	.337	.684	29	4
IF	Larry Kopf[b]	23	37	86	69	8	13	0	12	6	8	14	.188	.300	.275	.575	19	5
P	Bob Shawkey	23	38	90	83	6	17	0	5	0	4	22	.205	.241	.229	.470	19	4
P	Weldon Wyckoff	23	34	80	75	7	11	1	6	3	4	15	.147	.190	.187	.377	14	1
P	Bullet Joe Bush	21	38	80	74	6	14	1	8	0	2	25	.189	.211	.284	.494	21	4
P	Eddie Plank[a]	38	34	71	60	6	9	0	5	1	4	14	.150	.203	.183	.386	11	7
P	Chief Bender	30	28	70	62	4	9	1	8	0	4	13	.145	.197	.210	.407	13	4
P	Rube Bressler	19	29	60	51	6	11	0	4	0	6	7	.216	.310	.275	.585	14	2
P	Herb Pennock[b]	20	28	59	56	7	12	0	9	0	2	11	.214	.241	.286	.527	16	1
Team Totals		25.7	158	5,941	5,126	749	1,392	29	627	231	545	517		.348	.352	.699	1804	218
Rank in Eight AL Teams										3	3	8		1	1			1
Nonpitcher Totals		25.8	158	5,398	4,637	706	1,308	26	581	227	516	396		.360	.366	.726	1695	194
Pitcher Totals		24.9	158	543	489	43	84	3	46	4	29	121		.220	.223	.443	109	24

Note: Individual statistics include only those players who played in twenty or more games. Team statistics include all players. *Source:* http://www.baseball-reference.com.

a Bats left-handed
b Bats both

Table 5.4. Boston Braves 1914 Season Batting Statistics

Pos.	Player	Age	G	PA	AB	R	H	HR	RBI	SB	BB	SO	BA	OBP	SLG	OPS	TB	SH
C	Hank Gowdy	24	128	426	366	42	89	3	46	14	48	40	.243	.337	.347	.684	127	8
1B	Butch Schmidt[a]	27	147	613	537	67	153	1	71	14	43	55	.285	.350	.356	.706	191	23
2B	Johnny Evers[a]	32	139	612	491	81	137	1	40	12	87	26	.279	.390	.338	.728	166	31
SS	Rabbit Maranville	22	156	663	586	74	144	4	78	28	45	56	.246	.306	.326	.632	191	27
3B	Charlie Deal	22	79	293	257	17	54	0	23	4	20	23	.210	.270	.276	.546	71	15
OF	Larry Gilbert[a]	22	72	262	224	32	60	5	25	3	26	34	.268	.347	.371	.717	83	10
OF	Les Mann	21	126	425	389	44	96	4	40	9	24	50	.247	.292	.375	.668	146	11
OF	Joe Connolly[a]	30	120	469	399	64	122	9	65	12	49	36	.306	.393	.494	.886	197	13
UT	Possum Whitted	24	66	258	218	36	57	2	31	10	18	18	.261	.326	.376	.703	82	19
3B	Red Smith	24	60	251	207	30	65	3	37	4	28	24	.314	.401	.449	.850	93	14
C	Bert Whaling	26	60	199	172	18	36	0	12	2	21	28	.209	.303	.250	.553	43	4
OF	Herbie Moran[a]	30	41	178	154	24	41	0	4	4	17	11	.266	.347	.299	.646	46	5
OF	Ted Cather	25	50	161	145	19	43	0	27	7	7	28	.297	.338	.400	.738	58	7
OF	Josh Devore[a]	26	51	151	128	22	29	1	5	2	18	14	.227	.327	.281	.608	36	4
UT	Oscar Dugey	26	58	122	109	17	21	1	10	10	10	15	.193	.267	.239	.505	26	2
OF	Jim Murray	36	39	121	112	10	26	0	12	2	6	24	.232	.277	.304	.581	34	2
3B	Jack Martin	27	33	94	85	10	18	0	5	0	6	7	.212	.264	.235	.499	20	3
OF	Wilson Collins	25	27	37	35	5	9	0	1	0	2	8	.257	.297	.257	.554	9	0
P	Dick Rudolph	26	43	137	120	10	15	0	8	1	11	19	.125	.205	.175	.380	21	5
P	Bill James	22	49	135	129	9	33	0	9	0	0	20	.256	.262	.279	.541	36	5
P	Lefty Tyler[a]	24	38	104	94	6	19	0	4	0	4	20	.202	.235	.213	.447	20	6
P	Dick Crutcher	24	33	59	54	5	8	0	3	1	4	15	.148	.207	.167	.374	9	1
P	Otto Hess[a]	35	31	48	47	5	11	1	6	0	1	11	.234	.250	.319	.569	15	2
Team Totals		25.7	158	5,979	5,206	657	1,307	35	572	139	502	617	.251	.323	.335	.658	1745	221
Rank in Eight NL Teams				1	2	4	3			8	1	3	4	3	5	4	4	
Nonpitcher Totals		25.8	158	5,412	4,687	617	1,208	34	535	137	478	509	.258	.333	.347	.680	1627	199
Pitcher Totals		25.2	158	567	519	40	99	1	37	2	24	108	.191	.229	.227	.457	118	22

Note: Individual statistics include only those players who played in twenty or more games. Team statistics include all players. *Source:* http://www.baseball-reference.com.
[a] Bats left-handed

Table 5.5. Philadelphia Athletics 1914 Season Pitching Statistics

Pos.	Pitcher	Age	W	L	ERA	G	GS	CG	SHO	SV	IP	H	R	ER	HR	BB	SO	WHIP	SO/BB
SP	Bob Shawkey	23	15	8	2.73	38	31	18	5	2	237.0	223	88	72	4	75	89	1.257	1.19
SP	Bullet Joe Bush	21	17	13	3.06	38	23	14	2	2	206.0	184	84	70	2	81	109	1.286	1.35
SP	Eddie Plank[a]	38	15	7	2.87	34	22	12	4	3	185.1	178	68	59	2	42	110	1.187	2.62
SP	Weldon Wyckoff	23	11	7	3.02	32	20	11	0	2	185.0	153	82	62	2	103	86	1.384	0.84
SP	Chief Bender	30	17	3	2.26	28	23	14	7	2	179.0	159	49	45	4	55	107	1.196	1.95
RP	Herb Pennock[a]	20	11	4	2.79	28	14	8	3	3	151.2	136	56	47	1	65	90	1.325	1.38
RP	Rube Bressler[a]	19	10	4	1.77	29	10	8	1	2	147.2	112	37	29	1	56	96	1.138	1.71
RP	Boardwalk Brown	25	1	5	4.09	15	7	2	0	0	66.0	64	34	30	1	26	20	1.364	0.77
	Byron Houck	22	0	0	3.27	3	3	1	0	0	11.0	14	9	4	0	6	4	1.818	0.67
	Willie Jensen	24	0	1	2.00	1	1	1	0	0	9.0	7	4	2	1	2	1	1.000	0.50
	Chick Davies[a]	22	1	0	1.00	1	1	1	0	0	9.0	8	4	1	0	3	4	1.222	1.33
	Jack Coombs	31	0	1	4.50	2	2	0	0	0	8.0	8	4	4	0	3	1	1.375	0.33
	Charlie Boardman	21	0	0	4.91	2	0	0	0	0	7.1	10	5	4	0	4	2	1.909	0.50
	Fred Worden	19	0	0	18.00	1	0	0	0	0	2.0	8	5	4	0	0	1	4.000	
	Team Totals	24.9	98	53	2.78	158	157	89	22	16	1,404.0	1,264	529	433	18	521	720	1.271	1.38
	Rank in Eight NL Teams	1	1	8	4		2	2	2	2	5	4	3	4	4	6	2		

Source: http://www.baseball-reference.com.
[a] Throws left-handed

Table 5.6. Boston Braves 1914 Season Pitching Statistics

Pos.	Pitcher	Age	W	L	ERA	G	GS	CG	SHO	SV	IP	H	R	ER	HR	BB	SO	WHIP	SO/BB
SP	Dick Rudolph	26	26	10	2.35	42	36	31	6	0	336.1	288	105	88	9	61	138	1.038	2.26
SP	Bill James	22	26	7	1.90	46	37	30	4	3	332.1	261	91	70	7	118	156	1.140	1.32
SP	Lefty Tyler[a]	24	16	13	2.69	38	34	21	5	2	271.1	247	113	81	7	101	140	1.283	1.39
SP	Otto Hess[a]	35	5	6	3.03	14	11	7	1	1	89.0	89	39	30	2	33	24	1.371	0.73
RP	Dick Crutcher	24	5	7	3.46	33	15	5	1	0	158.2	169	73	61	4	66	48	1.481	0.73
RP	Paul Strand[a]	20	6	2	2.44	16	3	1	0	0	55.1	47	23	15	1	23	33	1.265	1.43
RP	Gene Cocreham	29	3	4	4.84	15	3	1	0	0	44.2	48	30	24	2	27	15	1.679	0.56
	Iron Davis	24	3	3	3.40	9	6	4	1	0	55.2	42	25	21	1	26	26	1.222	1.00
	Hub Perdue	32	2	5	5.82	9	9	2	0	0	51.0	60	35	33	5	11	13	1.392	1.18
	Tom Hughes	30	2	0	2.65	2	2	1	0	0	17.0	14	7	5	0	4	11	1.059	2.75
	Dolf Luque	23	0	1	4.15	2	1	1	0	0	8.2	5	5	4	0	4	1	1.038	0.25
	Ensign Cottrell[a]	25	0	1	9.00	1	1	0	0	0	1.0	2	2	1	0	3	1	5.000	0.33
	Team Totals	25.0	94	59	2.74	158	158	104	18	6	1,421.0	1,272	548	433	38	477	606	1.231	1.27
	Rank in Eight NL Teams	1	8	4	1			2	1	2	3	3	3	5	7	6	4		

Source: http://www.baseball-reference.com.
[a] Throws left-handed

.850 winning percentage. He had pitched seven shutouts; at one point in the season, he won 14 straight times. In the previous five years, he had compiled a 91–31 record. He had won four straight World Series games, two in 1913.[76] Before the 1914 Series, F. C. Lane, a writer for *Baseball Magazine*, commented, "Bender, when it comes to pitching an individual game, has no equals. In a short series like the World Champions' contests, no pitcher in the business can excel Bender." The *Philadelphia North American* placed a simple, telling phrase under a picture of Bender: "The Greatest Money Pitcher in Baseball."[77]

The intimidating, six-foot, two-inch pitcher powered his delivery through leg strength. His high leg kick added subterfuge to an already deceptive motion. Biographer Tom Swift wrote of his delivery: "Charles Albert Bender's body remained closed, his arm hidden, until the last moment, and by the time he reached the release point, he was coming over the top."[78] In addition to his fastball, Bender might throw a sidearm pitch or a submarine fadeaway, a pitch similar to a screwball, fading away from left-handed batters. Bender talked about his "twisted slow one," a pitch that behaved remarkably like a knuckleball. To this rich repertoire of pitches he added a hard slider and a "slow ball," or changeup. According to teammate Bob Shawkey, Bender's great strength was his ability to change speeds: "I'd say his greatest success came on the changeup he threw off his fastball. They'd swing at his motion, and that ball would come floating up there."[79] And despite throwing the likes of a knuckleball, Bender kept the ball in the strike zone, often recording one of the lowest walk rates in baseball. Mack later reflected, "If I had all the men I've ever handled, and they were in their prime, and there was one game I wanted to win above all others, Albert would be my man."[80]

Any hitter who stepped into the batter's box encountered not only Bender's assortment of deliveries, pitches, and speeds, but also his pitching intelligence. Bender considered how each pitch would suit each batter. Explaining his calm, reflective approach to sportswriter Grantland Rice, Bender noted, "Tension is the greatest curse in any sport. I've never had any tension. You give the best you have—you win or lose. What's the difference if you give all you've got to give?" Having studied the batter, appearing calm and collected (although admitting to an internal nervousness), Bender, in the eyes of his contemporary, umpire Billy Evans, "knows how to pitch." When on the mound, "He takes advantage of every weakness, and once a player shows him a weak spot, he is marked for life by the crafty Indian."[81]

Evans intended "crafty" as a compliment, yet the compliment found its origins in misgivings, misjudgments, and stereotypes that whites held of Native Americans. The European American treatment of Native Americans took many forms at the turn of the twentieth century: paternalistic acceptance, disrespectful assimilation, or violent extermination. In 1890, when Bender was just seven years old, the U.S. Seventh Cavalry massacred 300 Lakota Sioux at the Battle of Wounded Knee. In 1907, two years after Bender had pitched his first World Series game, the U.S. Fifth Cavalry executed a surprise dawn raid on the Aneth Navajo in southern Utah. The Aneth Navajo had refused to follow the Roosevelt administration's assimilation policy and prevented their Indian children from attending boarding school, designed to acculturate Native Americans. In 1887, white assimilationists had enacted the Dawes Severalty Act, legislation that required the dispersal of collective Indian lands to individual native farmers. The law allowed "surplus land" to be purchased by land speculators, and Indians subsequently lost millions of acres. Indian boarding schools had preceded the Dawes Act, and these schools were often founded on the assumption held by writer Hamlin Garland, an advisor to Theodore Roosevelt, who claimed that Indians were "like children."[82] They were also built according to Richard Henry Pratt, who believed that whites should eliminate Indian culture: "A great general has said that the only good Indian is a dead one. . . . In a sense, I agree with the sentiment, but only in this: that all the Indian there is in the race should be dead. Kill the Indian in him, and save the man."[83]

During his youth, Bender had attended the Lincoln Institution in Pennsylvania, and he later volunteered for the most noted Native American boarding school founded by Pratt, the Carlisle Indian Industrial School. A strong student who contributed to the Lincoln Institution athletic program, a program noted for its excellence in football, Bender caught the attention of pro scouts when he played as a teenager in summer semipro baseball leagues. Later, when he pitched for the Harrison Athletic Club, Connie Mack discovered his talents.[84]

Bender, who grew to understand the workings of European American culture, had hoped that Americans would recognize him simply for his great skills as a pitcher. He asserted, "I do not want my name to be presented to the public as an Indian, but as a pitcher."[85] Yet, European Americans rarely respected his cultural identity. "Chief," the cultural tag regularly attached to Bender and other Native American ballplayers, resembled, according to Swift, "calling a black man 'boy.'"[86] Scientific racism, popularized in Madison Grant's 1916 book *The Passing of the Great Race*, rested on the assumption that the "Nordic Race," a biological race responsible for advancing the human condition, stood atop other inferior races. Grant's views had been accepted in the world of baseball, where blacks were denied entry into the major leagues, and Native Americans like Bender were judged inferior. Charles Zuber of *Sporting Life* wrote about Charles Bender after the 1905 World Series:

> Bender, according to reports, is a typical representative of his race, being just sufficiently below the white man's standard to be coddled into doing anything that his manager might suggest, and to the proper exercise of this influence on the part of manager Connie Mack much of the Indian's

success as a twirler is due. Like the Negro on the stage who . . . will work himself to death if you jolly him, the Indian can be "conned" into taking up any sort of burden.[87]

Sports cartoonists, players, and fans shared similar racial attitudes. Although Connie Mack always addressed him as "Albert," cartoonists drew caricatures of Bender as a tomahawk-wielding, headdress-wearing warrior. Players jockeying from the bench oftentimes yelled, "Back to the reservation!" Fans would mimic Indian signals, scream battle cries, and, to his displeasure, shout "Chief."[88] Bender, appearing and acting calm, sometimes protested, stating, "Foreigners! Foreigners!" Yet, taunting wounded him, and Bender reflected that while he was cool "on the outside, I was nervous, just like anyone else— maybe twice as nervous—but I couldn't let it out. Indians can't."[89]

REVVED FOR A PARTY

In the fall of 1914, Philadelphia fans held the highest of expectations for Bender and the Athletics. The A's were world champs and had won the pennant by eight and a half games. Bender, after all, was the championship pitcher, with the 14-game win streak. In the days before the game, lines overflowed with fans and ticket hawkers. Anticipating another great triumph for the city, the first Philadelphia fan lined up to buy reserved seats 26 hours before they went on sale. When the 5,000 tickets went on sale, Philadelphians bought them up in five hours. Thousands of fans were turned away, and if they returned to buy tickets for bleacher seats, they would need to begin queuing up at midnight. Such national magazines as *Sporting Life* saw no possibility of Boston winning except for the "improbable collapse of the Mack machine or the element of luck."[90] In recent World Series, the A's had defeated powerful clubs, including the Cubs and Giants. They now faced the inexperienced Braves, merely "a surprise, a wonder, and a problem," a team that had defied the law of averages to win. Athletics' fans sensed a victory that would arrive as easily as a July Fourth celebration. Ticket sales surpassed any previous Athletics' World Series.[91] As author Tom Swift noted, "Philadelphia fans were revved for this party as though they were about to celebrate another successful Revolution."[92]

TALKING SMACK

But George Stallings wanted to stifle the partygoers and took on a combative nature with the Philly fans. Tensions between fans and team members deepened as an out-of-town visitor, P. J. Callahan, tracked down Stallings at the Majestic Hotel and began relentlessly and brazenly taunting the Braves' players for two days, calling them "rotten" and claiming that the A's were going to "show them." Stallings tried to avoid Callahan and told the visitor to go about his business, but the fan never let up and, in fact, suggested that he could pulverize Stallings. Stallings, no longer able to endure Callahan, punched him in the face.[93] Braves' players, with the help of the hotel manager, hustled the fan out of the Majestic, and Stallings, exhibiting satisfaction, "strolled back to his post at the hotel desk and lighted a cigar."[94]

During the World Series, Stallings drove his players past the edge of baseball respectability, urging them to carry on another commonly practiced Deadball Era tactic: bench jockeying. Verbal harassment of opponents was common. John McGraw's New York Giants were particularly adept at the craft, but the Braves, under the guidance of Stallings, spewed out vitriol at an unmatched level. Stallings, according to Damon Runyon,

> harried them with verbal goad. . . . He spoke rudely of their personalities. He abused their ancestry. Invective fell from his tongue in a searing stream as he crouched there conning the field before him, his strong fingers folding and unfolding against his palms as if grasping the throat of enemy.[95]

Stallings combed the newspapers for bits of information that he could transform into verbal ammunition. The Braves attacked Rube Oldring for allegedly leaving his wife, and Eddie Collins for accepting a new moneymaking newspaper syndication. "Chief" Bender endured disparaging comments about his Native American ancestry. The A's might have grown accustomed to this old-school practice, and under Mack's code of sportsmanship the A's refrained from attacks while keeping their gentlemanly demeanor; still, the harshness of the Braves' verbal onslaught, especially as it was directed toward Bender, undoubtedly added pressure to an already strained atmosphere.[96] "Get in there and beat that big Indian!"[97] Stallings had ordered before the first game, and during the game, umpire Bill Dinneen admonished the Braves to ease up. But the Braves attacked relentlessly: "They reminded the Athletics of debts they owed, troubles in their families, and intimate personal shortcomings." The A's youthful catcher, Wally Schang, who received a torrent of invective, allowed the Braves to steal nine bases in four games.[98]

PLAY BALL!

Mack responded with guile and, just before the first game, instructed pitcher Eddie Plank to practice with the regulars; Bender, in the meantime, warmed up secretly under the stands. Yet, under the blue skies of October, Albert "Chief" Bender started the first game and, in his usual, masterful way, stifled the Braves in the first inning: Moran, Evers, and Connolly made three quick outs. When the Athletics first brought their overpowering lineup to bat, the Braves, in the opinion of T. H. Murinane, looked "anxious."[99] Braves pitcher Dick Rudolph's anxiety grew out of not only World Series first-game pressures, but also events going on in his personal life: Rudolph's wife, back home in New York, was expected to deliver the couple's first child on game day (she delivered the following day). Rudolph allowed Eddie Murphy to single to right; Oldring sacrificed Murphy to second; and Rudolph, hoping to set up a double play, intentionally walked Collins. Home Run Baker strode to the plate, but instead of matching his previous World Series heroics, he hit a high pop fly that floated near the Braves' dugout. Braves first baseman Butch Schmidt snared the ball and spotted Murphy, who, trying to catch the nervous Braves off-guard, tagged and charged to third. But Schmidt, calmly and alertly, threw to Charlie Deal at third for a double play.[100] As Stallings later mused,

> The double play was completed, and Deal's part in it was beautiful to look upon. I think that happening alone saved us considerable bother, for had the man advanced, a run might have counted, and with the Athletics in front, they would have been possessed of worlds of confidence.[101]

The Braves' anxiety fell sharply; the champs appeared vulnerable. As a *Boston Globe* reporter noted, the "Braves paused, sighed, and suspected that they had a chance."[102]

Shouting and jeering relentlessly at Braves' hitters, Philadelphia fans expected Bender to succeed, as he had so often before in the World Series. In the second inning, the Braves' Possum Whitted worked the count and earned a walk, sparking a "kick" from the usually composed Bender, who, consequently, provoked umpire "Big Bill" Dinneen. Braves first baseman Butch Schmidt flied out to Oldring in deep left, and then Hank Gowdy, the young, always smiling, although highly anxious catcher, steadied himself and, despite the taunting from the Philadelphia fans, worked the count to three and two, smashing a double to the fence and scoring Possum Whitted. Rabbit Maranville, so often a clutch hitter, then hit a single, driving Gowdy home for the second run of the inning. A Barry-to-Collins-to-McInnis double play ended the inning, but as the Braves took a 2–0 lead, Philadelphia fans quieted.[103]

Although the shouting coming from the Philadelphia fans diminished in the second inning, the Athletics' hitters began to live up to their reputation. McInnis drew a walk, and Strunk singled him to second base. When right fielder Herb Moran let the ball bounce through his legs, Stuffy McInnis scored, and Amos "The Flying Foot" Strunk sprinted all the way to third; however, the Braves, despite their inexperience, kept their composure: Rudolph struck out the dangerous "Black Jack" Barry. Team captain Johnny Evers now had his opportunity to perform in one of those pivotal, psychological moments of a baseball game, the game's crucial moment, which he had described years earlier in *Touching Second*: When Wally Schang lashed a grounder to second, Evers scooped up the ball and gunned down Strunk at the plate. The Phillies rally had stalled, and the Braves kept their lead.[104]

In the third and fourth innings, as the three o'clock sun shone directly into his eyes, Rudolph appeared distracted, but he mixed up his pitches: fastball, curveball, change, and spitball. Rudolph, known as a "wise pitcher," threw a "spitter occasionally, just often enough to remind the batter that he can expect a freak break once in a while."[105] He fooled Oldring into swinging at a pitch inches wide and high off the plate; he set up Baker to take a vicious cut at the ball, "missing it by a foot"; and he even struck out McInnis, the contact hitter who rarely received a K on the scorecard (in 1914, 27 strikeouts in 576 at bats). Rudolph created his own outs, striking out four batters in the third and fourth innings, and the Athletics, with a chance to score, gambled away their opportunity to add a run. In the fourth inning, Strunk tried to stretch a single into a double but was thrown out by left fielder Joe Connolly.[106]

In the fifth, the Braves added to their lead when Hank Gowdy drove the ball deep to the scoreboard in left center, deep enough that Gowdy, the slowest position player on the team, managed a triple. When Connie Mack told the infield to pull in, Rabbit Maranville blooped a single over McInnis's head into right, scoring Gowdy. The sixth began with a spectacular catch by Philadelphia's Jack Barry of a Herb Moran fly ball toward the third-base side. Barry sprinted and lunged, snagging the ball barehanded near the fence. At that point, Bender inexplicably stopped throwing his changeup, and Boston's batters waited on their pitch. His pitches now appeared far from Bender-like, his fastball down a notch in speed and his curve failing to break sharply. As Swift noted, "No one had ever seen Bender unravel before. Not in such an important contest. Not in such a complete manner."[107]

After Johnny Evers singled a sharply hit ball through Bender's legs and Joe Connolly walked, Possum Whitted, with a 1–0 count, thumped a Bender fastball to right center, tripling his teammates home. Whitted also scored after a single by Schmidt. Sensing that his World Series ace had lost his effectiveness, Mack, according to the *Boston Globe*, removed "Old Chief Bender from the game."[108] As the *New York Times* reported, inserting language that caricatured Bender's Ojibwe heritage, "With six runs in the Indian was escorted to his wigwam, while the young Braves from old Boston town had a quiet little war dance."[109]

THE ROYAL ROOTERS

The Braves' notorious fan support group, the Royal Rooters, burst into song and revelry—as if the Braves had already won the game. The Rooters, originally led by Michael T. "Nuf Ced" McGreevy of Boston's Third Base Saloon, were now directed by former mayor John F. "Honey Fitz" Fitzgerald. The Rooters chanted, cheered, and sang for their Boston team. Before the first game, seven train cars filled with Royal Rooters had trekked to Philadelphia, and the 300 passionate fans had paraded in the Philadelphia streets the night before.[110] Stallings understood their value "To us it certainly was inspiring to know that so many of our own fans had made the long journey to Philadelphia to help cheer us along."[111]

But the champion A's, the best team in baseball, persisted. Philadelphia started a comeback in the seventh: Baker reached base on a nearly uncatchable ball to Evers, and McInnis followed with a walk. Still, the Braves stood firm, their nervousness at a minimum. They played with the same skill and confidence they had maintained since late July. And when Strunk sent a sizzling grounder down the first-base line that looked like a double, Schmidt cut it off for an out. Then, with one out and men on second and third, Rudolph struck out the great clutch hitter Black Jack Barry, the batter Ty Cobb had called the "most feared hitter on the A's." Rudolph ended the inning when new catcher Jack Lapp hit a weak grounder back to the pitching mound. In the ninth, the A's launched another attack when Baker led off with a double, but Rudolph and the agile-fielding Braves stopped the rally. The Braves' final stand had appeared within the rhythm of the game: whenever Philadelphia threatened, the Braves put together a fielding gem, and if the game situation turned even more precarious, Rudolph shut down the A's. Stallings later commented on the Braves' determination, on their capacity to be "game," saying, "I have been in baseball for 25 years, and the present Boston club is the gamest baseball organization I have ever been connected with. Three times third was occupied, once with none out and again with only one out, yet they failed to score."[112] James Isaminger, of the *Philadelphia Inquirer*, stressed the Braves' tenacity: "Boston beat, whipped, licked, tormented, maltreated, belabored, walloped, smashed, gashed, bruised, mangled, and wrecked us."[113]

GAME TWO

The Braves turned to their best pitcher, Bill James, for the second game. Considered the best pitcher in the National League, James had earned the second spot in pitcher WAR, with 8.2, the second-lowest ERA, with 1.90, and the highest winning percentage, with .788. With 26 victories and seven defeats, James had a nearly impeccable second half of the season, winning 19 and losing one since early July. He gained victories against every National League club. Three teams had beat him only once, and two never won against him. He could endure, even pitching extra innings—13—in a winning effort on June 2, against Brooklyn. He would pitch on two days' rest; he might pitch nine innings and then throw relief the following day. In addition to winning 26 games, he saved three. In the Deadball Era, managers exploited their pitchers as needed. In 1914, the 22-year-old's last good year, he pitched 332 innings.[114]

For the second game, Mack chose Eddie Plank, one of his college-trained players (Gettysburg), and a lefty, who threw a fastball and curve, delivering the ball with his cross-fire delivery. The cross fire confused batters because the pitcher, instead of moving the front foot toward the batter, swung the foot to the side and threw with a large, sweeping motion. In other words, Plank threw across his body, landing his right foot on the first-base side of the mound. Although this motion added deception, only a few pitchers could use it and maintain control. Left-handed cross-fire pitchers with control were a rarity, and few batters could handle him.[115] As Eddie Collins once observed, "He was not the trickiest, and not the possessor of the most stuff. He was just the greatest."[116]

By 1914, Plank was so great that he had already won 284 games, averaging more than 20 games a season and winning 64 percent of the time. He had shut out his opponents 59 times and won 15 games. At 38, Plank still had a lively arm, one that would place him among the winningest left-handers of all time. When a batter confronted Plank, he faced not only the unorthodox delivery of an experienced, crafty left-hander, he endured a time-consuming, annoying set of rituals. "Human rain delay," a term later associated with Mike Hargrove, first baseman for the Cleveland Indians, applied to Plank's pitching-mound decorum. After he received the catcher's signal, he put his cap back in place, tucked his shirt, tugged at his sleeve, pulled up his trousers, and then, perhaps, asked for another ball, one that he might rub with dirt—before starting the entire ritual again. Plank provoked anxiety among fans, writers, and even his own teammates. The time between Plank's pitches appeared eternal, in part because of his annoying ritual, and in part because games in the Deadball Era lasted just more than two hours. Baseball was an efficient game during in the early 1900s, unless Eddie Plank was on the mound.[117]

Plank had pitched only 185 innings in 1914. Five times in his career he had pitched 300 or more innings, including 346 innings in 1905. And with his brilliant pitching in the 1913 World Series, Mack would expect another outstanding effort. In 1913, Plank dueled Christy Mathewson in two of the most illustrious pitching contests in World Series history. In Game Two of the World Series, Plank and Mathewson pitched nine scoreless innings, and in a controversial move, Mack sent Plank to the plate with the bases loaded in the bottom of the ninth. Plank's fielder's choice contributed to a scoreless inning. Although Plank lost the game by giving up three runs in the 10th, he came back to battle against Mathewson in Game Five, throwing a two-hitter to clinch the series.[118]

And the Eddie Plank–led A's still displayed all the confidence of dynastic champions, especially in front of raucous, fanatically supportive Philadelphia fans. Before the game, "[t]he Athletics were full of pepper . . . and brought the crowd to its feet by some remarkable infield practice . . . the team looked full of fight and determined to regain lost ground." With another highly skilled, experienced pitcher, the champion A's still remained clear favorites over the youthful Braves.[119]

Plank dominated the Braves for eight innings, shutting down the Boston players at every turn. In the first inning, he allowed two Braves to reach base. When the hot-hitting Hank Gowdy, the Braves' top batter in Game One, stepped to the plate, Plank forced Gowdy to hit a harmless fly to center. Plank allowed two men on with two men out in the fourth, only to have Barry brilliantly spear a ball for the last out. In the sixth, Plank walked Gowdy and hit Maranville, probably trying to keep Rabbit from knocking the ball to right field, but the inning ended when Deal hit a harmless grounder to Baker at third.[120]

James pitched masterfully, just as effectively as he had been pitching since July. Baker and Strunk swung wildly at his pitches; the A's often swung at James's first pitch, hitting harmless grounders. In fact, no Athletic managed a hit until the sixth inning, when, with one out, Schang smashed a James fastball down the left-field line for a double. And with Plank up to bat, Gowdy dropped a James pitch for a short passed ball. Schang darted for third, and Gowdy drilled a strike to Deal for an out—just one of umpire Bill "Lord" Byron's controversial calls. The A's wasted a rare scoring opportunity when Plank, a .206 lifetime hitter, grounded out weakly, finishing off the inning. The A's, now under duress, complained, moaned, and "kicked" much more than their usual gentlemanly selves.[121] According to a *Boston Globe* reporter, "I had never seen so much kicking at the umpiring in a World's Series game," with the Athletics kicking "five times."[122] The A's, for instance, groused loudly in the seventh inning when James picked off Eddie Collins at first base, snuffing out another potential rally.[123]

Although Plank stopped the Braves from scoring for eight innings, and although "the $100,000 infield" executed spectacular play after spectacular play, Plank could not prevent the Braves from lengthy at bats, the type that wear down pitchers. Plank had thrown more than 120 pitches by the end of the eighth inning, and the Braves in the ninth, after Maranville grounded out to first, stood ready to execute small-ball tactics to earn a run. Deal, who had been relentlessly criticized as a weak hitter, smashed a fly to center that Strunk misjudged. Deal reached second and, during the next at bat, toyed with Plank, a pitcher whose "biggest weakness," according to Ty Cobb, was his inability to hold runners.[124] Deal stretched his lead at second, and catcher Wally Schang threw a pickoff attempt to shortstop Barry. Deal, who had no intention of returning to second, instead scampered to third. Barry—and there are conflicting accounts on the next moment—inexplicably failed to throw to third. James stepped to the plate (no thought of a relief pitcher) and struck out. But Leslie Mann, placed in the lineup for his prowess against left-handers, popped a soft hit to right field that glanced off Collins's glove, scoring Deal. As A's scout Al Maul described it,

> Collins turned his back, ran as I have never seen a man do, and then, if he had measured the distance and had electric timers, could not have turned and leaped into the air, yes, leaped backward, at a more exact instant. His glove just tipped the ball. It looked like Collins had come up out of a cellar in the ballpark, so unexpected was his appearance. For one fraction of a second I thought that he had the ball, then I saw him tumble to the earth, and Deal shot over the plate. . . . I never expected to see any living man come so close to the impossible.[125]

Near misses do not count in baseball; the Braves had scored.

BEANTOWN FOLLOWS EVERY PLAY

In Boston, 12,000 fans packed Copley Square near the *Boston Globe* scoreboard. With traffic shut down from 1:30 p.m. until 4:00 p.m., when the final score was announced, Boston fans, as part of a true community event, kept track of the game via telegraph. The crowd learned the verdict from telegraph operators a full minute before the score went up. "They whiled the time bandying all kinds of remarks, guying, laughing, fidgeting."[126] Telegraph runners dispersed throughout the crowd in front of the *Globe* office interpreted every message that came across the ticker—and the crowd noise whirred and droned throughout the square. A runner might yell out, "Mann knocked a single," or "Deal scored for the Braves." The crowd would yell, and, if in the next inning, a "goose egg" appeared, the crowd would roar.[127]

In the last inning, James seemed to be tiring. Barry had walked and reached second when Gowdy dropped the ball; Walsh batted for Plank and also drew a walk. When right fielder Eddie Murphy strode to the plate, Johnny Evers, as both second baseman and manager on the field, clearly perceived left-handed-hitting Murphy's tendency to pull the ball. Evers knew that Murphy had not hit into a double play all year and ordered an infield shift. With James ready to pitch, Evers called time out.

"Get closer to the bag," Evers yelled at Maranville, who moved closer to second, five feet from the bag.

With James set to pitch, Evers called time out again. "Come over. What's the matter, you deaf? He is a dead right hitter and never hits to the left offside of the diamond. Get nearer to second base."

Always the diplomat, Maranville retorted, "You fathead. I'm almost on second base now."

Evers just barked, "Get closer," and commanded third baseman Charlie Deal to play at shortstop. The captain of the Braves, the on-field director, then ordered James to pitch. Murphy smashed the ball between James's legs, and Maranville performed his magic.[128] According to a reporter,

> The count down to three and two, Murphy hit a fast grounder that Maranville picked up on the dead run, touched the base just ahead of Walsh, and then while out of position and being interfered with by the runner. The Rabbit overcame all obstacles as if he were inhuman and shot the ball to first, and the game was over.[129]

Said Clark Griffith, president of the Washington Senators, "It was the greatest play I ever saw in my years of baseball."[130] James's spitball pitching, Evers's baseball intelligence, and Maranville's talent in the field, an unbeatable force since August, secured triumph for the Braves once again.

BOSTON ERUPTS

The now-15,000 fans on "Newspaper Row" in front of the *Globe* office on Washington and Milk Streets went wild in the ninth when the number 1 went up for the Braves and 0 for the A's. "Hats and caps and newspapers were flung in the air, and that intense exultant shout went up and lasted for some minutes." A reporter for the *Globe*, aware of how a pleasant World Series victory contrasted with events taking place across the Atlantic, wrote:

> Troubles and cares and war and the high cost of living were all forgotten— had been forgotten for two hours—by the crowd. Antwerp had fallen— what of it? The Braves had won the second game in the World Series, and Boston is the "home of the Braves." So who can expect Boston to consider

international war or peace at such a moment? Tush! Such things are very trivial compared with battle between the Braves and the Athletics.[131]

A day later, an artist from a St. Louis newspaper drew a globe, half of which was a baseball, and, in the western sphere, precisely in Boston, one found an American flag hoisted atop a baseball bat, with hats and derbies floating through a cloud. The eastern sphere of the same globe was adorned with a black casket bunting, falling from Europe, a part of the world covered with artillery pieces and smoke.[132]

Thousands of fans jammed the *Globe*'s telephone lines for hours. Many disbelieved the telephone operator, who, for two hours, had said the score was nothing to nothing. But when the Braves won, fans offered chocolates and other gifts to the operators.

Gaining a second victory against the champions, nearly eliminating the home-field advantage, and knowing that they could win in the closest of games, the Braves, as they left the field, reveled in the cheering of their most loyal fans, the Royal Rooters. In the game's final act, the Royal Rooters marched across the field behind a brass band: Johnny Evers and former Boston mayor Honey Fitzgerald led the band. Fitzgerald, whose eldest daughter Rose had married Joseph P. Kennedy Sr. on October 7, just two days earlier, could now continue festivities in Boston.[133] Stallings ordered the equipment manager to ship the road uniforms back to Boston. "We won't be coming back here," he boasted.[134] On the night of October 11, Boston fans waited all night to buy tickets. Lines had formed around Fenway before dark. As a *Globe* reporter notes, "Boston, last evening, was surcharged with a suppressed excitement in anticipation of the great battle which will be renewed at 2 this afternoon."[135]

A 70-piece brass band and the city's most prominent politicians greeted the Braves upon their arrival in Boston. The Braves were now comforted by the hometown advantage and heartened by the knowledge that one more victory just might form a barrier too imposing, even for a great team like the Philadelphia Athletics. By 1914, only one team, the 1907 Detroit Tigers, had faced a 0–3 deficit, and the Tigers had fallen to a hot-hitting (.471 average) Johnny Evers and the Cubs.[136] Both the Braves, now captained by Evers, and the Athletics understood that a 3–0 advantage would be overpowering. (Of course, they did not know that no team would ever come back from a 0–3 deficit in the World Series.)

The Royal Rooters, usually associated with the Red Sox, formed the cornerstone of the Braves' cheering section. "Nuf Ced" McGreevy, the founding father of the Rooters, owned the Third Base Saloon near the Huntington Avenue Grounds—the stadium used by the Red Sox prior to Fenway. The Third Base Saloon, the "last stop before home," was a precursor to the twenty-first-century sports bar. It included, a "life-sized statue of a player, baseball paraphernalia, lights cast in the shape of balls, sports pictures, and a clock that keeps time with a pendulum made from a ball and a bat."[137] McGreevy, the absolute monarch of the Third Base Saloon, issued final judgment on matters baseball and otherwise; the finality of his judgments had earned him the title "Nuf Ced."

The Rooters, with a brass band at the front, would march to their special seats and then chant out "Tessie," a song they had sung to the Red Sox as they battled the Pirates in the 1903 World Series. The Rooters sang special versions of "Tessie" to members of the Red Sox. Instead of singing, "Tessie you know I love you madly," they would belt out lyrics for individual Red Sox players, for instance, "Jimmy you know I love you madly." The Rooters would alter lyrics for the opposing players, and their singing was such an annoyance that Tommy Leach, who played for the Pirates against the Red Sox in the 1903 World Series, once quipped, "I think those Boston fans actually won that Series for the Red Sox."[138] Although stiffly attired in suits, ties, starched collars, and bowlers, the Rooters zealously expressed their likes and dislikes. They also refused to back down to any opposition, and in the 1912 Boston–New York World Series, when deprived of their regular seats, they nearly rioted when approached by the Boston Mounted Police.[139]

GAME THREE

Pregame festivities before the third game inspired the Rooters and stirred the 35,000 (some estimates say 40,000) fans entering Fenway Park. Guided by mounted policemen, the Rooters paraded in front of both teams' benches. Boston mayor James Michael Curley gave a gilded bat and gold ball to Gowdy and Maranville. Wearing a silk hat and frock coat, Honey Fitzgerald presented Stallings with a diamond stickpin. Stallings, breaking his superstitious tradition of refusing gifts before games, accepted. The crowd turned to Johnny Evers, who had won the Chalmers Award, judged by baseball writers as the "most important and useful player to the club and to the league." (Maranville finished in second place.) Recipients received a Chalmers Model 30, a luxury car. To the delight of the Boston fans, Evers took delivery of the automobile right before the game, driving it around the field.[140] Buoyed by two victories in Philadelphia, backed by the wildly cheering Royal Rooters, ready to support their pitcher Lefty Tyler, and inspired by their MVP hero Johnny Evers, the gritty, "game" Braves stood ready to battle the Athletics.

Yet, the Braves would now face a pitcher, the Athletics' Bullet Joe Bush, who had achieved accolades a year earlier in the World Series as a young

David overpowering a formidable Goliath, the New York Giants. Bush, a small-town Minnesota ballplayer whose mother was an immigrant from Poland, had skyrocketed to the major leagues. Bullet Joe had attained heroic stature when, as a 20-year-old, in Game Three of the 1913 World Series, he had subdued John McGraw's Giants. Bush threw, according to Mack, one of the best fastballs in the league. Grunting with each pitch, pirouetting with the singular "Joe-Bush-Twist-Around" delivery, the right-hander mixed an occasional curve with his vicious fastballs. In Game Two of the 1913 World Series, Christy Mathewson and the Giants had slowed Philadelphia's momentum, pitching a 10-inning, 3–0 shutout in Philadelphia. But a day later, they faced Bush's blazing fastball and fell 8–2. "Giants Slain by Mere Boy," proclaimed the October 10, 1913 edition of the *Boston Globe*.[141] Bullet Joe, clearly not a one-game wonder, pitched with great success in 1914, amassing a 16–13 record and 3.06 ERA. If Bush could pitch up to his standards, if he could replicate his 1913 World Series heroics, and if the A's could swing their potent bats, they could turn the World Series around and repeat as champions.

In the third game, Bush pitched skillfully, and the A's batters, for the first time in the World Series, hit the ball sharply, as they had all season. They scored in the first inning, as Murphy doubled and Oldring sacrificed him to second. The Braves' Joe Connolly, playing in left field, just a few yards in front of the rowdy, screaming, "Tessie"-singing Royal Rooters, dropped a Collins fly ball, allowing Murphy to score. But the Braves came back when, with two outs, Rabbit Maranville stole second and Hank Gowdy smashed a double into the section where the Royal Rooters were seated.[142]

Mr. and Mrs. Horace Gowdy, Hank Gowdy's parents, cheered on their son—without his knowledge of their presence. The young, self-effacing Gowdy suffered from extreme nervousness and subsequent poor play every time he learned that his parents were observing him. During the summer, Boston had traveled to Hank's home state of Ohio to play the Cincinnati Reds. In the first game of a doubleheader, Hank, unaware of his parents' presence, slugged three hits and fielded brilliantly. Between games he learned that his parents were in attendance and then played miserably. Performing poorly when his parents were there to watch him had evolved into a pattern, and his mother revealed that a visit to Hank in grammar school had resulted in "shaking knees and white lips." The Gowdys, as loyal parents and Braves fans, slipped into Boston under assumed names, only telling George Stallings—their source of tickets—of their venture. And Gowdy, "unburdened of the responsibility of having two pair of found eyes turned on him from the grandstand and believing his parents a few hundred miles away in Columbus, came across with the 'wallop' every time it was needed."[143]

In the fourth, the A's regained the lead as McInnis doubled into the left-field bleachers, and outfielder Jimmy Walsh singled him home. Nonetheless, when McInnis hit the ball to left, Connolly sprinted toward the foul line and plunged recklessly into the seats, inspiring the crowd, his teammates, and manager George Stallings. Stallings exulted that Connolly, by taking a "chance breaking his neck," had "claimed the fighting spirit of the Braves." Christy Mathewson, observing from the press box, called the Braves the "gamest club" he had ever seen, adding that he had "seen some game ones battling the old Giants, the Athletics, and the old Cubs."[144]

When back at the plate, the Braves once again fought back: Schmidt singled, took second on a grounder to second, and then watched as Rabbit Maranville ignored the seriousness of the moment and treated the Fenway fans to one of his lighthearted antics. Maranville had hit a Texas leaguer into right field, just out of reach of Collins, McInnis, and Murphy. Although the ball was judged foul, Rabbit, seeing a chance to please the fans, happily circled the bases. The fans cheered and the Braves' momentum never waned. Maranville usually combined playfulness with superb performances, and after his return to home plate, he inspired fans again, this time stroking a single that brought home Schmidt for the tying run.[145]

STRONG DEFENSE AND "TESSIE"

The game proceeded as so many Deadball Era games did: a defensive battle with great pitching. The crucial defensive play transpired in the eighth inning, when pitcher Bush ripped the ball hard down the first-base line. The ball went over the bag and was spinning toward the right-field line, probably for a triple; however, Butch Schmidt blocked the ball, allowing his momentum to carry him two strides beyond it.[146] But he dove back—"like a cat after mouse"—fielded the ball, and tossed it to a lightning-quick Lefty Tyler, who "had come over to first simply on speculation." *Globe* reporters judged it "one of the greatest plays ever pulled off on a ball field."[147]

Between each inning and when the Braves came to bat, the Royal Rooters played noisily, belting out "Tessie" amidst a "jumble of drums, brasses, and cymbals." They made music when Gowdy faced Bush and hit a home run. A *Boston Globe* reporter noted that the band, overwhelmed with excitement, blared out "indistinct" sounds, music that merely showed a "suspicion of Tessie emanating from the horns." The Royal Rooters "cared little whether they were playing, 'Tessie,' 'Sweet Adeline,' or 'Michigan,' as long as they were playing 'Tessie.'"[148] In the 12th inning, "everybody was madly, blindly waving pennants, hats, scorecards, and caps, and hoarse to a whisper, they endeavored to send words of appreciation to the lanky backstop." The crowd was passionate, intensifying its cries as the Athletics threatened to score in every inning until the fifth. The "lust-lunged shouters" sang "Tessie" with such enthusiasm that the *Globe* noted that "Connie Mack and Eddie Collins declared that it was 'Tessie' and not the Braves that beat them," that the "incessant repetition of the song caused Bush to weaken in the crucial final inning," and that "'Tessie' ought to be barred at World Series games, anyway."[149]

EVERS'S BONER

The game played out as a tight pitcher's duel until the 10th. The A's, still fighting like proud champions, loaded the bases in small-ball style: Schang singled, Murphy beat out a bunt, and the two runners moved up on a fielder's choice to Evers. Collins walked, and the bases were full. (Early in the inning, Mack had sent his pitcher, Bush, to the plate. Bush, only 21 years old, had batted .189 and pitched 206 innings during the regular season. Still, Mack considered him his best bet as a pitcher and kept him in. Bush struck out.)[150] With the bases loaded at a pivotal moment in the series, Mack would have bet that Johnny Evers would pull through, but when Baker hit a sizzler to Evers at second, the "meanest ball I ever handled," he fumbled it, allowing Schang to score, and then, letting loose his inner torments and anxieties, Evers began cursing at the ball. Philadelphia's Murphy, quick to notice the distracted, hesitant Evers, dashed across home plate, giving the A's a 4–2 lead. Evers lamented, "What did I do but stand there plumb dumb. . . . I wished the ground had swallowed me."[151]

The Braves rolled back the A's attack as Possum Whitted snared an Eddie Collins fly for the last out of the inning. Boston fans feared the worst (Evers knew he might have committed the new "Merkle's Boner" or "Snodgrass Muff"). But the hero of the World Series up until that point, Hank Gowdy, strode to the plate in the bottom of the 10th. Gowdy had already smashed a double in the second inning, a blast into the Royal Rooter section that had knocked in Maranville. Two days earlier, a writer for the *Philadelphia Press* had praised Gowdy for a "smile that knows no quit," adding, "When you're down on your luck and feeling fit for the hospital or the grave, just think of a chap who wouldn't quit, Hank Gowdy, the Boston Brave."[152]

Not dispirited by Evers's serious mental lapse, and not bothered by a two-run deficit to the world champs, Gowdy knocked a Bush fastball into Fenway's center-field seats for a home run. Some pessimistic Boston fans who had shifted close to the exits moved back to the seats. Josh Devore batted for Lefty Tyler but went down swinging. Maranville, in a practice common for Deadball Era players, took over as first-base coach: He began to wave, yell, and jeer at Bush. "Maranville," Christy Mathewson observed, "slid up and down the coaching box on all parts of his anatomy and turned somersaults and threw dirt into his hair and acted like a tumbler, hollering as if he were crazy all the time." The Braves' players, reaching insufferable levels, taunted Bush and the A's: "The whole Boston team seemed to go insane in an instant."[153]

Bush, apparently reacting to the frenzied Bostonians, walked Moran. And Evers, with a chance to redeem himself, whacked a single to right, advancing Moran to third. The Chalmers Award winner had lifted his World Series batting average to above .400. Connolly knocked a fly to the outfield, and Moran scored the tying run for the Braves on their 1914 signature play, the sacrifice. Maranville, displaying his unique first-base coaching style, "turned somersaults, and the crowd went crazy."[154]

DESPERATION AT SUNSET

A subdued, October twilight cast a glow on Fenway. Bill James, the season's pitching hero and winner of Game Two in Philadelphia, entered as a reliever in the 11th inning. He stopped the A's for two innings, despite yielding three walks. When the Braves took their turn to bat in the 12th, Gowdy advanced confidently to the plate; "the conviction seemed to filter through the multitude that the beginning of the end was at hand."[155] Bush pitched cautiously to Gowdy, getting him to foul off a couple of pitches. But Gowdy, who Mathewson judged to be hitting like a "demon," slugged a Bush changeup for a double into the left-field bleachers.[156]

George Stallings, fearing that the game might be called because of darkness and sensing a pivotal moment in the series, acted in desperation. He substituted for both his star player and his star pitcher, replacing Gowdy with the former track star Les Mann, and sending Larry Gilbert to the plate for James. After Bush walked Gilbert, leaving men on first and second, Moran put down a catchable sacrifice bunt, but Bush charged toward the third-base line, fielded the bunt, and, anticipating the speedy Mann's charge toward third, hurriedly threw the ball away from Baker into left field. Moran scored the winning run.[157]

That run produced the "complete intoxification of the Royals" and, it seemed, thousands of Boston fans.[158] The Royal Rooters, clutching blue and white pennants, fought their way over the low fence in left field and pushed their way to the front of the crowd. The band burst into Yale's famous "Boola," or the "Undertaker's Song," and Honey Fitzgerald led the crowd in "Sweet Adeline." The Rooters worked their way through swarming fans. They moved past the Athletics' bench, beyond the grandstand, and out through the gate by the first-base bleachers. Boston's 35,000 fans flowed across Fenway, a "glorious ending of a perfect day and a great game."[159]

CONFIDENCE

Mack sensed the importance of the game and later reminisced, "[I]f we had won it, we would have won the series."[160] With the Braves ahead, 3–0, Stallings's confidence swelled. He ordered the traveling secretary, Herman Nickerson, to cancel the Braves' train reservations to Philadelphia, scheduled after the fourth game. Nickerson, although beset with anxiety and doubt, complied. He then prayed for one more Braves victory.[161]

Nickerson, undoubtedly, was not the only Bostonian who prayed. Baseball fans well understood that the Athletics were champions, and that the Athletics, especially if hitters like Collins, Baker, and Schang became untracked, could still win it all. The Athletics possessed stellar pitching, capable of carrying the team through win streaks. The A's had experienced highs and lows all summer, and their highs—their win streaks—punctuated the entire season: On nine occasions the A's had won three in a row; two times four games in a row; three times five in a row; twice seven; and, most impressively, a 12-game winning streak in July. The Braves had manufactured their phenomenal comeback, catching the Giants in July and August. Yet, in August, the Athletics had attained even higher winning percentages than the Miracle Braves. While the Braves went 19–6 (.760) in August, the Athletics went 23–5 (.821). The A's, probably more than any other team, could recover momentum, overcome the deficit, and surprise baseball fans everywhere.[162] In addition, they had one of baseball's greatest minds leading them: Connie Mack. Before the fourth game, Mack, having lost faith in his former World Series stalwart, Albert Bender, shrewdly turned to 23-year-old Bob Shawkey, a second-year pro with a 15–8 record.

GAME FOUR

Mack's gamble appeared to work. Shawkey, a fastball and curveball pitcher, stymied the Braves for three innings. In the first three innings, the Braves managed four groundouts, two flyouts, and a walk to Gowdy. Before walking in the second inning, Gowdy, now a superstar in the eyes of Boston fans, thrilled the crowd for one brief moment, when he blasted a ball into the left-field bleachers, but foul. Up against the Braves' Dick Rudolph, the Athletics' Eddie Collins singled sharply to center in the first; Jimmy Walsh knocked a double to the outfield railing in the second; and Rube Oldring managed his first hit of the World Series, a single, in the third.

But the Braves' defense always tightened, stifling the Athletics' struggle to fight back and foiling Mack every time. After his single with two outs in the third, Oldring bolted toward second, but Gowdy thwarted his steal attempt with a perfect throw to Maranville. With one out in the fourth inning, Baker reached first after he smashed a liner down the first-base line that smacked Schmidt in the face, bloodying his nose. With the hit-and-run on, McInnis hit a single to left. As Baker rounded toward third, McInnis, "slow as a turtle," headed toward second and was gunned down: Connolly to Deal to Evers.[163] In the bottom of the fourth, patience and luck rewarded the Braves. Evers, waiting and waiting on each pitch, drew a walk. Connolly hit a hard bounder to Collins, who, despite his reputation as one of the greatest second basemen of all time, bobbled the ball. Although he tossed out Connolly at first, his slight mistake allowed Evers to move on to second. Whitted smashed a grounder toward Collins, a sharp hit into the hole in right, and Collins blocked the ball with his shins, injuring his leg. Collins had prevented Evers from scoring, but the Braves' captain stood on third. Collins limped, gaining his composure during a time-out. The tall, powerful Butch Schmidt, in typical Braves' fashion, "pulled something of a squeeze play," and hacked the ball into the ground at short as Evers raced home.[164] A's shortstop Jack Barry could only throw out Schmidt at first for the second out. Gowdy later grounded out, but the Braves took the lead, 1–0.[165]

The A's battled back in the fifth, when Barry, knocking his first hit of the series, reached on an infield hit, a sizzling grounder to third that Maranville gloved behind Deal and fired—too late—to first. Schang dribbled a fielder's choice to Evers that pushed Barry to second, and Shawkey, waiting on a Rudolph changeup, walloped a ball for a two-run double to center, scoring Barry. But the inning fizzled as Murphy grounded out, and Oldring went down swinging. Still, the A's remained in the game. The "Great White Elephants," although wounded, were still standing strong.

In the bottom half of the fifth inning, the Braves' fortune rose once more, and on "came the Braves with their characteristic rush."[166] After Maranville grounded out to Barry, his counterpart at short, and Deal to his fellow third baseman, Baker, Braves' pitcher Dick Rudolph knocked a clean hit to center. Moran smoked a ball into left center for a double, sending Rudolph to third. With Moran on second and Rudolph on third, Boston's captain, the "nervous and irritable" Johnny Evers, strode to the plate and "matched his years of experience against Connie Mack's last hope."[167] Evers worked the count to 3–2, waiting for his "groove ball," and then the "tricky batsman" smashed a single to center that scored two runs and put the Braves on top, 3–1.[168] The "crowd certainly did howl," offering its approval for the Chalmers Award winner.[169]

But the 1913 World Series victors never yielded. Shawkey picked off an unsuspecting Evers for the final out of the fifth. In the top of the sixth, Eddie Collins led off with a vicious liner through the mound, impossible for the pitcher to grab and looking like a "sure hit," but Maranville speared the ball "as it came sizzling off the ground" and threw Collins out by 15 feet. "Eddie," a *Boston Globe* reporter observed, was "dumbfounded and almost paralyzed when he saw the play come off. The crowd just stood up and howled and howled."[170]

In the bottom of the sixth, Mack replaced Shawkey with Herb Pennock, the smooth, collected left-hander who had finished the season with five straight victories, achieving an 11–4 record. Stallings, in turn, replaced left-handed-hitting Connolly with the right-handed, defensive-minded Les Mann. Mann flied out to center, but Pennock, who, according to Grantland Rice, usually pitched each game "with the ease and coolness of a practice session," faltered. Possum Whitted reached first on a hot grounder to Baker at third. Schmidt "banged a rap at Collins, which nearly knocked Eddie over," and drove Possum to third.[171] With Schmidt at first and Whitted at third with two outs, Stallings boldly called for a delayed double steal—one of the most thrilling Deadball Era tactics. With one out and two strikes on Gowdy, Schmidt broke for second, and Whitted then began a dash down the third-base line. Gowdy, for the first time in the series, struck out, and Collins intercepted the throw from Schang, tossing out Schmidt as he attempted to get back to first. No run scored, but the Braves still held the lead, and they were still attacking relentlessly.[172]

In the seventh inning, proud champion A's tried to come back again as Walsh walked and took second on a Rudolph wild pitch. The Braves stifled the rally with crafty pitching and smart defense: Rudolph struck out two of Philadelphia's best clutch hitters, Barry and Schang, and Gowdy whipped a strike to Evers, who, with a one-handed stab, caught Walsh on second. In the eighth, Murphy crushed a long fly ball to left center for the A's, a ball that looked as if it would go for extra bases, but Les Mann, Stallings's defensive replacement for Connolly, sprinted after it for the catch. The A's went down in order as they managed a groundout and weak fly ball for the other two outs.[173]

ACCORDING TO REPORTS

Reporters at the game witnessed the A's battling up until the eighth but approaching the ninth as a defeated team. Perhaps the struggling A's in the ninth left the impression that they lacked determination, but sportswriters composed their stories through the prism of hindsight. Reporters who offered their description of the game, and they all wrote their remarks after the Braves won, saw a listless A's team. The colorful, perceptive Hearst papers' baseball writer, Damon Runyon, said of the A's approach to Game Four, "They had little spirit. They have acted all along as if they were carrying the championship in a gallon bucket and were afraid of spilling it. Only on one or two occasions have they displayed the fighting expected of champions."[174] Philadelphia reporter James Isaminger, relating a more visceral metaphor, concluded that the Athletics "didn't exhibit any more enthusiasm than a missionary being led up to a cannibal king's soup pot."[175]

In the ninth, Mack sent up the heart of the A's order: Collins, Baker, and McInnis. But the confident American League MVP (Chalmers Award) Eddie Collins struck out on four pitches; Home Run Baker hit a slow grounder to Evers; and Stuffy McInnis, a lifetime .307 hitter, ended the series with a groundout to Deal at third. Perhaps the A's lessened their intensity, but the crafty Dick Rudolph fooled the A's as he had deceived opponents all year. He mixed his fastball, change, and spitter, often seeming to throw a spitter when tossing another pitch, and he was always one or two steps ahead of the batter. The Braves, with their craftiness, boldness, and "gameness," actively fought and won the last inning of the last game of the 1914 World Series.

The A's faded swiftly in the last inning, and with the final out, thousands swarmed toward the dugout. Stallings addressed the fans, and Maranville, dragged out of the locker room shirt undone, spoke to spectators. Then Boston politicians took their turn. Mayor James Michael Curley and former mayor Honey Fitzgerald, who had briefly battled as political rivals in 1913, spoke to the crowd. Boston fans cheered them both, saving their most enthusiastic applause for the redoubtable Honey Fitz, the leader of the Royal Rooters and their band. The band, amongst thousands of fans, paraded around the field singing "Tessie," and it then wound its way from the Fen to Huntington Avenue and Copley Square, where they sang to the defeated Athletics as they packed their bags at the Copley Plaza Hotel.[176]

THE MIRACLE BRAVES

In October 1914, Damon Runyon praised the Braves, offering a grand tribute: "One of the greatest and gamest ball clubs of all time. There can be no question as to the status of the Braves now. They go into history . . . with the memory of . . . all the other great clubs that have risen to high power over the baseball world." It was, indeed, the greatest comeback story in sports history, or, as Runyon offered, the "greatest feat in baseball history."[177] The "Miracle

Braves," as they were now being called, had suffered through abysmal season after abysmal season in the first 12 years of the twentieth century, seven times suffering more than 100 losses. In early 1914, they plunged into the cellar with their 4–18 start. They languished in last place as late as July 18. In mid-July, they had even suffered defeat to a minor-league team. Yet, they battled back to reach the top, struggling against such talented teams as Chicago and St. Louis, and most notably John McGraw's imposing New York Giants, finishing the season with a 51–16 record.[178] As the *New York Times* noted,

> The all-conquering spirit of this Boston team carried it through the storm-iest campaign baseball has ever known. Inspired by its own ability, the Braves accomplished something no team has ever accomplished before in a World's Series since the National Commission assumed charge in 1905. It captured four straight games in as many played. It turned the whole real world of baseball upside down. In a year of reversals in sport, the Boston team accomplished a task, which a few days before looked impossible. A ball club which started the season as a joke reached the perch deluxe in baseball in a blaze of glory.[179]

HEROES OF THE MODERN GAME

The Boston team, "inspired by its own ability," embodied the great tale of the American dream, the Horatio Alger story. In a typical Alger story, a poor boy, through hard work, courage, and honesty, rises up and achieves Victorian respectability. Alger stories had achieved popularity with the publication of *Ragged Dick* in 1868. But after Alger's death in 1899, his books sold in the millions, and in the early 1900s, baseball writers, including Gilbert Patten (pen name: Burt Standish) produced another version of the Alger tales: the immensely popular Frank Merriwell stories. In a Patten sports novel, Merriwell, a young man of integrity, attends school, fends off bullies, and then leads a struggling team in victory over a traditional, dominant rival, often securing a last-second victory. Merriwell, who fought for "truth, faith, justice, the triumph of right," represented to many Americans "muscular Christianity," where vigorous, masculine role models succeeded because of their gentlemanly, Christian values. Merriwell, although not poor, was impeccably modest, and through strength of mind and character could snatch victory when defeat seemed imminent.[180] The Boston Braves, although not always modest, exemplified the grit of a Merriwell character, earning the accolade from countless writers as being "game." Even Connie Mack remarked, "They are a game club, and they deserve to win."[181] Echoing the characters from boys' fiction, the Braves, tough and never yielding, shot up from last place to defeat baseball's perennial victors: the New York Giants and the Philadelphia Athletics.

And the Braves had accomplished this feat as part of a new, legitimized national pastime. Victorian Americans had judged baseball players as unsavory. Davy Jones, who played for 15 years during the Deadball Era, commented that "baseball wasn't a very respectable occupation back then." The parents of his intended girlfriend concluded that baseball was in such ill repute that they forbade their daughter from dating him.[182] Americans, imbued with a Puritan work ethic, slowly accepted such new leisure pursuits as baseball. As historian Michael McGerr observes, Victorian Americans often disliked ballplayers because "professional athletes seemed to devote their lives to pleasure instead of production, to dissipation instead of self-control."[183]

Christy Mathewson's mother had hoped that her son would train for the ministry; baseball, she feared, offered little career satisfaction. But Mathewson transformed himself into an apostle for the game of baseball, validating the sport as a "Christian gentleman." He, like the fictional Merriwell, was an exemplar of "muscular Christianity." While the Braves had their rough side—Stallings's language, Evers's anger, and Maranville's antics—fans and journalists recognized their determination, their "never-say-die" spirit. Catcher Hank Gowdy, the humble, determined hero of the World Series, could have been mistaken for Frank Merriwell. Soon after the World Series ended, fans throughout the country feted the Braves as national celebrities. The Miracle Braves paraded through the streets of Boston as World Series champions. Throughout the winter, Braves players were toasted at banquets. Rudolph, Gowdy, and Evers returned to their hometown as heroes. Two days after the World Series, Dick Rudolph, a Fordham alumnus, attended the Fordham–Middlebury football game and amid parades, "college yelling," and speechmaking, "received the greatest ovation ever accorded to a former Fordham athlete."[184] When Hank Gowdy returned to his hometown of Columbus, Ohio, in late October, thousands marched, escorting him from the train station to the Ohio Statehouse.[185] In Troy, New York, 5,000 citizens, including several drum corps, 10 marching bands, and torch-bearing fans, cheered the National League's Most Valuable Player, baseball's Horatio Alger character, Johnny Evers.[186]

The Braves' victory validated the new, modern ball game of the new, modern country. When Johnny Evers, a rags-to-riches ballplayer on a rags-to-riches team, drove his Chalmers automobile in Fenway Park, a high-tech concrete and steel ballpark, he signaled how well the American dream matched modern, Progressive America. The season of 1914 formed a bridge to a modern era. Evers exemplified the modern progressive player. He systematically studied every dimension of the game in the way his Progressive

Era counterparts had examined education, government, public health, and philanthropic giving. Progressives had promoted systematic charitable giving, not merely random, emotional, heartfelt gifts to the poor; they endorsed "scientific baseball," not semiskilled players performing in front of raucous gamblers. Evers and his manager George Stallings represented the "revolution in values," the shift from small-town mores to sophisticated business-like thinking. Plant managers in the 1910s stressed time studies to improve worker efficiency; baseball managers studied hitting lanes so that players reached first more frequently.

This shift in perspective corresponded to the transformation of base-ball venues. Before 1909, the A's had played in a wooden stadium that held 13,000; by 1914, they were playing in Shibe Park, the first stadium built with concrete and steel (1909). Shibe, with a Beaux-Arts cupola at the entrance and a French Renaissance façade, could hold 32,000.[187] The Braves played Opening Day 1914 at the Huntington Grounds, a broken-down wooden stadium that could hold 11,000. They left the field as World Series victors in Fenway Park, a permanent edifice that could hold more than 35,000. Owners invested in the new parks, with the newest technologies: telephones and electric-powered elevators.[188] In 1914, fan territory near the ballparks radiated outward, with streetcar lines and roads for automobiles. Indeed, Henry Ford's assembly line, the quintessential modern apparatus, began producing Model Ts just four months before Opening Day 1914. Americans could buy toasters and blenders; they would have to stop their Model Ts at stoplights as they headed toward the newest retail space, the supermarket.[189] They could even drive to the ballpark.

Industrialized technology influenced Americans at precisely the same moment that modern warfare experienced a transformation. As the Braves earned victories in August and September 1914, Europeans, with their steel helmets, machine guns, airplanes, submarines, and eventually poison gas and tanks, rushed into devastating battles, not comprehending the destructive powers of their new technologies. While Americans celebrated the exploits of the Braves, Europeans would soon lament the abhorrent conditions of incessant trench warfare. The day the Braves won the World Series, readers read the following headlines in the *New York Times*: "The Western Front, Germans Pressing On to Capture Ostend" and "Belgian Government Flees to France." Americans read about events farther east: "The Russians Fall Back" and "Warsaw Is Threatened."

As the Braves and their fans celebrated, thousands of refugees fled Belgium for the Netherlands. In Europe, the "August Madness" had transformed itself into a level of death and destruction the world had never before seen. In August and September 1914, hundreds of thousands of German, Russian,

French, British, and Belgian soldiers fell to their deaths. But in that same year, the United States refrained from engagement, somewhat oblivious to the anguish of war. One reporter, failing to observe the disjunction between sports and war, observed after the World Series that the Braves had "fought harder than the Belgians at Liege."[190] The Miracle of the Marne, the successful last-ditch defense by hundreds of thousands of French troops to stop the German offensive, took place in the summer of 1914; the battle held no comparison to the Braves' miracle. That summer, Americans, still peaceful, played baseball, a sport now recognized as a national pastime, but in Boston, as the last game of the World Series ended, as Charlie Deal threw across the diamond to Butch Schmidt, "fans were pouring over the fences in a torrent," swarming the dugout, "until one wondered how such a great multitude had ever been compressed into the seating space."[191] The Braves, the Boston fans, and all Americans could pause and celebrate.

· *Appendix* ·
1914 World Series Statistics

GAME 1: BOSTON BRAVES 7, PHILADELPHIA ATHLETICS 1; FRIDAY, OCTOBER 9, 1914; (D) SHIBE PARK

Table A.1. 1914 World Series Game 1 Statistics

										R	H	E
BOS N	0	2	0	0	1	3	0	1	0	7	11	2
PHI A	0	1	0	0	0	0	1	0	0	1	5	0

BATTING Braves	AB	R	H	RBI	BB	SO	PO	A
Moran RF	5	0	0	0	0	1	0	0
Evers 2B	4	1	1	0	0	1	2	2
Connolly LF	3	1	1	0	1	1	0	1
Whitted CF	3	2	1	2	1	0	2	0
Schmidt 1B	4	1	2	1	0	0	11	1
Gowdy C	3	2	3	1	1	0	9	1
Maranville SS	4	0	2	2	0	1	2	3
Deal 3B	4	0	0	0	0	0	1	2
Rudolph P	4	0	1	0	0	1	0	3
Totals	34	7	11	6	3	5	27	13

FIELDING
DP: 1. Schmidt-Deal
E: Moran (1), Evers (1)

BATTING
2B: Gowdy (1, off Bender)
3B: Gowdy (1, off Bender); Whitted (1, off Bender)
GDP: Deal 2 (2, off Bender, off Wyckoff); Whitted (1, off Bender)
Team LOB: 3

BASERUNNING
SB: Moran (1, 2nd base off Wyckoff/Lapp); Schmidt (1, home off Wyckoff/Lapp); Gowdy (1, 2nd base off Wyckoff/Lapp)

BATTING A's	AB	R	H	RBI	BB	SO	PO	A
Murphy RF	4	0	1	0	0	1	0	0

	AB	R	H	BB	SO	PO	A
Oldring LF	3	0	0	0	2	2	0
Collins 2B	3	0	0	1	0	2	2
Baker 3B	4	0	1	0	1	3	4
McInnis 1B	2	1	0	2	1	10	1
Strunk CF	4	0	2	0	0	0	0
Barry SS	4	0	0	0	2	3	3
Schang C	2	0	0	0	1	3	0
Lapp C	1	0	0	0	0	2	1
Bender P	2	0	0	0	0	1	3
Wyckoff P	1	0	1	0	0	1	0
Totals	30	1	5	3	8	27	14

FIELDING

DP: 5. Barry-Collins-McInnis, Bender-Barry-McInnis, Bender-McInnis, Baker-McInnis, Lapp-Baker

BATTING

2B: Wyckoff (1, off Rudolph); Baker (1, off Rudolph)

SH: Oldring (1, off Rudolph)

Team LOB: 6

PITCHING

Boston Braves	IP	H	R	ER	BB	SO	HR	BFP
Rudolph W (1–0)	9	5	1	0	3	8	0	34
Philadelphia A's								
Bender L (0–1)	5.1	8	6	6	2	3	0	23
Wyckoff	3.2	3	1	1	1	2	0	14
Totals	9	11	7	7	3	5	0	37

Umpires: HP—Bill Dinneen, 1B—Bill Klem, 2B—Lord Byron, 3B—George Hildebrand

Time of Game: 1:58

Attendance: 20,562

Source: http://www.retrosheet.org.

GAME 2: BOSTON BRAVES 1, PHILADELPHIA ATHLETICS 0; SATURDAY, OCTOBER 10, 1914; (D) SHIBE PARK

Table A.2. 1914 World Series Game 2 Statistics

BOS N	0	0	0	0	0	0	0	0	1	1	7	1
PHI A	0	0	0	0	0	0	0	0	0	0	2	1

BATTING Braves	AB	R	H	RBI	BB	SO	PO	A
Mann RF	5	0	2	1	0	1	0	0
Evers 2B	4	0	2	0	1	0	0	3
Cather LF	5	0	0	0	0	1	2	0
Whitted CF	3	0	0	0	1	0	1	0
Schmidt 1B	4	0	1	0	0	0	12	1
Gowdy C	2	0	0	0	2	0	8	1
Maranville SS	2	0	1	0	0	0	2	4
Deal 3B	4	1	1	0	0	0	2	4
James P	4	0	0	0	0	4	0	3
Totals	33	1	7	1	4	6	27	14

BATTING
2B: Deal (1, off Plank)
SH: Maranville (1, off Plank)
HBP: Maranville (1, off Plank)
Team LOB: 11

FIELDING
DP: 1. Maranville-Schmidt
E: Maranville (1)

BASERUNNING
SB: Deal 2 (2, 2nd base off Plank/Schang, 3rd base off Plank/Schang)
CS: Evers (1, 2nd base by Plank/Schang)

BATTING A's	AB	R	H	RBI	BB	SO	PO	A
Murphy RF	3	0	0	0	0	1	0	0

	AB	R	H	BB	SO	PO	A
Oldring LF	3	0	0	0	2	2	0
Collins 2B	3	0	1	1	0	2	2
Baker 3B	3	0	0	0	1	3	3
McInnis 1B	3	0	0	2	1	10	0
Strunk CF	3	0	0	0	0	0	0
Barry SS	2	0	0	0	2	3	5
Schang C	3	0	1	0	1	3	2
Plank P	2	0	0	0	0	2	1
Walsh PH	0	0	0	0	0	1	0
Totals	25	0	2	3	8	27	13

BATTING
2B: Schang (1, off James)
GDP: Murphy (1, off James)
Team LOB: 1

FIELDING
E: Barry (1)
PB: Schang (1)

BASERUNNING
SB: Barry (1, 2nd base off James/Gowdy)

PITCHING

Boston Braves	IP	H	R	ER	BB	SO	HR	BFP
James W (1–0)	9	2	0	0	3	8	0	28

Philadelphia A's	IP	H	R	ER	BB	SO	HR	BFP
Plank L (0–1)	9	7	1	1	4	6	0	39

HBP: Plank (1, Maranville)

Umpires: HP—George Hildebrand, 1B—Lord Byron, 2B—Bill Klem, 3B—Bill Dinneen
Time of Game: 1:56
Attendance: 20,562

Source: http://www.retrosheet.org.

GAME 3: BOSTON BRAVES 5, PHILADELPHIA ATHLETICS 4; MONDAY, OCTOBER 12, 1914; (D) FENWAY PARK

Table A.3. 1914 World Series Game 3 Statistics

PHI A	1	0	0	1	0	0	0	0	2	0	0	4	8	2
BOS N	0	1	0	1	0	0	0	0	2	0	1	5	9	1

BATTING A's	AB	R	H	RBI	BB	SO	PO	A
Murphy RF	5	2	2	0	1	0	2	0
Oldring LF	5	0	0	0	0	1	1	0
Collins 2B	4	0	1	1	1	0	1	4
Baker 3B	5	0	2	2	1	2	4	4
McInnis 1B	5	1	1	0	1	0	18	0
Walsh CF	4	0	1	1	1	0	1	0
Barry SS	5	0	0	0	0	0	0	7
Schang C	4	1	1	0	1	0	6	1
Bush P	5	0	0	0	0	2	0	5
Totals	42	4	8	4	6	5	33	21

FIELDING
E: Schang (1), Bush (1)

BATTING
2B: Murphy 2 (2, off Tyler 2); McInnis (1, off Tyler); Baker (2, off Tyler)
SH: Oldring (2, off Tyler)   SF: Collins (1, off Tyler)
GDP: Baker (1, off Tyler)   IBB: Walsh (1, by Tyler); Baker (1, by James)
Team LOB: 10

BASERUNNING
SB: Collins (1, 2nd base off Tyler/Gowdy)

BATTING Braves	AB	R	H	RBI	BB	SO	PO	A
Moran RF	4	1	0	0	1	0	2	0
Evers 2B	5	0	3	0	0	0	3	5
Connolly LF	4	0	0	1	0	0	1	0
Whitted CF	5	0	0	0	0	1	2	0
Schmidt 1B	5	1	1	0	0	1	17	1
Deal 3B	5	0	1	0	0	0	2	3
Maranville SS	4	1	1	1	1	0	2	3
Gowdy C	4	1	3	2	1	0	6	0

Mann PR	0	1	0	0	0	0	0	0
Tyler P	3	0	0	0	0	1	1	5
Devore PH	1	0	0	0	0	1	0	0
James P	0	0	0	0	0	0	0	2
Gilbert PH	0	0	0	0	1	0	0	0
Totals	40	5	9	4	4	4	36	19

FIELDING
DP: 1. Evers-Maranville-Schmidt
E: Connolly (1)

BASERUNNING
SB: Evers (1, 2nd base off Bush/Schang)
Maranville 2 (2, 2nd base off Bush/Schang 2)
CS: Maranville (1, home by Bush/Schang)

BATTING
2B: Gowdy 2 (3, off Bush 2); Deal (2, off Bush)
HR: Gowdy (1, 10th inning off Bush 0 on 0 out)
SH: Moran (1, off Bush)
SF: Connolly (1, off Bush)
IBB: Connolly (1, off Bush)
IBB: Gilbert (1, by Bush)
Team LOB: 8

PITCHING

Philadelphia A's	IP	H	R	ER	BB	SO	HR	BFP
Bush L (0–1)	11	9	5	4	4	4	1	46

Bush faced 3 batters in the 12th inning
IBB: Bush (1, Gilbert)

Boston Braves	IP	H	R	ER	BB	SO	HR	BFP
Tyler	10	8	4	4	3	4	0	41
James W (2–0)	2	0	0	0	3	1	0	9
Totals	12	8	4	4	6	5	0	50

IBB: Tyler (1, Walsh); James (1, Baker)

Umpires: HP—Bill Klem, 1B—Bill Dinneen, 2B—Lord Byron, 3B—George Hildebrand
Time of Game: 3:06
Attendance: 35,520

Source: http://www.retrosheet.org.

GAME 4: BOSTON BRAVES 3, PHILADELPHIA ATHLETICS 1; TUESDAY, OCTOBER 13, 1914; (D) FENWAY PARK

Table A.4. 1914 World Series Game 4 Statistics

	1	2	3	4	5	6	7	8	9	R	H	E
PHI A	0	0	0	0	0	0	1	0	0	1	7	0
BOS N	0	0	0	0	1	0	0	2	X	3	6	0

BATTING A's	AB	R	H	RBI	BB	SO	PO	A
Murphy RF	4	0	0	0	0	0	0	0
Oldring LF	4	0	1	0	0	1	3	0
Collins 2B	4	0	1	0	0	1	1	4
Baker 3B	4	0	1	0	0	0	1	4
McInnis 1B	4	0	1	0	0	0	15	0
Walsh CF	2	0	1	0	1	1	1	0
Barry SS	3	1	1	0	0	1	0	5
Schang C	3	0	0	0	0	2	3	1
Shawkey P	2	0	1	1	0	1	0	3
Pennock P	1	0	0	0	0	0	0	0
Totals	31	1	7	1	1	7	24	17

FIELDING
PB: Schang (2)

BASERUNNING
CS: Oldring (1, 2nd base by Rudolph/Gowdy)

BATTING
2B: Walsh (1, off Rudolph); Shawkey (1, off Rudolph)
Team LOB: 4

BATTING Braves	AB	R	H	RBI	BB	SO	PO	A
Moran RF	4	1	0	0	1	0	2	0
Evers 2B	5	0	3	0	0	0	3	5

	AB	R	H	RBI	PO	A
Connolly LF	4	0	0	1	1	0
Whitted CF	5	0	0	0	2	0
Schmidt 1B	5	1	1	0	17	1
Deal 3B	5	0	1	0	2	3
Maranville SS	4	1	1	1	2	3
Gowdy C	4	1	3	2	6	0
Mann PR	0	1	0	0	0	0
Tyler P	3	0	0	0	1	5
Devore PH	1	0	0	0	0	0
James P	0	0	0	0	0	2
Gilbert PH	0	0	0	0	0	0
Totals	40	5	9	4	36	19

FIELDING
DP: 1. Gowdy-Evers

BATTING
2B: Moran (1, off Shawkey)
Team LOB: 5

PITCHING

Philadelphia A's	IP	H	R	ER	BB	SO	HR	BFP
Shawkey L (0–1)	5	4	3	2	2	0	0	20
Pennock	3	2	0	0	2	3	0	12
Totals	8	6	3	2	4	3	0	32

Boston Braves

	IP	H	R	ER	BB	SO	HR	BFP
Rudolph W (2–0)	9	7	1	1	1	7	0	32

WP: Rudolph (1)

Umpires: HP—Lord Byron, 1B—George Hildebrand, 2B—Bill Klem, 3B—Bill Dinneen
Time of Game: 1:49
Attendance: 34,365

Source: http://www.retrosheet.org.

Notes

INTRODUCTION

1. Thomas H. O'Connor, *The Hub: Boston Past and Present* (Boston: Northeastern University Press, 2000), 158–203.

2. O'Connor, *The Hub*, 185–86. James J. Connolly dismisses the boss-against-reformer stereotype of Progressive urban politics. See James J. Connolly, *The Triumph of Ethnic Progressivism: Urban Political Culture in Boston, 1900–1925* (Cambridge, MA: Harvard University Press, 1998).

3. Steven A. Riess, *Touching Base: Professional Baseball and American Culture in the Progressive Era* (Urbana: University of Illinois Press, 1999), 11–20.

4. Steven A. Riess, *Sport in Industrial America: 1850–1920* (Wheeling, IL: Harlan Davidson, 1995), 165.

5. "President Woodrow Wilson Baseball Game Attendance Log," *Baseball-Almanac.com*, accessed January 3, 2014, http://www.baseball-almanac.com/prz_cww .shtml.

CHAPTER 1

1. *New York Times*, May 10, 1914.

2. Charles C. Alexander, *John McGraw* (New York: Penguin Books, 1988), 5–6.

3. Harold Kaese, *The Boston Braves* (New York: G. P. Putnam's Sons, 1948), 152–53. Kaese includes a quote from Johnny Evers stating that the Braves lost an exhibition game to a "soap-company" team, but records indicate that the Braves played an International League team.

4. Bob Klapisch and Peter Van Wieren, *The World Champion Braves: 125 Years of America's Team* (Atlanta, GA: Turner Publishing, 1996), 34–35; Edwin Pope, *Baseball's Greatest Managers: Twenty of the All-Time Greats, Past and Present* (New York:

Doubleday, 1960), 241; Martin Kohout, "George Tweedy Stallings," in *Deadball Stars of the National League*, ed. Tom Simon (Washington, DC: Brassey's, 2004), 323–24.

5. George Will, *Men at Work: The Craft of Baseball* (New York: HarperCollins, 1990), 26.

6. Nancy Joan Weiss, *Charles Francis Murphy, 1858–1924: Respectability and Responsibility in American Politics* (Northampton, MA: Smith College, 1968); see also David C. Hammack, *Power and Society: Greater New York at the Turn of the Century* (New York: Russell Sage Foundation, 1982), 170–71.

7. Kaese, *The Boston Braves*, 129.

8. *New York Times*, August 18, 1932, in *Deadball Stars of the National League*, ed. Tom Simon (Washington, DC: Brassey's, 2004), 305–6. Donald Dewey and Nicholas Acocella, *Total Ball Clubs* (Toronto: Sports Classics Books, 2005), 57; Kaese, *The Boston Braves*, 128–29.

9. Pope, *Baseball's Greatest Managers*, 250–51.

10. Pope, *Baseball's Greatest Managers*, 251.

11. Kaese, *The Boston Braves*, 138.

12. Kohout, "George Tweedy Stallings," 323.

13. Cait Murphy, *Crazy '08: How a Cast of Cranks, Rogues, Boneheads, and Magnates Created the Greatest Year in Baseball History* (New York: Smithsonian Books/HarperCollins, 2007), 274–75.

14. Pope, *Baseball's Greatest Managers*, 248.

15. Pope, *Baseball's Greatest Managers*, 248.

16. Pope, *Baseball's Greatest Managers*, 249; Kohout, "George Tweedy Stallings," 324.

17. Pope, *Baseball's Greatest Managers*, 248.

18. Kaese, *The Boston Braves*, 137; Klapisch and Van Wieren, *The World Champion Braves*, 35.

19. George Gmelch, "Superstition and Ritual in American Baseball," *Elysian Fields Quarterly* 11, no. 3 (1992): 25–36.

20. In 1914, National League teams averaged 3.8 runs per game, as opposed to 4.45 runs per contest in 2005. See Bill James, *The New Bill James Historical Baseball Abstract* (New York: Free Press, 2001), 94–95, and David Jones, ed., Introduction, in *Deadball Stars of the American League* (Dulles, VA: Potomac Books, 2006), cclxxvii.

21. Pope, *Baseball's Greatest Managers*, 249.

22. Kohout, "George Tweedy Stallings," 324.

23. Michael Lewis, *Moneyball: The Art of Winning an Unfair Game* (New York: W. W. Norton and Company, 2003), 127–28. Podesta constructed a "model for predicting run production that was more accurate than any he knew of. In this model an extra point of on-base percentage was worth three times an extra point of slugging percentage."

24. Charles C. Alexander, *Our Game: An American Baseball History* (New York: Henry Holt and Company, 1991), 101, 216; Bill James, *The New Bill James Historical Baseball Abstract* (New York: Free Press, 2001), 117.

25. Jonah Keri, ed. *Baseball between the Numbers: Why Everything You Know about the Game Is Wrong* (New York: Basic Books, 2006), 348–51.

26. Will, *Men at Work*, 37.

27. Pope, *Baseball's Greatest Managers*, 249.

28. Eric Rolfe Greenberg, *The Celebrant* (Lincoln: University of Nebraska Press, 1983), 144.

29. Martin Kohout, "Hal Chase," in *Deadball Stars of the American League*, ed. David Jones (Dulles, VA: Potomac Books, 2006), 712–14.

30. Geoffrey C. Ward and Ken Burns, *Baseball: An Illustrated History* (New York: Alfred A. Knopf, 1994), 133; Alexander, *Our Game*, 118. Alexander notes that players would ask the same question.

31. Alexander, *Our Game*, 118.

32. Pope, *Baseball's Greatest Managers*, 250.

33. Ward and Burns, *Baseball*, 8; Alexander, *Our Game*, 89.

34. "Seven Ways to Compute the Relative Value of a U.S. Dollar Amount, 1774 to Present," *MeasuringWorth.com*, http://www.measuringworth.com/uscompare/ (accessed November 29, 2013).

35. Alexander, *Our Game*, 116–17.

36. Pope, *Baseball's Greatest Managers*, 260.

37. Quoted in Alexander, *Our Game*, 116.

38. Kaese, *The Boston Braves*, 139–40.

39. John J. Evers and Hugh S. Fullerton, *Touching Second* (Jefferson, NC: McFarland, 2005; originally published in 1910 by Reilly and Britton), 229.

40. Lewis, *Moneyball*, 170–73.

41. "Innings Pitched," *Baseball-Almanac.com*, http://www.baseball-almanac.com/pitching/piinnp4.shtml (accessed April 12, 2009); Bill James, "E = M CY Squared," in Bill James and Rob Neyer, *The Neyer/James Guide to Pitchers: An Historical Compendium of Pitching, Pitchers, and Pitches* (New York: Simon & Schuster, 2004), 470.

42. Evers and Fullerton, *Touching Second*, 227–28.

43. Evers and Fullerton, *Touching Second*, 228.

44. Michael McGerr, *A Fierce Discontent: The Rise and Fall of the Progressive Movement in America, 1870–1920* (New York: Free Press, 2003), 242–43.

45. Murphy, *Crazy '08*, 145, 296.

46. Evers and Fullerton, *Touching Second*, 241; Gil Bogen, *Tinker, Evers, and Chance: A Triple Biography* (Jefferson, NC: McFarland, 2003), 72. According to Murphy, Tinker hit .400 against Mathewson in 1906, .364 in 1907, and .421 in 1908. Murphy, *Crazy '08*, 121.

47. Evers and Fullerton, *Touching Second*, 240.

48. Evers and Fullerton, *Touching Second*, 225–27. In *Men at Work*, Will describes a turning point of the 1988 World Series, when Jose Conseco's third-inning grand slam caused the A's to lose their competitive edge (it was not really Kirk Gibson's game-ending homer that altered the series). Will, *Men at Work*, 48.

49. Pope, *Baseball's Greatest Managers*, 248–49.

50. Harold Kaese, *The Boston Braves*, 152; Kaese, 138, relates the story that Stallings as a minor league coach in Buffalo lashed out at a pitcher who, having walked the bases loaded, walked in two runs, "Go on to the clubhouse and burn your uniform!" When a player alerted him to the smoke rising from the clubhouse chimney, Stallings responded angrily but was surprised at the depth of the pitcher's reaction.

51. Gil Bogen, *Tinker, Evers, and Chance*, 105–6.

52. Alexander, *John McGraw*, 127, 119–20.

53. Alexander, *John McGraw*, 4.

54. Frank Deford, *The Old Ball Game: How John McGraw, Christy Mathewson, and the New York Giants Created Modern Baseball* (New York: Grove Press, 2005), 108–9.

55. *New York Times*, October 14, 1914.

56. *New York Times*, October 14, 1914.

57. *New York Times*, October 12, 1914.

58. Kaese, *The Boston Braves*, 153. See Alexander, *John McGraw*, 145.

59. Klapisch and Van Wieren, *The World Champion Braves*, 36.

60. Murphy, *Crazy '08*, 14.

61. Robert Wiebe, *The Search for Order: 1877–1920* (New York: Hill & Wang, 1967); McGerr, *A Fierce Discontent*, xiii–xvi.

62. Nell Irvin Painter, *Standing at Armageddon: The United States, 1877–1919* (New York: W. W. Norton and Company, 1989), 177.

63. Frederick Winslow Taylor, *The Principles of Scientific Management,* Chapter II, 1911, *Ibiblio.org*, http://www.ibiblio.org/eldritch/fwt/t2.html (accessed August 10, 2013).

64. Ward and Burns, *Baseball*, 127.

65. Deford, *The Old Ball Game*, 173; Murphy, *Crazy '08*, 15–16.

66. Evers and Fullerton, *Touching Second*, 189.

67. Evers and Fullerton, *Touching Second*, 190.

68. Evers and Fullerton, *Touching Second*, 190–91.

69. Evers and Fullerton, *Touching Second*, 189–99.

70. Evers and Fullerton, *Touching Second*, 192, 197.

71. Evers and Fullerton, *Touching Second*, 198.

72. Evers and Fullerton, *Touching Second*, 199–201.

73. Evers and Fullerton, *Touching Second*, 202, 206.

74. *Boston Globe*, March 8, 1914.

75. Pope, *Baseball's Greatest Managers*, 251.

76. *Boston Globe*, March 8, 1914.

77. Kaese, *The Boston Braves*, 152.

78. David Jones, "Bill James," in *Deadball Stars of the National League*, ed. Tom Simon (Washington, DC: Brassey's, 2004), 325–26.

79. Dick Leyden, "Dick Rudolph," in *Deadball Stars of the National League*, ed. Tom Simon (Washington, DC: Brassey's, 2004), 327–28; Bob Klapisch and Pete Van Wieren, *The Braves: An Illustrated History of America's Team* (Atlanta, GA: Turner Publishing, 1995), 36; Al Hirshberg, *The Braves: The Pick and the Shovel* (Boston: Waverly House, 1948), 14.

80. "Lefty Tyler," *Baseball-Reference.com*, http://www.baseball-reference.com/players/t/tylerle01.shtml (accessed March 13, 2009).

81. "Hub Perdue," *Baseball-Reference.com*, http://www.baseball-reference.com/players/p/perduhu01.shtml (accessed May 27, 2013).

82. "Gene Cocreham," *Baseball-Reference.com*, http://www.baseball-reference.com/players/c/cocrege01.shtml (accessed May 25, 2009); "Dick Crutcher," *Baseball-Reference.com*, http://www.baseball-reference.com/players/c/crutcdi01.shtml (accessed May 25, 2009); "Ensign Cottrell," *Baseball-Reference.com*, http://www.baseball-reference.com/players/c/cottren01.shtml (accessed May 25, 2009); "Paul Strand," *Baseball-Reference.com*, http://www.baseball-reference.com/players/s/stranpa01.shtml (accessed May 25, 2009); Kaese, *The Boston Braves*, 151.

83. "Otto Hess Stats," *Baseball-Almanac.com*, http://www.baseball-almanac.com/players/player.php?p=hessot01 (accessed March 13, 2009); Kaese, *The Boston Braves*, 151. Dick Leyden, "Dick Rudolph," in *Deadball Stars of the National League*, ed. Tom Simon (Washington, DC: Brassey's, 2004), 327–28.

84. Dennis Auger, "Joe Connolly," in *Deadball Stars of the National League*, ed. Tom Simon (Washington, DC: Brassey's, 2004), 329–30; "Joe Connolly," *Baseball-Reference.com*, http://www.baseball-reference.com/players/c/connojo04.shtml (accessed November 29, 2013).

85. Kaese, *The Boston Braves*, 149; "Les Mann Stats," *Baseball-Almanac.com*, http://www.baseball-almanac.com/players/player.php?p=mannle01 (accessed May 27, 2013).

86. *Boston Globe*, March 23, 1914; "Larry Gilbert," *Baseball-Reference.com*, http://www.baseball-reference.com/players/g/gilbela01.shtml (accessed May 27, 2013).

87. Frank Ceresi and Carol McMains, "Hank Gowdy," in *Deadball Stars of the National League*, ed. Tom Simon (Washington, DC: Brassey's, 2004), 317–19.

88. The term *rookie* defined in "Rookie of the Year Award/Jackie Robinson Award," *Baseball-Almanac.com*, http://www.baseball-almanac.com/awards/aw_roy.shtml (accessed May 27, 2013).

89. "Charlie Deal Stats," *Baseball-Almanac.com*, http://www.baseball-almanac.com/players/player.php?p=dealch01 (accessed May 27, 2013); Kaese, *The Boston Braves*, 147.

90. *Boston Globe*, March 9, 1914; "Butch Schmidt Stats," *Baseball-Almanac.com*, http://www.baseball-almanac.com/players/player.php?p=schmibu01 (accessed May 27, 2013).

91. Kaese, *The Boston Braves*, 146, 147; Hirshberg, *The Braves*, 14.

92. *Boston Globe*, March 9, 1914; Schmidt showed up a day before spring practice in "fine shape."

93. Dick Leyden, "Rabbit Maranville," in *Deadball Stars of the National League*, ed. Tom Simon (Washington, DC: Brassey's, 2004), 320–23; Klapisch and Van Wieren, *The Braves*, 37; Walter "Rabbit" Maranville, *Run, Rabbit, Run: The Hilarious and Mostly True Tales of Rabbit Maranville* (Cleveland, OH: Society for American Baseball Research, 1991), 5–7.

94. Leyden, "Rabbit Maranville," 321–22.

95. Klapisch and Van Wieren, *The World Champion Braves*, 37; David Shiner, "Johnny Evers," in *Deadball Stars of the National League*, ed. Tom Simon (Washington, DC: Brassey's, 2004), 99–102; Kaese, *The Boston Braves*, 146.

96. *Boston Globe*, March 26, 1914.

CHAPTER 2

1. See Baseball Hall of Fame John J. Evers clippings. Evers explains to the press that "Eh-vers" is the best pronunciation, but "EE-vers" is acceptable.

2. Cait Murphy, *Crazy '08: How a Cast of Cranks, Rogues, Boneheads, and Magnates Created the Greatest Year in Baseball History* (New York: Smithsonian Books/HarperCollins, 2007), 186–87.

3. "Christy Mathewson," *Baseball-Reference.com*, http://www.baseball-reference.com/players/m/mathech01.shtml (accessed August 2, 2013).

4. Murphy, *Crazy '08*, 188; Gil Bogen, *Tinker, Evers, and Chance: A Triple Biography* (Jefferson, NC: McFarland, 2003), 88–89.

5. "1908 National League Team Statistics and Standings," *Baseball-Reference.com*, http://www.baseball-reference.com/leagues/NL/1908.shtml (accessed June 16, 2013).

6. Stuart Schimler, "Jack Pfiester," in *Deadball Stars of the National League*, ed. Tom Simon (Washington, DC: Brassey's, 2004), 121.

7. Schimler, "Jack Pfiester," 122.

8. Murphy, *Crazy '08*, 189–90; Schimler, "Jack Pfiester," 122.

9. Murphy, *Crazy '08*, 186; Trey Strecker, "Fred Merkle," in *Deadball Stars of the National League*, ed. Tom Simon (Washington, DC: Brassey's, 2004), 61–62.

10. Ken Burns, *Baseball: An Illustrated History* (New York: Alfred A. Knopf, 1994), 92.

11. Murphy, *Crazy '08*, 189–91.

12. Major League Baseball Rules, Section 4.09, http://mlb.mlb.com/mlb/downloads/y2008/official_rules/04_starting_ending_game.pdf (accessed August 5, 2013).

13. Murphy, *Crazy '08*, 193–94; see also John J. Evers, Baseball Hall of Fame clippings.

14. Murphy, *Crazy '08*, 191.

15. Murphy, *Crazy '08*, 191–95.

16. Deford, 145.

17. Murphy, *Crazy '08*, 198; Frank Deford, *The Old Ball Game: How John McGraw, Christy Mathewson, and the New York Giants Created Modern Baseball* (New York: Grove Press, 2005), 144–47; Michael Foster, "Smoky Joe Wood," David, Jones ed. *Deadball Stars of the American League*, 442.

18. Murphy, *Crazy '08*, 191.

19. Gil Bogen, *Tinker, Evers, and Chance*, 20, 132; "Tom Evers," *Baseball-Reference.com*, http://www.baseball-reference.com/players/e/eversto01.shtml (accessed June 16, 2013).

20. Tim Layden, "Tinker to Evers to Chance . . . to Me," *SI Vault*, December 3, 2012, http://sportsillustrated.cnn.com/vault/article/magazine/MAG1206500/3/index.htm (accessed August 11, 2013); Deford, *The Old Ball Game*, 18.

21. Deford, *The Old Ball Game*, 18.

22. Jules Tygiel, *Past Time: Baseball as History* (New York: Oxford University Press, 2000), 36–37.

23. Bogen, *Tinker, Evers, and Chance*, 21.

24. Bogen, *Tinker, Evers, and Chance*, 23.

25. Layden, "Tinker to Evers to Chance . . . to Me."

26. Bogen, *Tinker, Evers, and Chance*, 20–25. The $100 offered to Evers in 1902 would have been worth $2,611.77 in 2012. See Inflation Calculator, http://www.westegg.com/inflation/infl.cgi (accessed September 20, 2013).

27. Bogen, *Tinker, Evers, and Chance*, 41–42.

28. Bogen, *Tinker, Evers, and Chance*, 45–46.

29. David Shiner, "Johnny Evers," in *Deadball Stars of the National League*, ed. Tom Simon (Washington, DC: Brassey's, 2004), 99.

30. See John Shiffert, "Tossing Bobby Cox and the SABR Baseball List and Record Book," *Baseballlibrary.com*, June 5, 2007, http://www.baseballlibrary.com/columns/column.php?id=25 (accessed August 7, 2013). "Bad Bill" Dahlen played from 1891 to 1911, and he managed the Dodgers from 1910 to 1913. Dahlen was tossed a total of 65 games. Evers's ejections appear to be the second highest in baseball history.

31. Layden, "Tinker to Evers to Chance . . . to Me."

32. John J. Evers and Hugh S. Fullerton, *Touching Second* (Jefferson, NC: McFarland, 2005; originally published in 1910 by Reilly and Britton), editor's note, 3.

33. Shiner, "Johnny Evers," 100.

34. Shiner, "Johnny Evers," 100; Evers and Fullerton, *Touching Second*, editor's note, 3.

35. Evers and Fullerton, *Touching Second*, 150.

36. Bogen, *Tinker, Evers, and Chance*, 109–10.

37. "Something Like a War, 1900–1910," Volume 2 (1994), DVD, *Baseball*, Ken Burns, PBS Broadcasting.

38. Bill James, *The New Bill James Historical Baseball Abstract* (New York: Free Press, 2001), 441.

39. Evers and Fullerton, *Touching Second*, editor's note, 3.

40. Len Jacobson, "Joe Tinker," in *Deadball Stars of the National League*, ed. Tom Simon (Washington, DC: Brassey's, 2004), 97.

41. James, *The New Bill James Historical Baseball Abstract*, 499.

42. Walter Maranville, *Run, Rabbit, Run: The Hilarious and Mostly True Tales of Rabbit Maranville* (Cleveland, OH: Society for American Baseball Research, 1991), 17.

43. George Will, *Men at Work: The Craft of Baseball* (New York: HarperCollins, 1990), 240.

44. Murphy, *Crazy '08*, 145.

45. Bogen, *Tinker, Evers, and Chance*, 112.

46. Jacobson, "Joe Tinker," 97.

47. Bogen, *Tinker, Evers, and Chance*, 53.

48. Ward and Burns, *Baseball*, 80.

49. Shiner, "Johnny Evers," 100.

50. Bogen, *Tinker, Evers, and Chance*, 61.

51. Joe Tinker, *Chicago Daily News* (July 27, 1948) quoted in Bogen, 61.

52. Bogen, *Tinker, Evers, and Chance*, 111.

53. Bogen, *Tinker, Evers, and Chance*, 113–14; "Baseball Off the Field," *Encyclopedia.com*, 2001, http://www.encyclopedia.com/doc/1G2-3468300653.html (accessed August 8, 2013).

54. F. C. Lane, *Baseball Magazine*, September 1913, quoted in Bogen, *Tinker, Evers, and Chance*, 114.

55. Murphy, *Crazy '08*, 197.

56. Len Jacobson, "Charles Murphy," *SABR Baseball Biography Project*, http://bioproj.sabr.org/bioproj.cfm?a=v&v=l&pid=16915&bid=912 (accessed August 8, 2013).

57. Lane, quoted in Bogen, *Tinker, Evers, and Chance*, 114.

58. Lane, quoted in Bogen, *Tinker, Evers, and Chance*, 114.

59. Layden, "Tinker to Evers to Chance . . . to Me."

60. Lane, quoted in Bogen, *Tinker, Evers, and Chance*, 115–16.

61. Lane, quoted in Bogen, *Tinker, Evers, and Chance*, 116.

62. Shiner, "Johnny Evers," 102.

63. Lane, quoted in Bogen, *Tinker, Evers, and Chance*, 116.

64. Bogen, *Tinker, Evers, and Chance*, 123–25.

65. Lane, quoted in Bogen, *Tinker, Evers, and Chance*, 116–17.

66. Michael McGerr, *A Fierce Discontent: The Rise and Fall of the Progressive Movement in America, 1870–1920* (New York: Free Press, 2003), 164–66.

67. Quoted in Douglas Brinkley, *Wheels for the World: Henry Ford, His Company, and a Century of Progress* (New York: Viking, 2003), 155.

68. Brinkley, *Wheels for the World*, 151–56.

69. Evers and Fullerton, *Touching Second*, 7.

70. Evers and Fullerton, *Touching Second*, 8.

71. Evers and Fullerton, *Touching Second*, 24.

72. Evers and Fullerton, *Touching Second*, 24.

73. Evers and Fullerton, *Touching Second*, 24, 28.

74. Evers and Fullerton, *Touching Second*, 24.

75. Evers and Fullerton, *Touching Second*, 28.

76. Evers and Fullerton, *Touching Second*, 212.

77. Evers and Fullerton, *Touching Second*, 212.

78. Evers and Fullerton, *Touching Second*, 32.

79. Lawrence Ritter, *The Glory of Their Times: The Story of the Early Days of Baseball Told by the Men Who Played It* (New York: Perennial, 2002), 93–94.

80. Evers and Fullerton, *Touching Second*, 88.

81. Evers and Fullerton, *Touching Second*, 88.

82. Bill James and Rob Neyer, *The Neyer/James Guide to Pitchers: An Historical Compendium of Pitching, Pitchers, and Pitches* (New York: Simon & Schuster, 2004), 5.

83. Evers and Fullerton, *Touching Second*, 101.

84. Evers and Fullerton, *Touching Second*, 102.

85. Evers and Fullerton, *Touching Second*, 168.

86. Evers and Fullerton, *Touching Second*, 168.

87. Evers and Fullerton, *Touching Second*, 61.

88. Evers and Fullerton, *Touching Second*, 63.

89. Evers and Fullerton, *Touching Second*, 64.

90. Deford, *The Old Ball Game*, 129–30.

91. Evers and Fullerton, *Touching Second*, 19, 67.

92. Quoted in Bogen, *Tinker, Evers, and Chance*, 129.

93. Quoted in Bogen, *Tinker, Evers, and Chance*, 131.

94. Shiner, "Johnny Evers," 102; Bogen, *Tinker, Evers, and Chance*, 134–36.

95. Ward and Burns, *Baseball*, 121–27.

96. Charles C. Alexander, *Our Game: An American Baseball History* (New York: Henry Holt and Company, 1991), 102–3.

97. Shiner, "Johnny Evers," 102; Bogen, *Tinker, Evers, and Chance*, 134–36. The Cubs received second baseman Bill Sweeney.

98. Bogen, *Tinker, Evers, and Chance*, 126; Layden, "Tinker to Evers to Chance . . . to Me."

99. Thomas H. O'Connor, *The Hub: Boston Past and Present* (Boston: Northeastern University Press, 2000), 176–77.

100. "The History Place: The Irish Potato Famine," *HistoryPlace.com*, http://www. historyplace.com/worldhistory/famine/america.htm (accessed June 22, 2010).

101. Noel Ignatiev, *How the Irish Became White* (New York: Routledge, 1995), 170–203.

102. O'Connor, *The Hub*, 163.

103. Doris Kearns Goodwin, *The Fitzgeralds and the Kennedys: An American Saga* (New York: Simon & Schuster, 1987), 65; O'Connor, *The Hub*, 165.

104. O'Connor, *The Hub*, 164–65; Goodwin, *The Fitzgeralds and the Kennedys*, 94–95.

105. O'Connor, *The Hub*, 161, 170.

106. Michael Gershman, *Diamonds: The Evolution of the Ballpark from the Elysian Fields to Camden Yards* (Boston: Houghton Mifflin, 1993), 47, 55, 56, 110; "Sports Temples of Boston: South End Grounds," *Boston Public Library*, http://www.bpl.org/ collections/online/sportstemples/temple.php?temple_id=13 (accessed September 8, 2013); "Braves Field," *Ballparksofbaseball.com*, http://www.ballparksofbaseball.com/ past/BravesField.htm (accessed September 8, 2013).

107. *Boston Globe*, May 2, 1914.

108. *Boston Globe*, April 17, 1914.

109. *Boston Globe*, April 16, 1914.

110. *Boston Globe*, April 18, 1914; *Boston Globe*, April 23, 1914.

111. *Boston Globe*, April 19, 1914.

112. *Boston Globe*, April 20, 1914; Robert W. Creamer, *Babe: The Legend Comes to Life* (New York: Simon & Schuster, 1974), 71–83.

113. *Boston Globe*, April 26, 1914.

114. *Boston Globe*, April 26, 1914.

115. *Boston Globe*, April 23, 1914. David Jones, ed., Introduction, *Deadball Stars of the American League* (Dulles, VA: Potomac Books, 2006), ccclxxvii.

116. *Boston Globe*, May 25, 1914; *Boston Globe*, June 1, 1914; David Jones, ed., Introduction, in *Deadball Stars of the American League* (Dulles, VA: Potomac Books, 2006), cclxxvii.

117. *Boston Globe*, May 2, 1914.

118. *Boston Globe*, May 3, 1914.

119. "Yearly League Leaders and Records for Home Runs," *Baseball-Reference. com*, http://www.baseball-reference.com/leaders/HR_leagues.shtml (accessed September 8, 2013).

120. *Boston Globe*, May 10, 1914.

121. *Boston Globe*, April 27, 1914.

122. *Boston Globe*, May 8, 1914.

123. *Boston Globe*, May 8, 1914.

124. *Boston Globe*, May 9, 1914.

125. *Boston Globe*, May 25, 1914.

126. *New York Times*, May 8, 1914.

127. *Boston Globe*, June 2, 1914.

128. *New York Times*, June 2, 1914.

129. *New York Times*, June 3, 1914.

130. *Boston Globe*, May 27, 1914.

131. *Boston Globe*, June 20, 1914.

132. *Boston Globe*, May 20, 1914.

133. *Boston Globe*, May 21, 1914. The *Globe* describes his pitching as "peculiar and deliberate."

134. Peter C. Bjarkman, "Dolf Luque," *SABR Baseball Biography Project*, http://bio proj.sabr.org/bioproj.cfm?a=v&v=l&bid=2734&pid=8525 (accessed August 8, 2013).

135. *Boston Globe*, May 27, 1914.

136. *Boston Globe*, May 30, 1914.

137. Nate Silver, "Lies, Damned Lies: The Greatest Pennant Race Comebacks," *Baseball Prospectus*, October 4, 2007, http://www.baseballprospectus.com/article. php?articleid=6793 (accessed September 28, 2013).

138. "The 1914 Boston Braves Schedule," *Baseball-Almanac.com*, http://www.base ball-almanac.com/teamstats/schedule.php?y=1914&t=BSN (accessed August 13, 2013).

139. *New York Times*, July 5, 1914.

CHAPTER 3

1. Walter "Rabbit" Maranville, *Run, Rabbit, Run: The Hilarious and Mostly True Tales of Rabbit Maranville* (Cleveland, OH: Society for American Baseball Research, 1991), 17.

2. Bob Klapisch and Peter Van Wieren, *The World Champion Braves: 125 Years of America's Team* (Atlanta, GA: Turner Publishing, 1996), 37; New York Times, July 19, 1914.

3. *Boston Globe*, July 2, 1914.

4. Cait Murphy, Crazy '08: *How a Cast of Cranks, Rogues, Boneheads, and Magnates Created the Greatest Year in Baseball History* (New York: Smithsonian Books/Harper-Collins, 2007), 90.

5. *Boston Globe*, July 2, 1914.

6. Klapisch and Van Wieren, *The World Champion Braves*, 37.

7. Harold Kaese, *The Boston Braves* (New York: G. P. Putnam's Sons, 1948), 152–53.

8. Kaese, *The Boston Braves*, 153.

9. Kaese, *The Boston Braves*, 152–53.

10. "1914 Boston Braves Schedule," *Baseball-Almanac.com*, http://www.baseball-almanac.com/teamstats/schedule.php?y=1914&t=BSN (accessed August 17, 2013).

11. *Boston Globe*, July 5, 1914.

12. *New York Times*, July 5, 1914.

13. *Boston Globe*, July 7, 1914.

14. *New York Times*, July 8, 1914.

15. "Paul Strand Stats," *Baseball-Almanac.com*, http://www.baseball-almanac.com/players/player.php?p=stranpa01 (accessed August 17, 2013); *New York Times*, July 8, 1914.

16. Joseph M. Overfield, "How Losing an Exhibition Sparked Miracle Braves," *Baseball Digest* 20, no. 4 (May 1961): 83–85.

17. Klapisch and Van Wieren, *The World Champion Braves*, 37.

18. "Smoky Joe Wood," *Baseball-Reference.com*, http://www.baseball-reference.com/players/w/woodjo02.shtml (accessed August 17, 2013); "Red Sox History," *MLB.com*, http://boston.redsox.mlb.com/bos/history/ (accessed August 17, 2013).

19. David Southwick, "Cy Young," *SABR Baseball Biography Project*, http://sabr.org/bioproj/person/dae2fb8a (accessed August 17, 2013).

20. Don Jensen, "Tris Speaker," in *Opening Fenway Park in Style: The 1912 Boston Red Sox*, ed. Bill Nowlin (Phoenix, AZ: Society for American Baseball Research, 2012), 1026–32.

21. Quoted in Jensen, "Tris Speaker," 1023.

22. Jensen, "Tris Speaker," 1033.

23. Michael Foster, "Smoky Joe Wood," David, Jones ed. *Deadball Stars of the American League*, 442.

24. Michael Foster, "Smoky Joe Wood," David, Jones ed. *Deadball Stars of the American League*, 441.

25. Michael Foster, "Smoky Joe Wood," in *Deadball Stars of the American League*, ed. David Jones (Dulles, VA: Potomac Books, 2006), 441–42; Glenn Stout, *Fenway, 1912: The Birth of a Ballpark, a Championship Season, and Fenway's Remarkable First Year* (Boston: Houghton Mifflin, 2011), 210–12. In 1912, Wood, like many major-league pitchers, experienced a meteoric rise, and, soon thereafter, a burnout.

26. Saul Wisnia, "Getting to Fenway: How Baseball's Most Storied Ballpark Came to Be," in *Opening Fenway Park in Style: The 1912 Boston Red Sox*, ed. Bill Nowlin (Phoenix, AZ: Society for American Baseball Research, 2012), 31–38.

27. Roger Angell, *Once More around the Park: A Baseball Reader* (Chicago: Ivan R. Dee, 1988), 73.

28. Wisnia, "Getting to Fenway," 24–60; Stout, *Fenway, 1912*, xii, 111, 74–77.

29. Bill Nowlin, ed., Introduction, in *Opening Fenway Park in Style: The 1912 Boston Red Sox* (Phoenix, AZ: Society for American Baseball Research, 2012), 18.

30. Allan Wood, "George Herman 'Babe' Ruth" David, Jones ed. *Deadball Stars of the American League*, 457.

31. Robert W. Creamer, *Babe: The Legend Comes to Life* (New York: Simon & Schuster, 1974), 41–83; Allan Wood, "George Herman 'Babe' Ruth," in *Deadball Stars of the American League*, ed. David Jones (Dulles, VA: Potomac Books, 2006), 457–60.

32. *Boston Globe*, July 12, 1914.

33. *Boston Globe*, July 18, 1914.

34. Creamer, *Babe*, 91–92.

35. "Hub Perdue," B*aseball-Reference.com*, http://www.baseball-reference.com/players/p/perduhu01.shtml (accessed August 17, 2013); *New York Times*, June 30, 1914.

36. "George 'Possum' Whitted," *Findagrave.com*, http://www.findagrave.com/cgi-bin/fg.cgi?page=gr&GRid=6139602 (accessed August 17, 2013).

37. "Ted Cather Stats," *Baseball-Almanac.com*, http://www.baseball-almanac.com/players/player.php?p=cathete01 (accessed September 7, 2013); "1914 National League Team Statistics and Standings," *Baseball-Reference.com*, http://www.baseball-reference.com/leagues/NL/1914.shtml (accessed September 7, 2013).

38. "Josh Devore Stats," *Baseball-Almanac.com*, http://www.baseball-almanac.com/players/player.php?p=devorjo01 (accessed August 19, 2013); "Josh Devore," *Baseball-Reference.com*, http://www.baseball-reference.com/players/d/devorjo01.shtml (accessed August 19, 2013).

39. "Larry Gilbert," *Baseball-Reference.com*, http://www.baseball-reference.com/players/g/gilbela01.shtml (accessed August 19, 2013); "Joe Connolly," *Baseball-Reference.com*, http://www.baseball-reference.com/players/c/connjo04.shtml (accessed August 19, 2013); Dennis Auger, "Joey Connolly," in *Deadball Stars of the National League*, ed. Tom Simon (Washington DC: Brassey's, 2004), 329–30; *Boston Globe*, July 4, 1914.

40. Kaese, *The Boston Braves*, 154.

41. "1914 Boston Braves Schedule," *Baseball-Almanac.com*, http://www.baseball-almanac.com/teamstats/schedule.php?y=1914&t=BSN (accessed August 19, 2013).

42. Lawrence Ritter, *The Glory of Their Times: The Story of the Early Days of Baseball Told by the Men Who Played It* (New York: Perennial, 2002), 56.

43. David Jones, ed., Introduction, in *Deadball Stars of the American League* (Dulles, VA: Potomac Books, 2006), ccclxxviiii.

44. H. H. Westlake, quoted in Bill James and Rob Neyer, *The Neyer/James Guide to Pitchers: An Historical Compendium of Pitching, Pitchers, and Pitches* (New York: Simon & Schuster, 2004), 56.

45. James and Neyer, *The Neyer/James Guide to Pitchers*, 57.

46. Murphy, *Crazy '08*, 209.

47. Ritter, *The Glory of Their Times*, 123.

48. Dick Leyden, "Dick Rudolph," in *Deadball Stars of the National League*, ed. Tom Simon (Washington DC: Brassey's, 2004), 327.

49. Quoted in Leyden, "Dick Rudolph," 327.

50. Quoted in James and Neyer, *The Neyer/James Guide to Pitchers*, 366.

51. Leyden, "Dick Rudolph," 328.

52. Quoted in James and Neyer, *The Neyer/James Guide to Pitchers*, 366.

53. Leyden, "Dick Rudolph," 328.

54. Wayne McElreavy, "George 'Lefty' Tyler," in *Deadball Stars of the National League*, ed. Tom Simon (Washington DC: Brassey's, 2004), 315–16.

55. Quoted in David Jones, "George 'Bill' James," in *Deadball Stars of the National League*, ed. Tom Simon (Washington DC: Brassey's, 2004), 325.

56. Donald Honig, *The Greatest Shortstops of All Time* (Dubuque, IA: Brown & Benchmark, 1992), 14.

57. Maranville, *Run, Rabbit, Run*, 13.

58. Dick Leyden, "Rabbit Maranville," in Tom Simon, ed. *Deadball Stars of the National League*, 320.

59. Dick Leyden, "Rabbit Maranville," in *Deadball Stars of the National League*, ed. Tom Simon (Washington DC: Brassey's, 2004), 320; Maranville, *Run, Rabbit, Run*, 14; Honig, *The Greatest Shortstops of All Time*, 15–18.

60. Maranville, *Run, Rabbit, Run*, 13.

61. Leyden, "Rabbit Maranville," 320.

62. Maranville, *Run, Rabbit, Run*, 5.

63. Honig, *The Greatest Shortstops of All Time*, 13–14.

64. Dan Holmes, "Germany Schaefer," in *Deadball Stars of the American League*, ed. David Jones (Dulles, VA: Potomac Books, 2006), 551–52.

65. Maranville, *Run, Rabbit, Run*, 25–27.

66. Honig, *The Greatest Shortstops of All Time*, 14.

67. Honig, *The Greatest Shortstops of All Time*, 14; Maranville, *Run, Rabbit, Run*, 16–17.

68. Chris Jaffe, "Baseball's Most Exciting Play," *Hardball Times*, June 1, 2009, http://www.hardballtimes.com/main/article/baseballs-most-exciting-play/ (accessed August 21, 2013).

69. Honig, *The Greatest Shortstops of All Time*, 15–18; Leyden, "Rabbit Maranville," 320–22.

70. "Top Shortstops," *BaseballPage.com*, http://www.thebaseballpage.com/content/top-shortstops (accessed July 15, 2012).

71. Bill James, *The New Bill James Historical Baseball Abstract* (New York: Free Press, 2001).

72. Quoted in Maranville, *Run, Rabbit, Run*, 77.

73. Leyden, "Rabbit Maranville," 320.

74. Steven A. Riess, *Touching Base: Professional Baseball and American Culture in the Progressive Era* (Urbana: University of Illinois Press, 1999), 185.

75. Quoted in Leyden, "Rabbit Maranville," 320.

76. Maranville, *Run, Rabbit, Run*, 18; Klapisch and Van Wieren, *The World Champion Braves*, 37–38.

77. Maranville, *Run, Rabbit, Run*, 18–19.

78. *Boston Globe*, July 13, 1914; "Standings and Games on Monday, July 13, 1914," Baseball-Reference.com, http://www.baseball-reference.com/games/standings.cgi?year=1914&month=7&day=13&submit=Submit+Date (accessed August 25, 2013).

79. *Boston Globe*, July 21, 1914.

80. *Boston Globe*, July 21, 1914.

81. *Boston Globe*, July 19, 1914.

82. Maranville, *Run, Rabbit, Run*, 18.

83. Murphy, *Crazy '08*, 125–28.

84. *Boston Globe*, July 14, 1914.

85. *Boston Globe*, July 12, 1914.

86. *Boston Globe*, July 24, 1914.

87. "1914 Boston Braves Schedule," *Baseball-Almanac.com*, http://www.baseball-almanac.com/teamstats/schedule.php?y=1914&t=BSN (accessed August 24, 2013).

88. Maranville, *Run, Rabbit, Run*, 20–23.

89. Maranville, *Run, Rabbit, Run*, 21.

90. Maranville, *Run, Rabbit, Run*, 20–23.

91. Paul Michel Taillon, "What We Want Is Good, Sober Men: Masculinity, Respectability, and Temperance in the Railroad Brotherhoods, c. 1870–1910," *Journal of Social History* 36, no. 2 (Winter 2002), 319–38, http://www.jstor.org/stable/3790113.

92. Maranville, *Run, Rabbit, Run*, 21.

93. Maranville, *Run, Rabbit, Run*, 21.

94. Maranville, *Run, Rabbit, Run*, 22.

95. Maranville, *Run, Rabbit, Run*, 22.

96. Maranville, *Run, Rabbit, Run*, 22.

97. Maranville, *Run, Rabbit, Run*, 20–23. "Boston Braves 5, Pittsburgh, 4," *Retrosheet.org*, August 6, 1914, http://www.retrosheet.org/boxesetc/1914/B08060BSN1914.htm (accessed August 24, 2013).

98. Brian Stevens, "Charles 'Babe' Adams," in *Deadball Stars of the National League*, ed. Tom Simon (Washington DC: Brassey's, 2004), 171–72.

99. "Career Leaders and Records for Hit by Pitch," *Baseball-Reference.com*, http://www.baseball-reference.com/leaders/HBP_career.shtml (accessed August 24, 2013). This website lists all three men in the top 250 of all time; Fletcher and Herzog are in the top 50.

100. Maranville, *Run, Rabbit, Run*, 23–24. The box score for that game, played on August 22, does not quite square with Maranville's account. See *Retrosheet.org*, August 6, 1914, http://www.retrosheet.org/boxesetc/1914/B08222PIT1914.htm (accessed August 24, 2013).

101. "Johnny Evers," *BaseballPage.com*, http://www.thebaseballpage.com/players/eversjo01/bio (accessed August 24, 2013).

102. William A. Phelon, "Review of the Month in Baseball," *Baseball Magazine* 12, no. 4 (February 1914): 19. Available online at LA84 Foundation, Digital Library Collection, http://library.la84.org/SportsLibrary/BBM/1914/bbm4e.pdf (accessed August 24, 2013).

103. Hew Strachan, *The First World War* (London: Penguin Books, 2003) 8–18; *The First World War*, produced by Jonathan Lewis (Chatsworth, CA: Channel 4, 2004), DVD; John Keegan, *The First World War* (New York: Vintage Books, 2000), 48–72.

104. "Topics in Chronicling America: World War I Declarations," *Library of Congress Newspaper and Current Periodical Reading Room*, http://www.loc.gov/rr/news/topics/ww1declarations.html (accessed August 25, 2013).

CHAPTER 4

1. Jeffrey Verhey, *The Spirit of 1914: Militarism, Myth, and Mobilization in Germany* (New York: Cambridge University Press, 2000), 1–11, 52–55. Although the flag-waving crowds were not representative of European societies as a whole, the idea of the "August Madness" persisted throughout the war years and beyond. *War Land on the Eastern Front: Culture, National Identity, and German Occupation in World War I*, by Vejas Gabriel Liulevicius (New York: Cambridge University Press, 2000), 1–53, shows how the Eastern Front contrasts with the more well-known Western Front.

2. John Keegan, *The First World War* (New York: Vintage Books, 2000), 71–73; "Great War Resources," *PBS.org*, http://www.pbs.org/greatwar/resources/casdeath_pop.html (accessed July 15, 2012); "Source List and Detailed Death Tolls for the Primary Megadeaths of the Twentieth Century: World War I," *Historical Atlas of the Twentieth Century*, http://necrometrics.com/20c5m.htm (accessed July 24, 2012).

3. Hew Strachan, *The First World War* (London: Penguin Books, 2003), xvii.

4. *The First World War*, produced by Jonathan Lewis (Chatsworth, CA: Channel 4, 2004), DVD; Strachan, *The First World War*, 52; J. Rickard, "Battle of the Frontiers of France, 20–24 August 1914," *History of War*, August 15, 2007, http://www.historyofwar.org/articles/battles_frontiers_of_france.html (accessed November 29, 2013).

5. Strachan, *The First World War*, 48–51; *The First World War*, DVD; Keegan, *The First World War*, 80–85.

6. David Stevenson, *1914–1918: The History of the First World War* (London: Allen Lane, 2004), 92–93; *The First World War*, DVD; *New York Times*, August 29, 1914; *New York Times*, August 31, 1914.

7. Keegan, *The First World War*, 140–50. Hastings, Max. *Catastrophe 1914: Europe Goes to War* (New York: Alfred A. Knopf, 2013), 531.

8. *Boston Globe*, August 11, 1914.

9. *Boston Globe*, August 15, 1914.

10. "1914 National League Team Statistics and Standings," *Baseball-Reference.com*, http://www.baseball-reference.com/leagues/NL/1914.shtml (accessed July 24, 2013); *Boston Globe*, August 14, 1914.

11. *Boston Globe*, August 13, 1914.

12. Roger Angell, *Once More around the Park: A Baseball Reader* (Chicago: Ivan R. Dee, 1988), 15–16.

13. "The 1914 Season," *Retrosheet.org*, http://www.retrosheet.org/boxesetc/1914/Y_1914.htm (accessed September 14, 2013); *Boston Globe*, August 5, 1914; *Boston Globe*, August 6, 1914.

14. Major League Baseball, "MLB Season History, 1914," *ESPN.com*, http://espn.go.com/mlb/history/season/_/year/1914 (accessed July 23, 2013).

15. *Boston Globe*, August 2, 1914; Harold Kaese and Braves historians have noted a later date for the first Fenway game. See Harold Kaese, *The Boston Braves* (New York: G. P. Putnam's Sons, 1948), 156.

16. *Boston Globe*, August 2, 1914.

17. *Boston Globe*, August 2, 1914; *Boston Globe*, August 3, 1914; *Boston Globe*, August 4, 1914.

18. "3,000 Hits Club," *Baseball-Almanac.com*, http://www.baseball-almanac.com/hitting/hi3000c.shtml (accessed September 14, 2013).

19. *Boston Globe*, August 4, 1914.

20. Gil Bogen, *Tinker, Evers, and Chance: A Triple Biography* (Jefferson, NC: McFarland, 2003), 159; Tim Layden, "Tinker to Evers to Chance . . . to Me," *SI Vault*, December 3, 2012, http://sportsillustrated.cnn.com/vault/article/magazine/MAG1206500/3/index.htm (accessed July 24, 2013).

21. Quoted in Bogen, *Tinker, Evers, and Chance*, 159.

22. *Boston Globe*, August 7, 1914.

23. *Boston Globe*, August 8, 1914.

24. *Boston Globe*, August 11, 1914.

25. Kaese, *The Boston Brave*s, 155; "1914 Boston Braves Schedule," *Baseball-Almanac.com*, http://www.baseball-almanac.com/teamstats/schedule.php?y=1914&t=BSN (accessed July 24, 2013).

26. "Christy Mathewson," *Baseball-Reference.com*, http://www.baseball-reference.com/players/m/mathech01.shtml (accessed July 24, 2013).

27. Quoted in Richard Adler, *Mack, McGraw, and the 1913 Baseball Season* (Jefferson, NC: McFarland, 2008), 39.

28. Frank Deford, *The Old Ball Game: How John McGraw, Christy Mathewson, and the New York Giants Created Modern Baseball* (New York: Grove Press, 2005), 3.

29. Charles C. Alexander, *John McGraw* (New York: Penguin Books, 1988), 10.

30. Charles C. Alexander, *John McGraw*, 10–13; Deford, *The Old Ball Game*, 73–74; Adler, *Mack, McGraw, and the 1913 Baseball Season*, 40.

31. Alexander, *John McGraw*, 16–17.

32. Alexander, *John McGraw*, 18; Adler, *Mack, McGraw, and the 1913 Baseball Season*, 41.

33. Alexander, *John McGraw*, 19; Adler, *Mack, McGraw, and the 1913 Baseball Season*, 41; Deford, *The Old Ball Game*, 7–8.

34. Cait Murphy, *Crazy '08: How a Cast of Cranks, Rogues, Boneheads, and Magnates Created the Greatest Year in Baseball History* (New York: Smithsonian Books/HarperCollins, 2007), 16–29; Adler, *Mack, McGraw, and the 1913 Baseball Season*, 43–45.

35. Murphy, *Crazy '08*, 19; Deford, *The Old Ball Game*, 25–26.

36. Alexander, *John McGraw*, 30.

37. Alexander, *John McGraw*, 41.

38. Adler, *Mack, McGraw, and the 1913 Baseball Season*, 42–44; Deford, *The Old Ball Game*, 135; Robert Weintraub, *The House That Ruth Built: The Untold Story of Babe Ruth's Yankees, John McGraw's Giants, and the Extraordinary Baseball Season of 1923* (Hachette Digital, 2011).

39. Adler, *Mack, McGraw, and the 1913 Baseball Season*, 44; Deford, *The Old Ball Game*, 135; Weintraub, *The House That Ruth Built*.

40. Murphy, *Crazy '08*, 18; Alexander, *John McGraw*, 47, 54.

41. Deford, *The Old Ball Game*, 76.

42. Adler, *Mack, McGraw, and the 1913 Baseball Season*, 50.

43. Adler, *Mack, McGraw, and the 1913 Baseball Season*, 54.

44. Deford, *The Old Ball Game*, 46, 56; Adler, *Mack, McGraw, and the 1913 Baseball Season*, 56.

45. Deford, *The Old Ball Game*, 21.

46. Adler, *Mack, McGraw, and the 1913 Baseball Season*, 168.

47. Alexander, *John McGraw*, 102.

48. "Christy Mathewson Stats," *Baseball-Almanac.com*, http://www.baseball-almanac.com/players/player.php?p=mathech01 (accessed July 27, 2013).

49. Deford, *The Old Ball Game*, 127; Tim Morris, "Guide to Juvenile Baseball Books," *University of Texas at Arlington*, http://www.uta.edu/english/tim/baseball/juv/chadwick.html (accessed July 20, 2013).

50. Quoted in Deford, *The Old Ball Game*, 126.

51. Quoted in Lawrence Ritter, *The Glory of Their Times: The Story of the Early Days of Baseball Told by the Men Who Played It* (New York: Perennial, 2002), 96.

52. Deford, *The Old Ball Game*, 3.

53. Deford, *The Old Ball Game*, 36–37, 131; Michael S. Kimmel and Amy Aronson, *Men and Masculinities: A Social, Cultural, and Historical Encyclopedia, Volume 1* (Santa Barbara, CA: ABC-CLIO), 558.

54. Deford, *The Old Ball Game*, 66, 130.

55. Alexander, *John McGraw*, 102, on vaudeville, 167.

56. Quoted in Alexander, *John McGraw*, 4.

57. "Manager Records," *Baseball-Almanac.com*, http://www.baseball-almanac.com/rb_mgr.shtml (accessed July 28, 2013).

58. Quoted in Deford, *The Old Ball Game*, 109.

59. Deford, *The Old Ball Game*, 32–33.

60. Alexander, *John McGraw*, 44, 47, 51.

61. Quoted in Deford, *The Old Ball Game*, 66.

62. Deford, *The Old Ball Game*, 67.

63. John McGraw, *Scientific Baseball* (New York: Richard K. Fox, 1913), 8, 9–14.

64. Quoted in Ritter, *The Glory of Their Times*, 14.

65. Ritter, *The Glory of Their Times*, 14–15.

66. Ritter, *The Glory of Their Times*, 91.

67. Ritter, *The Glory of Their Times*, 100.

68. "Jeff Tesreau," *Baseball-Reference.com*, http://www.baseball-reference.com/players/t/tesreje01.shtml (accessed October 18, 2013); "Rube Marquard," *Baseball-Reference.com*, http://www.baseball-reference.com/players/m/marquru01.shtml (accessed October 18, 2013); Larry Mansch, "Rube Marquard," in *Deadball Stars of the National League*, ed. Tom Simon (Washington, DC: Brassey's, 2004), 63–64; Ritter, *The Glory of Their Times*, 14.

69. Trey Strecker, "Fred Merkle," in *Deadball Stars of the National League*, ed. Tom Simon (Washington, DC: Brassey's, 2004), 58–60.

70. Gabriel Schechter, "Fred Snodgrass," in *Deadball Stars of the National League*, ed. Tom Simon (Washington, DC: Brassey's, 2004), 61–62.

71. R. J. Lesch, "Chief Meyers," in *Deadball Stars of the National League*, ed. Tom Simon (Washington, DC: Brassey's, 2004), 65–66.

72. R. J. Lesch, "Larry Doyle," in *Deadball Stars of the National League*, ed. Tom Simon (Washington, DC: Brassey's, 2004), 71–72.

73. *Boston Globe*, August 14, 1914.

74. *Boston Globe*, August 15, 1914.

75. *Boston Globe*, August 16, 1914; Bob Klapisch and Pete Van Wieren, *The World Champion Braves: 125 Years of America's Team* (Atlanta, GA: Turner Publishing, 1996), 39.

76. *Boston Globe*, August 16, 1914.

77. *Boston Globe*, August 27, 1914.

78. *Boston Globe*, August 28, 1914.

79. *Boston Globe*, August 30, 1914.

80. Klaplisch and Van Wieren, *The World Champion Braves*, 40.

81. Klapisch and Van Wieren, *The World Champion Braves*, 20–21; John Durant, *Baseball's Miracle Teams* (New York: Hastings House, 1975), 40–41.

82. Klaplisch and Van Wieren, *The World Champion Braves*, 41.

83. Kaese, *The Boston Braves*, 157.

84. *New York Times*, September 8, 1914.

85. Kaese, *The Boston Braves*, 157.

86. *Boston Globe*, September 17, 1914; Retrosheet.com, "September 16, 1914," http://www.retrosheet.org/boxesetc/1914/09161914.htm (accessed April 12, 2014).

87. *Boston Globe*, September 17, 1914. In September, the season turned so favorably for the Braves that seldom used pitcher George Davis pitched a no-hitter on September 9 against the Phillies.

88. *Boston Globe*, September 22, 1914; *Boston Globe*, September 23, 1914.

89. *Boston Globe*, September 22, 1914.

90. *Boston Globe*, September 24, 1914.

91. "1914 National League Fielding Leaders," *Baseball-Reference.com*, http://www.baseball-reference.com/leagues/NL/1914-fielding-leaders.shtml (accessed July 15, 2013).

92. *Boston Globe*, October 7, 1914.

93. *Boston Globe*, October 7, 1914.

94. "Joffre Gives Order to Attack," *History Channel*, http://www.history.com/this-day-in-history/joffre-gives-order-to-attack-at-the-marne (accessed October 18, 2013).

95. Strachan, *The First World War*, 52, 56.

96. Barbara W. Tuchman, *The Guns of August* (New York: Random House, 2005; originally published in 1962 by Tess Press), 513.

97. Strachan, *The First World War*, 51–58; Keegan, *The First World War*, 100–29.

98. Tuchman, *The Guns of August*, 38, 39.

99. Quoted in Tuchman, *The Guns of August*, 508.

CHAPTER 5

1. "1914 American League Team Statistics and Standings," *Baseball-Reference.com*, http://www.baseball-reference.com/leagues/AL/1914.shtml (accessed May 19, 2013);

"1914 National League Team Statistics and Standings," *Baseball-Reference.com*, http://www.baseball-reference.com/leagues/NL/1914.shtml (accessed May 19, 2013).

2. Al Hirshberg, *The Braves: The Pick and the Shovel* (Boston: Waverly House, 1948), 17; Doug Skipper, "Connie Mack" in *Deadball Stars of the American League*, ed. David Jones (Dulles, VA: Potomac Books, 2006), 583.

3. Norman Macht, *Connie Mack and the Early Years of Baseball* (Lincoln: University of Nebraska Press, 2007), 637.

4. Ted Davis, *Connie Mack: A Life in Baseball* (San Jose, CA: Writers' Club Press, 2001), 71; Macht, *Connie Mack and the Early Years of Baseball*, 637, 639.

5. Harold Kaese, *The Boston Braves* (New York: G. P. Putnam's Sons, 1948), 160–61.

6. Macht, *Connie Mack and the Early Years of Baseball*, 636–37; Kaese, *The Boston Braves*, 160–61; Edwin Pope, *Baseball's Greatest Managers: Twenty of the All-Time Greats, Past and Present* (New York: Doubleday, 1960), 260–61.

7. Macht, *Connie Mack and the Early Years of Baseball*, 636.

8. *Boston Globe*, October 8, 1914.

9. Quoted in Charles C. Alexander, *Ty Cobb* (New York: Oxford University Press, 1984), 312.

10. Pope, *Baseball's Greatest Managers*, 260.

11. Connie Mack, *My 66 Years in the Big Leagues: The Great Story of America's National Game* (Philadelphia, PA: John C. Winston Company, 1950), 3.

12. Bill James, *The New Bill James Historical Baseball Abstract* (New York: Free Press, 2001), 35, 49, 241; Charles C. Alexander, *Our Game: An American Baseball History* (New York: Henry Holt and Company, 1991), 229; "Cleveland Municipal Stadium Firsts," *Retrosheet.org*, http://www.retrosheet.org/ballparks/cleveland_stad.htm (accessed May 25, 2013).

13. Robert Smith, *Pioneers of Baseball* (Boston: Little, Brown and Company: 1978) 71; Bob Considine, "Mr. Mack," in *The Baseball Reader*, ed. Charles Einstein (New York: McGraw-Hill, 1982), 46–49.

14. Macht, *Connie Mack and the Early Years of Baseball*, 15, 17.

15. Mack, *My 66 Years in the Big Leagues*, 8–9.

16. Macht, *Connie Mack and the Early Years of Baseball*, 37, 92–94; Jules Tygiel, *Past Time: Baseball as History* (New York: Oxford University Press, 2000), 37; Mack, *My 66 Years in the Big Leagues*, 16.

17. Macht, *Connie Mack and the Early Years of Baseball*, 17; Robert Smith, Pioneers of Baseball (Boston: Little, Brown and Company, 1978), 71; Bob Considine "Mr. Mack" 48.

18. Considine, "Mr. Mack," 49 .

19. Davis, *Connie Mack*, 23.

20. Macht, *Connie Mack and the Early Years of Baseball*, 145.

21. Macht, *Connie Mack and the Early Years of Baseball*, 145.

22. Macht, *Connie Mack and the Early Years of Baseball*, 145; Richard Adler, *Mack, McGraw, and the 1913 Baseball Season* (Jefferson, NC: McFarland, 2008), 8.

23. Pope, *Baseball's Greatest Managers*, 153.

24. Geoffrey C. Ward and Ken Burns, *Baseball: An Illustrated History* (New York: Alfred A. Knopf, 1994), 74; Macht, *Connie Mack and the Early Years of Baseball*, 317–22.

25. Geoffrey C. Ward and Ken Burns, *Baseball: An Illustrated History* (New York: Alfred A. Knopf, 1994), 74; Macht, *Connie Mack and the Early Years of Baseball*, 317–22. Waddell led the American League in strikeouts for six consecutive years.

26. Pope, *Baseball's Greatest Managers*, 153; Macht, *Connie Mack and the Early Years of Baseball*, 121.

27. "The Homestead Strike," *Corporation for Public Broadcasting*, http://www.pbs.org/wgbh/amex/carnegie/peopleevents/pande04.html (accessed May 25, 2013).

28. Mack, *My 66 Years in the Big Leagues*, 146.

29. Ward and Burns, *Baseball*, 51.

30. Mack, *My 66 Years in the Big Leagues*, 141.

31. Frank Deford, *The Old Ball Game: How John McGraw, Christy Mathewson, and the New York Giants Created Modern Baseball* (New York: Grove Press, 2005), 43.

32. Pope, *Baseball's Greatest Managers*, 154.

33. Considine, "Mr. Mack," 49.

34. Considine, "Mr. Mack," 46–57.

35. Pope, *Baseball's Greatest Managers*, 151.

36. Pope, *Baseball's Greatest Managers*, 151.

37. Deford, *Old Ball Game*, 53–54.

38. Considine, "Mr. Mack," 50.

39. Considine, "Mr. Mack," 50–51; Pope, *Baseball's Greatest Managers*, 153; Macht, *Connie Mack and the Early Years of Baseball*, 280–81; Deford, *The Old Ball Game*, 118.

40. Quoted in Pope, *Baseball's Greatest Managers*, 155.

41. Quoted in George Will, *Men at Work: The Craft of Baseball* (New York: HarperCollins, 1990), 279.

42. Quoted in Pope, *Baseball's Greatest Managers*, 156.

43. Quoted in Will, *Men at Work*, 279–80.

44. Adler, *Mack, McGraw, and the 1913 Baseball Season*, 36.

45. *Washington Post*, March 31, 1912.

46. Ward and Burns, *Baseball*, 65–66; Deford, *The Old Ball Game*, 43–44.

47. Harvey Frommer, *Baseball's Greatest Managers* (New York: Franklin Watts, 1985), 185; Macht, *Connie Mack and the Early Years of Baseball*, 197–206; Adler, *Mack, McGraw, and the 1913 Baseball Season*, 10–11.

48. Lawrence Ritter, *The Glory of Their Times: The Story of the Early Days of Baseball Told by the Men Who Played It* (New York: Perennial, 2002), 121.

49. Considine, "Mr. Mack," 52.

50. Considine, "Mr. Mack," 55.

51. Ritter, *The Glory of Their Times*, 199.

52. Quoted in Pope, *Baseball's Greatest Managers*, 157.

53. Quoted in Davis, *Connie Mack*, 23.

54. Smith, *Pioneers of Baseball*, 75–76; Considine, "Mr. Mack," 48; Macht, *Connie Mack and the Early Years of Baseball*, 99.

55. Considine, "Mr. Mack," 48.

56. Pope, *Baseball's Greatest Managers*, 158.

57. Donald Honig, *Baseball's 10 Greatest Teams.* (New York: Macmillan, 1982), 14–28; Pope, *Baseball's Greatest Managers*, 164; "American League Batting Encyclo-

pedia," *Baseball-Reference.com*, http://www.baseball-reference.com/leagues/AL/bat.shtml (accessed May 25, 2013).

58. David Jones, "John Franklin Baker," in *Deadball Stars of the American League*, ed. David Jones (Dulles, VA: Potomac Books, 2006), 622.

59. Jones, "John Franklin Baker," 620–24.

60. Fred Lieb, *Baseball as I Have Known It* (New York: Coward, McCann & Geoghegan, 1977), 80.

61. David Jones, "John Franklin Baker," 620–24; Fred Lieb, *Baseball as I Have Known It* (New York: Coward, McCann & Geoghegan, 1977), 77–80, 85.

62. Paul F. Mittermayer, "Edward Trowbridge Collins," in *Deadball Stars of the American League*, ed. David Jones (Dulles, VA: Potomac Books, 2006), 610–14; Rob Neyer and Eddie Epstein, *Baseball Dynasties: The Greatest Teams of All Time* (New York: W. W. Norton & Company, 2000), 45–47.

63. Quoted in Norman Macht, "John Joseph Barry," in *Deadball Stars of the American League*, ed. David Jones (Dulles, VA: Potomac Books, 2006).

64. Quoted in Macht, "John Joseph Barry."

65. Macht, "John Joseph Barry," 625–26.

66. Quoted in Macht, "John Joseph Barry."

67. Aaron M. Davis and C. Paul Rogers, "John Phalen 'Stuffy' McInnis," in *Deadball Stars of the American League*, ed. David Jones (Dulles, VA: Potomac Books, 2006), 630; Honig, *Baseball's 10 Greatest Teams*, 17.

68. Davis and Rogers, "John Phalen 'Stuffy' McInnis," 629.

69. Davis and Rogers, "John Phalen 'Stuffy' McInnis," 630; Honig, *Baseball's 10 Greatest Teams*, 17. Baseball Reference, "Stuffy McInnis," notes 250 strikeouts in 8639 plate appearances http://www.baseball-reference.com/players/m/mcinnst01.shtml (accessed April 18, 2014).

70. Davis and Rogers, "John Phalen 'Stuffy' McInnis," 629.

71. John McMurray, "Amos Aaron Strunk," in *Deadball Stars of the American League*, ed. David Jones (Dulles, VA: Potomac Books, 2006), 627–28.

72. "Eddie Murphy," *Baseball-Reference.com*, http://www.baseball-reference.com/players/m/murphed02.shtml (accessed May 25, 2013).

73. Bill Bishop, "Reuben Nosher Oldring," in *Deadball Stars of the American League*, ed. David Jones (Dulles, VA: Potomac Books, 2006), 618–19. Right before the World Series began, Oldring publicly announced his engagement, but his former common-law wife read the news and filed charges of nonsupport and desertion. Boston Braves fans, not disposed to generosity, taunted him throughout the World Series.

74. Don Geiszler, "Walter Henry Schang," in *Deadball Stars of the American League*, ed. David Jones (Dulles, VA: Potomac Books, 2006), 632–34.

75. "1914 Philadelphia Athletics," *Baseball-Almanac.com*, http://www.baseball-almanac.com/teamstats/roster.php?y=1914&t=PHA (accessed September 12, 2012).

76. "Chief Bender," *Baseball-Almanac.com*, http://www.baseball-almanac.com/players/player.php?p=bendech01 (accessed March 9, 2013); "Chief Bender," *Baseball-Reference.com*, http://www.baseball-reference.com/players/b/bendech01.shtml (accessed March 9, 2013).

77. Quoted in Tom Swift, *Chief Bender's Burden: The Silent Struggle of a Baseball Star* (Lincoln: University of Nebraska Press, 2008), 3.

78. Tom Swift, "Charles Albert Bender," in *Deadball Stars of the American League,* ed. David Jones (Dulles, VA: Potomac Books, 2006), 607.

79. Bill James and Rob Neyer, *The Neyer/James Guide to Pitchers: An Historical Compendium of Pitching, Pitchers, and Pitches* (New York: Simon & Schuster, 2004), 131.

80. Swift, "Charles Albert Bender."

81. Quoted in Swift, "Charles Albert Bender," 607.

82. Michael McGerr, *A Fierce Discontent: The Rise and Fall of the Progressive Movement in America, 1870–1920* (New York: Free Press, 2003), 205, 207.

83. Charla Bear, "American Indian Boarding Schools Haunt Many," *NPR*, May 12, 2008, http://www.wbur.org/npr/16516865 (accessed March 8, 2013).

84. Swift, "Charles Albert Bender," 607.

85. Quoted in Swift, *Chief Bender's Burden*, 5.

86. Swift, *Chief Bender's Burden*, 5.

87. Quoted in Swift, *Chief Bender's Burden*, 7.

88. Swift, *Chief Bender's Burden*, 6.

89. Quoted in Swift, *Chief Bender's Burden*, 1.

90. *Sporting Life*, October 10, 1914.

91. Swift, *Chief Bender's Burden*, 2–4.

92. Swift, *Chief Bender's Burden*.

93. *New York Times*, October 10, 1914; *Boston Globe*, October 9, 1914.

94. *New York Times*, October 10, 1914. On obnoxious fans, see Cait Murphy, *Crazy '08: How a Cast of Cranks, Rogues, Boneheads, and Magnates Created the Greatest Year in Baseball History* (New York: Smithsonian Books/HarperCollins, 2007), 189–90.

95. Swift, *Chief Bender's Burden*, 77.

96. Macht, *Connie Mack and the Early Years of Baseball*, 633–35.

97. Swift, *Chief Bender's Burden*, 78.

98. Kaese, *The Boston Braves*, 161.

99. *Boston Globe*, October 9, 1914.

100. Harold Kaese Notes, Herman Kaese Collection, Box 17, Boston Braves Notes, Boston Public Library.

101. *Boston Globe* October 10, 1914.

102. *Boston Globe*, October 9, 1914.

103. *Boston Globe*, October 9, 1914.

104. *Boston Globe*, October 9, 1914.

105. James and Neyer, *The Neyer/James Guide to Pitchers*, 366.

106. *Boston Globe*, October 9, 1914.

107. Swift, *Chief Bender's Burden*, 215.

108. *Boston Globe*, October 9, 1914.

109. *New York Times*, October 10, 1914.

110. *Boston Globe*, October 10, 1914.

111. *Boston Globe*, October 10, 1914.

112. *Boston Globe*, October 10, 1914.

113. Quoted in Macht, *Connie Mack and the Early Years of Baseball*, 641.

114. *Boston Globe*, October 11, 1914; "Baseball Awards Voting, 1914," *Baseball-Reference.com*, http://www.baseball-reference.com/awards/awards_1914.shtml#ALmvp (accessed March 11, 2013).

115. Jan Finkel, "Edward Stewart Plank," in *Deadball Stars of the American League*, ed. David Jones (Dulles, VA: Potomac Books, 2006), 587–90.

116. James and Neyer, *The Neyer/James Guide to Pitchers*, 344.

117. Finkel, "Edward Stewart Plank," 587; Hal Bodley, "Baseball Wants Just a Few More Minutes," *USA Today Baseball*, February 26, 2004, http://usatoday30. usatoday.com/sports/baseball/columnist/bodley/2004-02-26-bodley_x.htm (accessed May 27, 2013); Murphy, *Crazy '08*, 190.

118. "Eddie Plank," *Baseball-Reference.com*, http://www.baseball-reference.com/players/p/planked01.shtml (accessed September 1, 2013); Finkel, "Edward Stewart Plank," 587–90.

119. *Boston Globe*, October 11, 1914.

120. *Boston Globe*, October 11, 1914; *Boston Post*, October 14, 1914.

121. *Boston Globe*, October 11, 1914; Macht, *Connie Mack and the Early Years of Baseball*, 641.

122. *Boston Globe*, October 11, 1914.

123. *Boston Globe*, October 11, 1914; Macht, *Connie Mack and the Early Years of Baseball*, 641.

124. James and Neyer, *The Neyer/James Guide to Pitchers*, 344.

125. Quoted in Macht, *Connie Mack and the Early Years of Baseball*, 642.

126. *Boston Globe*, October 9, 1914.

127. *Boston Globe*, October 9, 1914; *Boston Globe*, October 10, 1914; *Boston Globe*, October 11, 1914. At the South End Grounds, the usual ballpark for the Braves, and at parks throughout the city, fans would reproduce the game. Local bars received telegraph wires and then relayed the story to cheering fans.

128. Walter "Rabbit" Maranville, *Run Rabbit Run: The Hilarious Mostly True Tales of Rabbit Maranville*, 32; on this incident, see also Macht, *Connie Mack 632*; Kaese, *the Boston Braves*, 163.

129. *Boston Globe*, October 11, 1914.

130. *Boston Globe*, October 11, 1914; Kaese, *The Boston Braves*, 163; Macht, *Connie Mack and the Early Years of Baseball*, 632, 642; Walter "Rabbit" Maranville, *Run, Rabbit, Run: The Hilarious and Mostly True Tales of Rabbit Maranville* (Cleveland, OH: Society for American Baseball Research, 1991), 32.

131. *Boston Globe*, October 12, 1914.

132. *Boston Globe*, October 12, 1914.

133. *Boston Globe*, October 11, 1914; Doris Kearns Goodwin *The Fitzgeralds and the Kennedys*, 259.

134. Bob Klapisch and Pete Van Wieren, *The World Champion Braves: 125 years of America's Team* (Atlanta: Turner Publishing, 1996, 44.

135. *Boston Globe*, October 12, 1914.

136. "World Series History," *Baseball-Almanac.com*, http://www.baseball-almanac.com/ws/wsmenu.shtml (accessed September 1, 2013).

137. Murphy, *Crazy '08*, 126.

138. Ritter, *The Glory of Their Times*, 27.

139. Ward and Burns, *Baseball*, 66–67, 114.

140. Kaese, *The Boston Braves*, 164.

141. Quoted in "Bullet Joe Bush," *SABR Baseball Biography Project*, http://sabr.org/bioproj/person/30a2a3bd (accessed May 26, 2013).

142. Kaese, *The Boston Braves*, 164; *Boston Globe*, October 13, 1914; Gene Schoor, *History of the World Series* (New York: William Morrow and Company, 1990); Francis C. Richter, ed., *The Reach Official: American League Baseball Guide for 1914* (Philadelphia, PA: A. J. Reach, 1914).

143. *Boston Globe*, October 13, 1914.

144. *Boston Globe*, October 13, 1914.

145. *Boston Globe*, October 13, 1914; Richter, *The Reach Official*.

146. *Boston Globe*, October 13, 1914; Richter, *The Reach Official*.

147. *Boston Globe*, October 13, 1914.

148. *Boston Globe*, October 13, 1914.

149. *Boston Globe*, October 14, 1914.

150. Ron Anderson, "Joe Bush," *Baseball-Almanac.com*, http://www.baseball-almanac.com/ (accessed March 31, 2013); Richter, *The Reach Official*.

151. Macht, *Connie Mack and the Early Years of Baseball*, 642.

152. *Boston Globe*, October 14, 1914.

153. *Boston Post*, October 13, 1914. See also Macht, Connie Mack, 643.

154. *Boston Post*, October 13, 1914.

155. *Boston Globe*, October 13, 1914.

156. *Boston Post*, October 13, 1914.

157. *Boston Globe*, October 13, 1914; *Boston Globe*, October 14, 1914; Richter, *The Reach Official*.

158. *Boston Globe*, October 13, 1914.

159. *Boston Globe*, October 13, 1914.

160. Macht, *Connie Mack*, 642.

161. *Boston Globe*, October 13, 1914; *Boston Globe*, October 14, 1914; Macht, *Connie Mack and the Early Years of Baseball*; Kaese, *Boston Braves*, 165, 643.

162. "1914 Philadelphia Athletics Schedule," *Baseball-Almanac.com*, http://www.baseball-almanac.com/teamstats/schedule.php?y=1914&t=PHA (accessed May 27, 2013).

163. *New York Times*, October 14, 1914.

164. *Boston Globe*, October 14, 1914.

165. *Boston Globe*, October 14, 1914; Richter, *The Reach Official*; *New York Times*, October 14, 1914; Schoor, *History of the World Series*, 59.

166. *Boston Globe*, October 14, 1914.

167. *Boston Globe*, October 14, 1914.

168. *Boston Globe*, October 14, 1914.

169. *Boston Globe*, October 14, 1914; Richter, *The Reach Official*; *New York Times*, October 14, 1914.

170. *Boston Globe*, October 14, 1914.

171. Frank Vaccaro, "Herb Pennock," *SABR Baseball Biography Project*, http://sabr .org/bioproj/person/612bb457 (accessed September 1, 2013); *New York Times*, October 14, 1914.

172. *Boston Globe*, October 14, 1914; Richter, *The Reach Official*; *New York Times*, October 14, 1914.

173. *Boston Globe*, October 14, 1914; Richter, *The Reach Official*.

174. Damon Runyon, *Guys, Dolls, and Curveballs: Damon Runyon on Baseball* (New York: Carroll and Graf, 2005), 165.

175. Quoted in Macht, *Connie Mack and the Early Years of Baseball*, 643.

176. Kaese, *The Boston Braves*, 166; *Boston Post*, October 14, 1914; *New York Times*, October 14, 1914..

177. Runyon, *Guys, Dolls, and Curveballs*, 169.

178. Kaese, *The Boston Braves*, 152–60; "Atlanta Braves Team History," *Baseball-Reference.com*, http://www.baseball-reference.com/teams/ATL/ (accessed April 23, 2013).

179. *New York Times*, October 14, 1914.

180. Robert H. Boyle, "Frank Merriwell's Triumph: How Yale's Great Athlete Captured America's Fancy, or, Purified the Penny Dreadfuls and Became Immortal," *SI Vault*, December 24, 1962, http://si.com/vault/article/magazine/MAG1135102/ index.htm (accessed January 1, 2014); Deford, *The Old Ball Game*, 36–38.

181. *New York Times*, October 15, 1914.

182. Ritter, *The Glory of Their Times*, 38.

183. McGerr, *A Fierce Discontent*, 248.

184. *New York Times*, October 18, 1914.

185. *New York Times*, October 28, 1914.

186. *New York Times*, October 20, 1914.

187. "Shibe Park," *Ballparksofbaseball.com*, http://ballparksofbaseball.com/past/ ShibePark.htm (accessed May 27, 2013).

188. "Fenway Park," *Ballparksofbaseball.com*, http://www.ballparksofbaseball.com/ al/FenwayPark.htm (accessed May 27, 2013).

189. McGerr, *A Fierce Discontent*, 227–32.

190. *Boston Globe*, October 14, 1914.

191. *New York Times*, October 14, 1914.

Bibliography

CONTEMPORARY WORKS

Donovan, Tom, ed. *The Hazy Red Hell: Fighting Experiences on the Western Front, 1914–1918*. Staplehurst, England: Spellmount Publishers, 1999.

Evers, John J., and Hugh S. Fullerton. *Touching Second*. Jefferson, NC: McFarland, 2005. Originally published in 1910 by Reilly and Britton.

Harold Kaese Collection, Boston Public Library.

Lieb, Fred. *Baseball as I Have Known It*. New York: Coward, McCann & Geoghegan, 1977.

———. *Scientific Baseball*. New York: Richard K. Fox, 1913.

Mack, Connie. *My 66 Years in the Big Leagues: The Great Story of America's National Game*. Philadelphia, PA: John C. Winston Company, 1950.

Maranville, Walter "Rabbit." *Run, Rabbit, Run: The Hilarious and Mostly True Tales of Rabbit Maranville*. Cleveland, OH: Society for American Baseball Research, 1991.

Mathewson, Christy. *Pitching in a Pinch: Or Baseball from the Inside*. New York: Knickerbocker Press, 1912.

McGraw, John. *My Thirty Years in Baseball*. New York: Arno Press, 1974. Originally published in 1923 by Boni and Liveright.

Richter, Francis C., ed. *The Reach Official: American League Baseball Guide for 1914*. Philadelphia, PA: A. J. Reach, 1914.

Ritter, Lawrence. *The Glory of Their Times: The Story of the Early Days of Baseball Told by the Men Who Played It*. New York: Perennial, 2002.

Runyon, Damon. *Guys, Dolls, and Curveballs: Damon Runyon on Baseball*. New York: Carroll and Graf, 2005.

Sullivan, Dean A., ed. *Middle Innings: A Documentary History of Baseball, 1900–1948*. Lincoln: University of Nebraska Press, 1998.

Taylor, Frederick Winslow. *The Principles of Scientific Management*. Chapter II, 1911, *Ibiblio.org*, http://www.ibiblio.org/eldritch/fwt/t2.html (accessed August 10, 2013).

CONTEMPORARY PERIODICALS

Baseball Magazine
Boston Globe
Boston Post
New York Times
Sporting Life
"Topics in Chronicling America: World War I Declarations." *Library of Congress News-paper and Current Periodical Reading Room*, http://www.loc.gov/rr/news/topics/ww1declarations.html (accessed August 25, 2013).
Giamatti Research Center, National Baseball Hall of Fame Library, Cooperstown, New York, clipping files:
John J. Evers
James E. Gaffney
Walter "Rabbit" Maranville
George Stallings

SECONDARY BOOKS AND ARTICLES

Adair, Robert K. *The Physics of Baseball*. New York: Itbooks, 2003.
Adler, Richard. *Mack, McGraw, and the 1913 Baseball Season*. Jefferson, NC: McFarland, 2008.
Alexander, Charles C. *John McGraw*. New York: Penguin Books, 1988.
———. *Our Game: An American Baseball History*. New York: Henry Holt and Company, 1991.
———. *Ty Cobb*. New York: Oxford University Press, 1984.
Anderson, David. *More Than Merkle: A History of the Best and Most Exciting Baseball Season in Human History*. Lincoln: University of Nebraska Press, 2000.
Angell, Roger. *Once More around the Park: A Baseball Reader*. Chicago: Ivan R. Dee, 1988.
Asinof, Eliot. *Eight Men Out: The Black Sox and 1919 World Series*. New York: Holt Paperbacks, 1963.
Bell, Buddy, and Neal Vahle. *Smart Baseball: How Professionals Play the Mental Game*. New York: St. Martin's, 2005.
Bell, Christopher. *Scapegoats: Baseballers Whose Careers Are Marked by One Fateful Play*. Jefferson, NC: McFarland, 2002.
Bogen, Gil. *Tinker, Evers, and Chance: A Triple Biography*. Jefferson, NC: McFarland, 2003.
Boyle, Robert H. "Frank Merriwell's Triumph: How Yale's Great Athlete Captured America's Fancy, or, Purified the Penny Dreadfuls and Became Immortal." *SI Vault*, December 24, 1962, http://si.com/vault/article/magazine/MAG1135102/index.htm (accessed January 1, 2014).

Breslin, Jimmy. *Branch Rickey*. New York: Viking, 2011.

Brinkley, Douglas. *Wheels for the World: Henry Ford, His Company, and a Century of Progress*. New York: Viking, 2003.

Browning, Reed. *Cy Young*. Amherst: University of Massachusetts Press, 2000.

Burgos, Adrian, Jr. *Playing America's Game: Baseball, Latinos, and the Color Line*. Berkeley: University of California Press, 2007.

Burk, Robert F. *Only a Game: Players, Owners, and American Baseball to 1920*. Chapel Hill: University of North Carolina Press, 1994.

Clark, Christopher M. *The Sleep Walkers: How Europe Went to War in 1914*. New York: Penguin Books, 2012.

Cohen, Richard M., Jordan A. Deutsch, David S. Neft, and Roland T. Johnson. *World Series*. New York: Dial, 1976.

Connolly, James J. *The Triumph of Ethnic Progressivism: Urban Political Culture in Boston, 1900–1925*. Cambridge, MA: Harvard University Press, 1998.

Costa, Gabriel B., Michael R. Huber, and John T. Saccoman. *Understanding Sabermetrics: An Introduction to the Science of Baseball Statistics*. Jefferson, NC: McFarland, 2008.

Creamer, Robert W. *Babe: The Legend Comes to Life*. New York: Simon & Schuster, 1974.

Davis, Ted. *Connie Mack: A Life in Baseball*. San Jose, CA: Writers' Club Press, 2000.

Deford, Frank. *The Old Ball Game: How John McGraw, Christy Mathewson, and the New York Giants Created Modern Baseball*. New York: Grove Press, 2005.

Dewey, Donald. *Total Ballclubs: The Ultimate Book of Baseball Teams*. Wilmington, DE: Sports Media Publishing, 2005.

Dewey, Donald, and Nicholas Acocella. *The Biographical History of Baseball*. Chicago: Triumph Books, 2002.

———. *The Black Prince of Baseball: Hal Chase and the Mythology of Baseball*. Wilmington, DE: Sports Media Publishing, 2004.

———. *Total Ball Clubs*. Toronto: Sports Classics Books, 2005.

Dickey, Glenn. *The History of the World Series since 1903*. New York: Stein and Day, 1984.

Dickson, Paul. *Dickson's Baseball Dictionary*. New York: W. W. Norton & Company, 2009.

———. *The Hidden Language of Baseball: How Signs and Sign-Stealing Have Influenced the Course of Our National Pastime*. New York: Walker and Company, 2003.

Durant, John. *Baseball's Miracle Teams*. New York: Hastings House, 1975.

Echevarria, Roberto Gonzalez. *The Pride of Havana: A History of Cuban Baseball*. New York: Oxford University Press, 1999.

Einstein, Charles, ed. *The Baseball Reader*. New York: McGraw-Hill, 1982.

Enright, Jim. *Chicago Cubs*. New York: Routledge, 1975.

Frommer, Harvey. *Baseball's Greatest Managers*. New York: Franklin Watts, 1985.

Gay, Timothy M. *Tris Speaker: The Rough-and-Tumble Life of a Baseball Legend*. Guildford, CT: Lyons Press, 2007.

Gershman, Michael. *Diamonds: The Evolution of the Ballpark from the Elysian Fields to Camden Yards*. Boston: Houghton Mifflin, 1993.

Gillete, Gary, and Pete Palmer, eds. *The Ultimate Red Sox Companion: A Complete Statistical and Reference Encyclopedia.* Hingham, MA: Maple Street Press, 2007.

Ginsburg, Daniel. *The Fix Is In: A History of Baseball Gambling and Game-Fixing Scandals.* Jefferson, NC: McFarland, 2004.

Gmelch, George. "Superstition and Ritual in American Baseball." *Elysian Fields Quarterly* 11, no. 3 (1992): 25–36.

Goldman, Steven, ed. *Extra Innings: More Baseball between the Numbers from the Team at Baseball Prospectus.* New York: Basic Books, 2012.

———. *It Ain't Over 'Til It's Over: The Baseball Prospectus Pennant Race Book.* New York: Basic Books, 2007.

Goodwin, Doris Kearns. *The Fitzgeralds and the Kennedys: An American Saga.* New York: Simon & Schuster, 1987.

Greenberg, Eric Rolfe. *The Celebrant.* Lincoln: University of Nebraska Press, 1983.

Hammack, David C. *Power and Society: Greater New York at the Turn of the Century.* New York: Russell Sage Foundation, 1982.

Hartley, Michael. *Christy Mathewson: A Biography.* Jefferson, NC: McFarland, 2004.

Hastings, Max. *Catastrophe 1914: Europe Goes to War.* New York: Alfred A. Knopf, 2013.

Hirshberg, Al. *The Braves: The Pick and the Shovel.* Boston: Waverly House, 1948.

Hofstadter, Richard. *The Age of Reform: From Bryan to FDR.* New York: Vantage Books, 1955.

Hogan, Lawrence D. *Shades of Glory: The Negro Leagues and the Story of African American Baseball.* Washington, DC: National Geographic, 2006.

Holmes, Dan. *Ty Cobb: A Biography.* Westport, CT: Greenwood, 2004.

Honig, Donald. *Baseball America: The Heroes of the Game and Times of Their Glory.* New York: Macmillan, 1985.

———. *Baseball's 10 Greatest Teams.* New York: Macmillan, 1982.

———. *The Greatest Shortstops of All Time.* Dubuque, IA: Brown & Benchmark, 1992.

Ignatiev, Noel. *How the Irish Became White.* New York: Routledge, 1995.

James, Bill. *The Bill James Guide to Baseball Managers: From 1870 to Today.* New York: Scribner, 1997.

———. *The New Bill James Historical Baseball Abstract.* New York: Free Press, 2001.

James, Bill, and Rob Neyer. *The Neyer/James Guide to Pitchers: An Historical Compendium of Pitching, Pitchers, and Pitches.* New York: Simon & Schuster, 2004.

Jones, David, ed. *Deadball Stars of the American League.* Written by the Deadball Era Committee of the Society for American Baseball Research. Dulles, VA: Potomac Books, 2006.

Kaese, Harold. *The Boston Braves.* New York: G. P. Putnam's Sons, 1948.

Kanigel, Robert. *The One Best Way: Frederick Winslow Taylor and the Enigma of Efficiency.* New York: Viking, 1997.

Keegan, John. *The First World War.* New York: Vintage Books, 2000.

Kennedy, David M. *Over Here: The First World War and American Society.* New York: Oxford University Press, 2004.

Keri, Jonah, ed. *Baseball between the Numbers: Why Everything You Know about the Game Is Wrong.* New York: Basic Books, 2006.

Kimmel, Michael S., and Amy Aronson. *Men and Masculinities: A Social, Cultural, and Historical Encyclopedia, Volume 1.* Santa Barbara, CA: ABC-CLIO, 2003.

Klapisch, Bob, and Pete Van Wieren. *The Braves: An Illustrated History of America's Team.* Atlanta, GA: Turner Publishing, 1995.

———. *The World Champion Braves: 125 Years of America's Team.* Atlanta, GA: Turner Publishing, 1996.

Koppett, Leonard. *Koppett's Concise History of Major League Baseball.* Philadelphia, PA: Temple University Press, 1998.

———. *The Man in the Dugout: Baseball's Top Managers and How They Got That Way.* New York: Crown, 1993.

Layden, Tim. "Tinker to Evers to Chance . . . to Me." *SI Vault*, December 3, 2012, http://sportsillustrated.cnn.com/vault/article/magazine/MAG1206500/3/index.htm (accessed August 11, 2013).

Levy, Alan H. "The Right Myths at the Right Time: Myth Making and Hero Worship in Post-Frontier American Society—Rube Waddell vs. Christy Mathewson." In *The Cooperstown Symposium on Baseball and American Culture, 2001*, ed. Alvin L. Hall, 51–65. Jefferson, NC: McFarland, 2001.

———. *Rube Waddell: The Zany, Brilliant Life of a Strikeout Artist.* Jefferson, NC: McFarland, 2000.

Lewis, Michael. *Moneyball: The Art of Winning an Unfair Game.* New York: W. W. Norton & Company, 2003.

Lind, Michael. *Land of Promise: An Economic History of the United States.* New York: HarperCollins, 2012.

Littlefield, Bill, and Richard A. Johnson. *Fall Classics: The Best Writing about the World Series' First 100 Years.* New York: Three Rivers Press, 2003.

Liulevicius, Vejas Gabriel. *War Land on the Eastern Front: Culture, National Identity, and German Occupation in World War I.* New York: Cambridge University Press, 2000.

Macht, Norman. *Connie Mack and the Early Years of Baseball.* Lincoln: University of Nebraska Press, 2007.

Mansch, Larry D. *Rube Marquard: The Life and Times of a Baseball Hall of Famer.* Jefferson, NC: McFarland, 1998.

McGerr, Michael. *A Fierce Discontent: The Rise and Fall of the Progressive Movement in America, 1870–1920.* New York: Free Press, 2003.

Mills, Dorothy Seymour. *Chasing Baseball: Our Obsession with Its History, Numbers, People, and Places.* Jefferson, NC: McFarland, 2010.

"The Miracle Braves." *This Great Game*, http://www.thisgreatgame.com/1914-baseball-history.html (accessed November 2, 2013).

Mohl, Raymond A. *The New City: Urban America in the Industrial Age.* Arlington Heights, IL: Harlan Davidson, 1985.

Murphy, Cait. *Crazy '08: How A Cast of Cranks, Rogues, Boneheads, and Magnates Created the Greatest Year in Baseball History.* New York: Smithsonian Books/Harper Collins, 2007.

Nathanson, Mitchell. *A People's History of Baseball.* Urbana: University of Illinois Press, 2012.

Neyer, Rob. *Rob Neyer's Big Book of Baseball Legends: The Truth, Lies, and Everything Else.* New York: Fireside, 2008.

Neyer, Rob, and Eddie Epstein. *Baseball Dynasties: The Greatest Teams of All Time.* New York: W. W. Norton & Company, 2000.

Nowlin, Bill, ed. *Opening Fenway Park in Style: The 1912 Boston Red Sox.* Phoenix, AZ: Society for American Baseball Research, 2012.

O'Connor, Thomas H. *The Hub: Boston Past and Present.* Boston: Northeastern University Press, 2000.

Okrent, Daniel, and Harris Lewine, eds. *The Ultimate Baseball Book.* New York: Houghton Mifflin, 2000.

Okrent, Daniel, and Steve Wulf. *Baseball Anecdotes.* New York: Basic Books, 1989.

Overfield, Joseph M. "How Losing an Exhibition Sparked Miracle Braves." *Baseball Digest* 20, no. 4 (May 1961): 83–85.

Painter, Nell Irvin. *Standing at Armageddon: The United States, 1877–1919.* New York: W. W. Norton and Company, 1989.

Peary, Danny. *Cult Baseball Players: The Greats, the Flakes, the Weird, and the Wonderful.* New York: Simon & Schuster, 1990.

Peterson, Richard. "Slide, Kelly, Slide: The Irish in the Early History of Baseball." In *The Cooperstown Symposium on Baseball and American Culture, 1999*, ed. Peter M. Rutkoff, 177–86. Jefferson, NC: McFarland, 2000.

Peterson, Robert. *Only the Ball Was White: A History of Legendary Black Players and All-Black Professional Teams.* New York: Oxford University Press, 1970.

Piott, Steven L. *American Reformers, 1870–1920.* Lanham, MD: Rowman & Littlefield, 2006.

———. *Daily Life in the Progressive Era.* Santa Barbara, CA: Greenwood, 2011.

Pope, Edwin. *Baseball's Greatest Managers: Twenty of the All-Time Greats, Past and Present.* New York: Doubleday, 1960.

Porter, David L., ed. *Biographical Dictionary of American Sports: Baseball.* New York: Greenwood, 1987.

Puerzer, Richard J. "Engineering Baseball: Branch Rickey's Innovative Approach to Baseball Management." In *The Cooperstown Symposium on Baseball and American Culture, 2002*, ed. Alvin L. Hall, 81–94. Jefferson, NC: McFarland, 2002.

Rader, Benjamin G. *Baseball: A History of America's Game*, 3rd ed. Urbana: University of Illinois Press, 2008.

Riess, Steven A. *Sport in Industrial America: 1850–1920.* Wheeling, IL: Harlan Davidson, 1995.

———. *Touching Base: Professional Baseball and American Culture in the Progressive Era.* Urbana: University of Illinois Press, 1999.

Schoor, Gene. *History of the World Series.* New York: William Morrow and Company, 1990.

Seib, Philip. *The Player: Christy Mathewson, Baseball, and the American Century.* New York: Four Walls Eight Windows, 2003.

Seymour, Harold. *Baseball: The Golden Age.* New York: Oxford University Press, 1971.

Shatzkin, Mike, ed. *The Ballplayers: Baseball's Ultimate Biographical Reference.* New York: Arbor House, 1990.

Silver, Nate. "Lies, Damned Lies: The Greatest Pennant Race Comebacks." *Baseball Prospectus*, October 4, 2007, http://www.baseballprospectus.com/article .php?articleid=6793 (accessed September 28, 2013).

Simon, Tom, ed. *Deadball Stars of the National League*. Written by the Deadball Era Committee of the Society for American Baseball Research. Washington, DC: Brassey's, 2004.

Smith, Robert. *Pioneers of Baseball*. Boston: Little, Brown and Company, 1978.

Stein, Fred. *A History of the Baseball Fan*. Jefferson, NC: McFarland, 2005.

Stevenson, David. *1914–1918: The History of the First World War*. London: Allen Lane, 2004.

Stout, Glenn. *Fenway, 1912: The Birth of a Ballpark, a Championship Season, and Fenway's Remarkable First Year*. Boston: Houghton Mifflin, 2011.

Strachan, Hew. *The First World War*. London: Penguin Books, 2003.

Swift, Tom. *Chief Bender's Burden: The Silent Struggle of a Baseball Star*. Lincoln: University of Nebraska Press, 2008.

Taillon, Paul Michel. "What We Want Is Good, Sober Men: Masculinity, Respectability, and Temperance in the Railroad Brotherhoods, c. 1870–1910." *Journal of Social History* 36, no. 2 (Winter 2002), 319–38, http://www.jstor.org/stable/3790113.

Taylor, Frederick E. *The Runmakers*. Baltimore, MD: Johns Hopkins University Press, 2010.

Thorn, John. *Baseball in the Garden of Eden: The Secret History of the Early Game*. New York: Simon & Schuster, 2011.

Tuchman, Barbara W. *The Guns of August*. New York: Random House, 2005. Originally published in 1962 by Tess Press.

Turbow, Jason. *The Baseball Codes: Beanballs, Sign Stealing, and Bench-Clearing Brawls: The Unwritten Rules of America's Pastime*. New York: Pantheon, 2010.

Tygiel, Jules. *Past Time: Baseball as History*. New York: Oxford University Press, 2000.

Vaccaro, Mike. *The First Fall Classic: The Red Sox, the Giants, and the Cast of Players, Pugs, and Politicos Who Reinvented the World Series in 1912*. New York: Doubleday, 2009.

Verhey, Jeffrey. *The Spirit of 1914: Militarism, Myth, and Mobilization in Germany*. New York: Cambridge University Press, 2000.

Voigt, David Q. *America through Baseball*. Chicago: Nelson Hall, 1976.

———. *American Baseball, Volume II: From the Commissioners to Continental Expansion*. Norman: University of Oklahoma Press, 1970.

Ward, Geoffrey C., and Ken Burns. *Baseball: An Illustrated History*. New York: Alfred A. Knopf, 1994.

Weintraub, Robert. *The House That Ruth Built: The Untold Story of Babe Ruth's Yankees, John McGraw's Giants, and the Extraordinary Baseball Season of 1923*. Hachette Digital, 2011.

Weiss, Nancy Joan. *Charles Francis Murphy, 1858–1924: Respectability and Responsibility in American Politics*. Northampton, MA: Smith College, 1968.

White, Edward G. *Creating the National Pastime: Baseball Transforms Itself, 1903–1953*. Princeton, NJ: Princeton University Press, 1996.

Wiebe, Robert. *The Search for Order: 1877–1920.* New York: Hill & Wang, 1967.
Will, George. *Men at Work: The Craft of Baseball.* New York: HarperCollins, 1990.
Zoss, Joel, and John Bowman. *Diamonds in the Rough: The Untold History of Baseball.*
    Chicago: Contemporary Books, 1996.

WEBSITES

Baseball Almanac	http://www.baseball-almanac.com
Baseball Library	http://www.baseballlibrary.com
Baseball Page	http://www.thebaseballpage.com
Baseball Prospectus	http://www.baseballprospectus.com
Baseball Reference	http://www.baseball-reference.com
LA84 Foundation	http://www.la84.org
Retrosheet	http://www.retrosheet.org
SABR Baseball Biography Project	http://sabr.org/bioproject

Index

About the Author

J. Brian Ross earned a B.A. and an M.A. in history from the University of Michigan, and a Ph.D. from Case Western Reserve University. Born in Boston, Ross frequented Fenway Park, where he gained a lifelong devotion to Boston baseball. He acquired a passion for the 1880–1914 time period, the background years for the "Miracle Braves," when writing the "The New Philanthropy," a case study that looks at the politics of charity during the first two decades of the twentieth century. Ross has served as history teacher and department chair at Hawken School and Hathaway Brown School in northeast Ohio, as well as Collegiate School in Richmond, Virginia. He has researched baseball history since 1997, when, at Hathaway Brown School, in Shaker Heights, Ohio, he organized a history conference celebrating the 50th anniversary of Jackie Robinson's breaking the color barrier of the major leagues.